Date Due		
MAY 16 '66 OCT 1 '73		
AUG 9 '66 JUN 1 3 1975		
SEP 26 '66		
JAN 3 '67		
MAR 22 '67		
MAY 23 '67		
JUN 8 '67		
SEP 26 '67		
DEC 15 '67		

THE
PAGEANT OF
CANADIAN HISTORY

THE PAGEANT
OF
CANADIAN HISTORY

BY

ANNE MERRIMAN PECK

ILLUSTRATED WITH PHOTOGRAVURES
AND A MAP

SECOND EDITION

DAVID McKAY COMPANY, INC.
1963

For their courtesy in granting permission to use photographs, other than those taken by the author, sincere thanks are due to: Associated Screen News, Ltd.; Canada, Dept. of Mines and Resources, Ottawa; Canadian Pacific Air Lines; Canadian Pacific Railway; British Columbia, Government Travel Bureau; Leonard Frank; Hudson's Bay Co.; Don MacLean; Nicholas Morant; Quebec, Office du Tourisme; Saskatchewan, Bureau of Publications, Libraries and Archives, Regina; Max Sauer; Winnepeg, Dept. of Mines and Natural Resources, Travel and Publicity Bureau.

THE PAGEANT OF CANADIAN HISTORY

BY ANNE MERRIMAN PECK

First Edition November, 1943
Reprinted April, 1944
December, 1947
December, 1953
August, 1957
September, 1959
Second Edition 1963

LIBRARY OF CONGRESS CATALOG CARD NUMBER 63-16695

To E.J.

Best of Companions

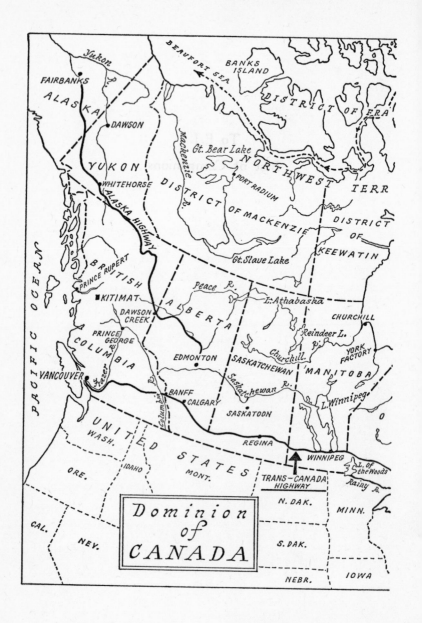

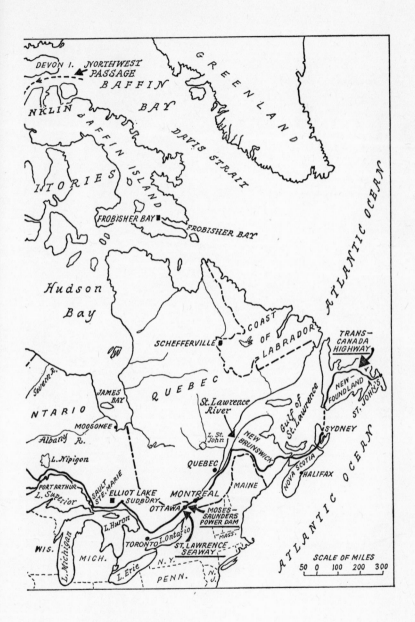

FOREWORD

THIS book was first written after a lengthy journey across Canada from sea to sea. I adopted its unconventional pattern because I saw the vigorous history of Canada in big sweeps of movement; the dramatic period of French exploration and the life of New France; the pursuit of fur which carried explorers and traders all the way to the Pacific; the growth of a few small British colonies into the Dominion of Canada; then the winning of the west and the advance to modern nationhood. I wished to make clear the motive power of ideas and ambitions that urged the people on from one period to another of their history. The book is a pageant, a story of the land and people, rather than a historian's study. Thanks and appreciation go to many Canadians of town and country who welcomed me with so much friendlines; to librarians and to officers of a variety of institutions who courteously gave their time and interest to help me with information. This 1962 revision of the book has become necessary because Canada, like other nations, has changed greatly in the years since World War II. I have studied these changes through up-to-date books, mostly written by Canadians; through magazine and newspaper articles, and through conversations with Canadian friends. It is my hope to present our northern neighbor and its people as they are today; members of a modern nation developing its resources, with an important place in the international councils of nations. This book is for my fellow Americans, to pass on my discoveries of the vivid history of our northern neighbors and my admiration for them. It is also offered to Canadians with the hope they will accept this interpretation of their story by an enthusiastic friend across the border.

ANNE MERRIMAN PECK

May, 1963
Tucson, Arizona

CONTENTS

V. GROWTH OF THE DOMINION

VI. CONTEMPORARY CANADA

ILLUSTRATIONS

[Between pages 178–179]

On the St. Lawrence; Notre Dame des Victoires, Quebec; Street Scene, Quebec.

Baude Street and City Hall, Quebec; Sous de Cap Street, Quebec; Old Houses Below the Château Frontenac, Quebec.

Porcupine Needlework; Old Silver; Old Wood Carving; Quebec Arts and Crafts — Habitant Bedspread and Wood Carving.

Place D'Armes, Montreal; Château de Ramezay, Montreal.

Old Mill, Île aux Coudres; An Outdoor Oven, Charlevoix County; Champlain Market, Quebec; Habitant; Old Houses, Île D'Orleans.

Government House, Halifax, N. S.; Ox Cart on Road, Digby, N. S.; Hackett's Cove, Nova Scotia.

Maude Lake in Schreiber District; School Car, Ontario; Cobalt, Ontario.

Reaping on the Prairies; Farmer in a Wheat Field, Alberta; Threshing on the Prairies.

Ukrainians' Greek Orthodox Church, Gonor; Hutterite Children, Manitoba; Manitoba Farmer; Harvesting Beets, Manitoba.

Lac les Arcs and Mount Longheed, Exshaw, Alberta; Indian Mother and Child; Indian Tepees near Banff.

Pulp Mill on British Columbia Coast; Totem Pole at Alert Bay, Vancouver Island; Prince Rupert, British Columbia.

Arrival of First Train at Vancouver; View of Vancouver Harbor.

Primitive North America and Its People

INCOMPARABLE in its spaciousness and beauty, North America was formed through geological ages to become the home of virile men. Wealth of forests, fertile soil, and metalliferous rocks awaited discoverers. The western side of the continent was ribbed with young, rugged mountain chains, lifting towering peaks crested with ice and snow to great heights. On the eastern side, the continent was also framed in mountains — older, more companionable ranges clothed in forests. Great river systems watered interior valleys and plains. In its main structural features North America was a whole.

From the Great Lakes to the eternal snow and ice of Arctic regions future inhabitants were to adjust themselves to a northern land, subject to long cold winters. Canada was once covered by the immense icecap of the Glacial Age and its present physical structure is to a great degree the work of glaciers. Rivers of ice pushed slowly over the land, changing contours and watercourses. As they melted, the glaciers scoured out the basins of great lakes or became the source of mighty rivers. Glacial deposits produced fertile soil in some regions while others were scraped to barren rock.

In later ages, under sun and rain and snow, verdure spread over the central plains and splendid forests clothed much of the land with the trees of a northern climate: spruce, hemlock, pine and cedar; birch, maple and elm. Warm sea currents off the northwest coast created a mild climate, with much rainfall, to nourish dense vegetation and enormous trees, from two to three hundred feet in height and of great girth.

A vast area of the most ancient rocks in the world, the Archean, discouraged human settlement in the northeast. This Pre-Cambrian or Laurentian Shield covers Labrador and eastern Quebec, northern and northwestern Ontario to Lake of the Woods, and extends around the shores of Hudson Bay. The rocks contain incalculable wealth in minerals, but the unproductive land, much of it treeless and covered with moss or bog, is unfriendly to human habitation.

Waterways and forests determined the course of exploration and settlement in Canada's share of North America: waterways, by which men might penetrate the wilderness ever westward toward the Pacific; waterways, such as the St. Lawrence River and chain of Great Lakes, making a highway to the interior of the continent; great rivers flowing north to the Arctic Ocean or Hudson Bay, and others forging their way through the western mountains to the Pacific.

Forests were the home of countless fur-bearing animals and the search for furs became the urge leading adventurers onward across the continent. Forests of giant cedar, spruce and Douglas fir in the west, and of birch, maple, spruce and hemlock in the east, were an inexhaustible source of timber for men's needs.

Prehistoric wanderers discovered this majestic land thousands of years ago. Anthropologists are still absorbed in the study of migrations which brought successive waves of nomads from Asia into northwestern North America. There may have been a land bridge between Siberia and Alaska, or the migrants may have crossed the fifty miles of Bering Strait in their crude boats. When these migrations began is still an open question, but many scientists believe that the first people came soon after the ice sheets of the Glacial Age had retreated.

Bands of migratory people spread throughout the western hemisphere, developing into countless tribes of differing customs, languages and cultural advancement. They are all believed to be of one basic race, now known as the American Indian.

The tribes who inhabited the northern half of the continent were men scarcely beyond the Stone Age in culture. They had no metal except a little copper, so that their tools, weapons and implements were of stone, bone or horn. They had no domesticated animal but the dog in prehistoric times, and none of them invented a wheeled vehicle to help in carrying burdens.

The tribes of forests, plains and seacoasts lived in a world of abundance. Inland waterways and the sea swarmed with fish of all kinds, wild fowl haunted the marshlands, and the forests were inhabited by many wild animals useful for food, whose skins provided clothing. There were berries and nuts, and some few of the tribes learned to cultivate the native maize, squash and beans. Yet, in spite of all that plenty, the people were often half-starved because of severe winters, long treks in search of food, and their inadequate weapons.

Everything that was needed for use in daily life must be made by long patient labor, but with admirable ingenuity the primitive people adapted the materials of their world to the uses of their simple lives.

Woodland tribes of the east invented the perfect craft for travel on the lakes and rivers of their country, the slim birchbark canoe, strong but light. Birchbark was used for the covers of their wigwams and to make containers for cooking. Trees were felled with stone axes to make poles for the wigwams and stockades for temporary villages. Wood was patiently fashioned with stone tools into canoe paddles, arrows and dishes. These Indians also invented the snowshoe and toboggan so that, with dog teams to haul the sleds, they could travel over the deep soft snow of winter forests. The men spent their summers fishing and their winters hunting and trapping deer, beaver, rabbits, moose and other wild animals.

The nomads of the western plains hunted elk and antelope for their skins, but depended chiefly on the buffalo for food and materials. In prehistoric times they hunted on foot but, after they had acquired horses, the spring roundups of buffalo herds were much more successful. Bands of hunters on horseback became very skillful in manipulating the animals, urging them toward pounds made of stakes, or driving them over steep places where they were easily slaughtered.

Buffalo tongues were the delicacy of springtime feasts after the hunts, but the mainstay of existence was the pemmican made by the women. They dried the buffalo meat in strips, pounded it up with berries and fat, and stored it in hide bags for winter use.

Hides of the animals with the hair left on made warm coverings for the winter, and, after the skins had been scraped, some were stretched over a framework of poles to make the temporary shelter, the tepee. Hides and sinews were used for many purposes.

When the western nomads were on the march their possessions were loaded on two poles tied together, hitched to horses. Just when these useful animals reached the Canadian plains is not known. Spaniards brought horses to what is now the southwestern United States and wild herds probably wandered northward, were caught and passed from tribe to tribe by barter. Men on horseback could range over a vast territory, and, with this freedom, small bands organized into powerful tribes who contended with one another for the best hunting grounds.

While the men of all the tribes exulted in their prowess in hunting and warfare, women labored patiently at interminable tasks. It was they who scraped and softened the hides of animals, fashioning them into leggings, moccasins and shirts. They had only bone awls with which to punch holes, bone needles and sinews to sew with, so that long hours were spent in making the family clothes. They found expression for their primitive love of beauty in decorating the garments with fringes of hide, or in painting designs on them with vegetable colors. Women's skilled fingers made use of dyed and flattened porcupine quills to adorn belts, moccasins and shirts with geometric patterns.

Savage warriors felt the need of ornament to enhance their prestige when they were dressed for ceremonies or tribal dances. Headdresses were made of feathers, the horns of beasts or whole animal heads, and necklaces of animal claws or shell beads were hung about their necks.

The men found time for games and gambling, for councils around the fires and ceremonial dances. For the women, however, life was eternal labor from youth to old age. They were the burden bearers, the mothers, the conservers of life in the wigwams and tepees. They must tend the fields when crops were raised, they must prepare the skins to make the clothes and shelters. Cooking, which was done by dropping hot stones into wood or bark containers filled with water, was painfully slow, so that the iron kettles introduced by white men became the most valued possessions of Indian women. When bands were on the move the women helped to paddle the canoes, carried burdens over the portages, and set up the temporary homes of poles covered with bark or hide.

Life was not reckoned in terms of time, but in the changing seasons, each with its occupations which were only interrupted by warfare. These aboriginal Canadians were children of nature, who interpreted their vast mysterious world in poetic imagery and beliefs. Most of them reverenced a great spirit who was to some of them a sky god, to others a god of thunder or the sun. There were multitudes of nature spirits, beings of the trees, mountains or great cataracts, and every animal had a soul more powerful than the creature itself. The people felt close to the beings of earth and sky and to the spirits of animals they hunted, addressing them in poetic chants.

With songs of war and religion, with rhythmic dances around their fires, primitive men expressed their emotions. Honored warriors inspired the young men before a war party set out with boastful recitals of their prowess against enemies. Oratory was the passion of these men. Individuals won prestige and power by their eloquence in the councils of warriors, crouched with their pipes around the lodge fires.

Europeans, invading this northern wilderness, did not find native kingdoms like those of Mexico and Peru, whose people were skilled in arts and strong in government. Canadian tribes with the exception of the Hurons and Iroquois were loosely organized, traveling mostly in small bands of family groups. In the lodges food was equally shared, and it was only by superior skill and bravery that chieftains held their position. There were no social classes except among the Pacific coast people, where membership in distinguished family clans created a nobility.

Most advanced in intelligence and talent for organization were the Iroquoian tribes of the east. They alone might be called nations, for the five strong tribes — Cayugas, Senecas, Oneidas, Onondagas and Mohawks — were banded together in a league governed by a council of chiefs chosen from the various tribes. This council made plans for wars of conquest and their unity made weaker tribes powerless before them. The Five Nations of the Iroquois were well on the way to creating an Indian empire, extending from the Great Lakes to the Atlantic, when their progress was checked by the arrival of the white men.

Iroquois warriors traced their descent from the mother's family instead of from the father, and women had influence in the councils. In the long tunnellike bark houses of Iroquois villages the women exercised a good deal of power over the men, although interminable tasks made their lives as laborious as those of other tribes.

These people and the Hurons, who had their territory near Lake Huron, had a semi-settled existence in villages protected by strong triple palisades of tree trunks. This gave the women opportunity to cultivate fields of maize, pumpkins, beans and tobacco so that they had better food than the tribes dependent on hunting and fishing alone.

An organization different from that of the Iroquois, and unlike anything else in North America, existed on the Pacific coast, extending into Alaska. These people had a character and culture quite distinct from that of the tribes of mountains, forests and plains. Proud family clans, tracing their descent from some supernatural being or powerful animal, ruled the villages and were surrounded with ceremony and a wealth of possessions. Below the nobility was a class of commoners, and slaves taken in war were the burden bearers for the people.

In their villages of large cedar-plank houses, strung along a beach or a river bank, the social life of the coast people was steeped in ceremonial observances and symbolism. Their artists created a bold, original type of design, expressive of their beliefs. They carved savage masks for dances of the secret societies and weird animal or human figures to uphold the roof beams of houses and to form the entrances to dwellings of chieftains. House fronts, canoe paddles, wooden chests and food containers were painted in earth colors with complex symbolic designs. The people of the northwest Pacific coast were the only artists among the Canadian tribes. Theirs was an exotic culture and a strange, exciting art, born of their response to an awe-inspiring world of forest and sea.

Since the people lived in villages, save for seasonal hunting excursions, they had time to enrich their lives with useful possessions. Ingenious use was made of materials around them, particularly wood which they handled in masterly fashion. With nothing but stone axes and wedges of wood the men managed to fell the huge cedar trees of the coast, split them into planks which they smoothed with a stone adze, and to build of them their large communal houses. Cedar trees were hollowed out by the use of fire and stone axes into great canoes with high carved prows. In these the men hunted sea otters, seals, and sometimes the great whales of the ocean. For trading and warfare the men paddled long distances in huge canoes.

Although people of the coast wore little clothing, the women made shirts of cedar bark split and woven, and important personages took pleasure in draping themselves in robes of soft sea-otter fur. They wore high conical hats of cedar roots, woven by the women. Excellent baskets were made of roots and fibers, so closely woven that they were watertight.

The tribes of the coast lived from the sea and the rivers, but the mainstay of their existence was the kingly salmon. Clever traps and weirs were set near the mouths of rivers, where the great fish came in the spring on their way up river to their spawning grounds. Ceremonies to honor the spirit of the salmon took place in the spring.

Even in the Arctic regions primitive people found homes for themselves. In appearance, customs and language these people, the Eskimo, were totally unlike other aboriginal people of North America. Most scientists consider them a distinct race whose origin is still a puzzle. It seems likely that they came from Siberia at a later period than other migrants from Asia. Recent discoveries reveal the fact that two branches of the Eskimo race entered America at different times.

The earliest groups, now vanished, were men of the sea who hunted the great whales. They built pit houses of boulders with roofs of skin and whale ribs. These stone house rings have been found in Greenland and some parts of the Arctic. Other Eskimo people came into the barren lands between the Mackenzie River basin and Hudson Bay, and lived a nomadic existence hunting the caribou. Eventually these bands of hunters went north to the Arctic shores, conquering and absorbing the earlier inhabitants of the coast.

The Eskimo, a strong, intelligent people, adapted themselves with ingenious skill to an existence along Arctic seas. Their food, their clothing of skins and furs, their snow houses for winter and skin tents for summer, were perfectly adapted to their environment. They seem to have brought with them to America a distinct culture, for their mythology and the poetic imagery of their songs are all their own.

For seal and walrus hunting they invented good weapons and the slim hunting boat of skin called a kayak. A larger craft, propelled by oars and called the umiak, was used for trading. With their skilled hands they made tools and weapons, stone cooking pots, and stone lamps in which seal oil was burned for heat and light. Bone and ivory were expertly carved in delicate etched patterns. During the long dark winters they enjoyed song and dance in their snow houses. Save for clashes in warfare they did not mingle with other native people, but lived a separate contented existence in their harsh land of ice and snow.

Among the aboriginal people of Canada, warfare and trade were twin pleasures. Spring and summer were the trading seasons. When forests and waterways were released from the grip of winter they trekked enormous distances to meet other tribes at accustomed places conveniently situated on lakes or rivers. By means of these barter parties useful and ornamental possessions and materials traveled far from their places of origin.

At the mouth of the Saguenay River tribes of the St. Lawrence country met those of the coast, exchanging skins and furs for corn, tobacco, and strings of shell beads called wampum. Belts and necklaces of wampum were the prized wealth of chieftains and were used in treaty making, while the beads were often used as currency. Copper, owned by tribes of Lake Superior, traveled all the way to the coast and tobacco traveled west.

To all the warriors tobacco was the solace of life and the mystic smoke of councils and treaties. Every man wore around his neck a skin pouch containing his pipe and tobacco. Tribes who had soapstone or other soft rock made carved pipe bowls for barter.

On the Pacific coast, copper of Alaska traveled south and shell beads went north. Men of the mountains followed a well-worn track called the Grease Trail to the coast to barter their furs and bear fat for fish and the oil of the candle fish, the oolahan.

Thus the people of seacoasts and those who could travel over inland waterways enlarged their experience by meeting tribes of differing languages and customs. They moved about in their vast primeval world to a surprising extent. Ever on the alert to obtain new articles by the pleasant game of barter, their first meeting with a strange white-skinned tribe, arriving in huge winged boats, seemed to them a rare opportunity for trade.

The first explorers from Europe introduced themselves to the natives through trade. They were welcomed with songs and dances because of the wonderful iron articles, blankets, guns and ornaments which they offered in exchange for Indian furs.

I. The French in North America

CHAPTER I

The Curtain Rises

[Sixteenth Century]

THE copper-skinned children of North America lived undisturbed in their magnificent land for many a long century. Most historians believe that Norsemen were the first
Europeans to reach the shores of the continent, five hundred
years before Columbus found the lovely islands in the Carib-
bean Sea and thought that he had discovered the Indies.

The Norsemen were adventurous seamen, sailing far from
home in northern waters beset by fogs, icebergs and storms. It
is certain that they had colonies in Iceland and Greenland during the ninth and tenth centuries A.D. from which they investigated the seas westward. Norse sagas tell of the explorations of heroes, particularly those of Leif, son of Eric the Red.

In 1000 A.D. this Viking hero sailed from Greenland in his
high-prowed ship to discover an inhospitable icy shore, probably Labrador. Onward he sailed southward, until he reached
a warm and pleasant land called Vineland by the Norse discoverers. This may have been Prince Edward Island, Cape
Breton or, as some believe, Cape Cod.

The sagas tell of visits to Vineland for timber, of meetings
and trade with savages. Small groups of Norsemen remained
on the shore of Vineland for a time, but settlements did not
last. The stories of Vineland may be merely a part of hero
sagas, but it seems likely that these men of the north really did

reach the continent and make use of what they found. Norse visits were of no particular importance to the future of North America because no permanent settlement resulted from them.

In the fifteenth century, European nations had advanced sufficiently that men's minds turned with curiosity to what might lie beyond their shores. They knew already of exotic Eastern lands through the travels of Marco Polo. Silks, spices and jewels came to Europe by long roundabout routes from lands that were called Cipangu and Cathay. Europeans were seeking routes to the East, other than those controlled by the Turkish Empire.

Daring navigators, having accepted the theory that the earth is round, were venturing westward, toward the close of the fifteenth century, into unknown seas.

Columbus was not the only Genoese who dreamed of reaching the fabled East by sailing west. A fellow Genoese, called John Cabot by the English, was an experienced navigator and geographer. Having failed to interest Spain and Portugal in his theories he, with his son Sebastian, came to England with a proposal for a voyage of discovery to the west. They reached Bristol at about the time when Columbus, having won the support of Queen Isabella, made his first voyage.

Bristol at that time was a seaport, second only to London in importance. Wealthy merchants of the town employed the fishing fleets to sail to Iceland for codfish to be sold in northern Europe. A Catholic population, having many meatless fast days, was a profitable market for fish, so that the merchants flourished and the seamen sailed farther and farther in search of new fishing grounds.

When the news of Columbus' discoveries burst on a startled Europe, John Cabot found a ready response to his proposals from the merchants of Bristol. They presented him to King

Henry VII who was willing to try for the discovery of new lands, provided he did not have to pay for it. He agreed to furnish a ship and crew for a voyage westward, but the expenses of fitting out an expedition were to be borne by the explorers.

Full of hope John Cabot with his three sons, Sebastian, Lewis and Sancius, set out in May, 1497, with a single ship and, after leaving Iceland, sailed westward into uncharted seas. They sighted the coast of Newfoundland in June, and sailing southward came to pleasant wooded shores, so delightful that Cabot was encouraged to think he was on the way to Cathay. He had probably reached Cape Breton Island. Lack of provisions prevented the explorers from following up their discovery and they reluctantly returned to England. They reported a fair land with useful timber and cod so plentiful they could be drawn up by the basketful.

John Cabot was made much of in England. Decked in fine robes he became a noted figure at Court and was given the title of the Great Admiral. Better yet, the king was sufficiently enthusiastic to give Cabot permission for another voyage, this time with six of the royal ships.

Confidently John and Sebastian Cabot set sail once more in the spring of 1498, but this time luck was against them. Voyaging southward from the forbidding shores of Labrador they probably skirted a good deal of the Atlantic coast, still searching for Cathay. There was no cartographer aboard, however, to map what they had seen. The ships were separated by storms and some were lost. John Cabot had no maps to show the king and, since he had found nothing more exciting than forests, Henry VII lost interest.

John Cabot, the first European after the Norsemen to set foot on North American soil, was no longer honored and disappeared in obscurity. His son Sebastian, however, became one of the great navigators of the age in the service of Charles I of Spain.   Cabot had raised the flag of England in North America, nevertheless, and from his discoveries England later based her claims to Nova Scotia.

His voyages had proved that the ocean could be crossed from northern Europe, so the fishing fleets sailed boldly westward, finding multitudes of codfish off the shores of what they called the New Found Island.   Fishermen of France and Portugal followed the English to the Grand Banks off Newfoundland during the early years of the sixteenth century, bringing back cod to fish-eating Europe, but paying little attention to inhospitable shores.   They entered the harbors to dry fish and repair their ships, but did not explore.

The Portuguese, who were the most successful navigators of the age, sailed to the north after they learned of John Cabot's voyages.   They had discovered a route to the fabled East by sailing around Africa, but the King of Portugal hoped to discover an easier route to the north.   Gaspar Corte-Real, a nobleman of the Azores, made voyages with his brother but both men were eventually lost at sea and Portugal gained from their explorations only further knowledge of the good fishing grounds off Newfoundland.

Francis I of France was the next monarch to take an interest in North America.   During the early part of the sixteenth century he and the Emperor Charles, who was also Charles I of Spain, were resplendent rulers, rivals for power and glory. Spanish explorers, following Columbus, were bringing to King Charles the golden wealth of Mexico and Francis I determined to try for a share of rich new lands.   For his first attempt he chose an Italian navigator, Giovanni da Verrazano, who followed with his small ships the Atlantic coastline, from North Carolina to the Penobscot River.   He was commissioned to find wealth for King Francis and to search for a passage to Asia and its treasures, through what men were then aware was a new continent. Portugal was already developing an eastern empire by her route around Africa and Spain controlled the Straits of Magellan, leading to the Pacific Ocean. Francis I hoped to find another route to the East north of Florida.

So, for the first time, appears the dream of the Northwest Passage. Verrazano's voyage was the beginning of the search for it, which was to occupy the minds of kings and explorers for centuries.

His report to King Francis described beautiful wooded shores and simple, unimpressive natives, but he had found no sign of gold. He did, however, discover Chesapeake Bay and jumped to the conclusion that it must be a sea leading to the Gulf of California, then called the Vermilion Sea. For some years maps were drawn showing the Sea of Verrazano occupying the central part of the continent.

No native empires had been discovered and Francis was so involved with wars and rivalries in Europe that he let ten years go by before making another attempt to claim part of the New World for France.

French mariners of Brittany and Normandy were as hardy and venturesome as any who sailed the seas at that time. From their little ports on the Channel they were already accustomed to crossing the Atlantic to fish for cod off Newfoundland. When Francis I decided on another voyage of discovery he chose for captain one of these men, an experienced navigator of the old Breton seaport of Saint Malo.

This man, Jacques Cartier, born of a seafaring family, was a master pilot of Saint Malo. There is no authentic portrait of the discoverer of Canada, but we may imagine him as a sturdy, weatherbeaten Breton. He was a man of courage and experience on the sea, who was devoted to the service of the king.

On April 20, 1534, Jacques Cartier, commanding two small ships, set sail from Saint Malo. He had doubtless made the western voyage before to the cod-fishing grounds, so the fogs and storms of those waters did not dismay him. The ships skirted the grim shores of Newfoundland, went through the rough passage between Newfoundland and Labrador, and sailed southwestward in the immense Gulf of St. Lawrence. To a man looking for exotic kingdoms the prospect was discouraging. "I believe this to be the land God allotted to Cain," Cartier wrote in the story of his voyage.

Soon, however, they sighted pleasant verdure-clad islands and passed into another large body of water. Frail bark canoes filled with savages, smeared with colored paints and draped in furs, came from the shores to swarm around the ships. Cartier cast anchor and went ashore with his men to meet the excited chattering natives. They willingly exchanged their fur robes for the strangers' knives, and the chief strutted proudly in the red cap Cartier set upon his head.

The Frenchmen were delighted with this land, so different from the rocky shores and islands they had first seen. In the sunshine their sea-weary eyes rejoiced in flowers and tall wild grasses while they feasted on juicy berries. Cartier explored the shores of the bay, hoping to find that it led into the continent, but to his disappointment it proved to be landlocked.

Naming it Baie de Chaleur for its pleasant warmth, the explorer sailed northward again in the wild green waters of the Gulf, trying to make his way around Gaspé Peninsula. Gales and storms blocked the little ships from continuing and they did not find the great river on the other side of the peninsula. They passed a tall cliff, jutting out into the sea like the prow of a ship, and took refuge in Gaspé Bay.

Jacques Cartier knew now that they had found new land for France. He and his men constructed a great cross of timber thirty feet high. They planted it in the earth, hanging on a cross beam a shield with the fleur-de-lis of France and the carved words "Vive le Roy de France." Then, kneeling about it with hands raised in prayer, these devout Frenchmen praised God for the land they had claimed for their king.

The chattering natives were awed into silence by this ceremony, but presently, their chief made a long harangue to Cartier, pointing out that the land belonged to him and his people. Nothing daunted, the explorer explained that the cross was intended to guide ships coming to trade. He gave point to his words by presenting the Indian with a hatchet. The chief could not resist such a wonderful weapon and the people were all beguiled by presents of wine and food. Cartier dressed two of the chief's sons in the irresistible red caps and French shirts. He indicated that he would like to take the boys with him to France and, strangely enough, the chief consented.

Presently the natives stood on the shore to watch the winged ships disappear, bearing two of their own people into the unknown. They had the strangers' knives, however, and the Frenchmen had their beaver and bear skins. The fur trade in North America had begun.

Storms and the lateness of the season forced Jacques Cartier to sail home with his tale of discovery, his trophies of furs and two Indian boys. There was excitement on the wharves of old Saint Malo when the sailors told the story of their voyage, and more interest the next year when ships were fitting out for another voyage to the new land.

Francis I commissioned Jacques Cartier to continue his explorations, this time with three little ships — the *Grande Hermine, Petite Hermine* and *Emerillon*. They set out on a voyage

of discovery as momentous as that of three other tiny ships —
the *Niña, Pinta* and *Santa Maria.*   Jacques Cartier expected to
find either a kingdom or the Northwest Passage.   He did not
know that he was to be the first white man to sail into the interior of the continent by its matchless gateway, the noble St.
Lawrence River.

With the explorer went the two Indians to act as interpreters.
Sophisticated they were now, speaking French, and wearing
French clothes.   When the ships had followed the route of the
first voyage into the gulf which Cartier named for St. Lawrence
the Indians guided the mariners past the Gaspé Peninsula into
the great river itself.

As the green salt waves hissed under the prow of his ship,
Cartier felt confident that he had found the way around the
continent to the riches of Asia.

They came to the mouth of the Saguenay River and saw bark
canoes full of savages dancing like dry leaves on the rough
foaming waters where the Saguenay meets the powerful St.
Lawrence.   The Indians had a rendezvous for fishing and trading at the spot they called Tadoussac, the junction of the two
rivers.   They were assembled there for the summer fishing.
Great was their astonishment at the sight of the ship and its
strange crew.   After venturing a little way up the dark, mysterious Saguenay, Cartier returned to the larger river.

On they went: three tiny ships lost on the vast bosom of a
waterway too mighty to be a river.   When they neared the
shore immense cliffs towered above them, or densely forested
mountainsides descended steeply to the water's edge.   They
saw white whales gambolling in the river and walruses on the
rocks.

The silence and solitude, the primeval grandeur of this fresh
new world, must have been overpowering to the Frenchmen,

used to the small compactness of their homeland. The landscape became more friendly as they advanced, and they passed
a long island so verdant and cheerful with its meadows, grape-
vines and beautiful trees that Cartier named it the Isle of Bac-
chus. Later it became the Île d'Orléans.

Beyond, they saw the river sweeping around a steep lofty headland. They were the first white men to set eyes upon the great
promontory of Quebec. At the foot of the cliffs they saw an
Indian village among the trees.

Indian warriors, befeathered and painted, paddled around the
ships while their chief, Donnacona, stood up in his canoe and
made a dramatic oration. Vociferous greetings burst out when
the Indians recognized Cartier's two young guides as members
of their tribe. The sailors handed down food and wine to the
canoes while Cartier distributed bright trinkets. The strangers
were properly introduced by the Indian interpreters and welcomed to the village of Stadacona. The Indians of this village
belonged to the Huron-Iroquois people.

Through his interpreters Cartier could now get the information he sought about this wondrous land. When he asked the
name of the country the Indians replied with a word which the
French understood as Canada. It was probably the Iroquois
word *kanata* meaning village, but the French accepted the name
and Canada the land became forthwith. Anxious to make an
impression on their visitors the Indians spoke vaguely of a rich
Kingdom of Saguenay somewhere in the wilderness, and said
that the river ran on farther than men had ever seen. Farther
up the stream, they told Cartier, there was another Indian town,
Hochelaga.

After building a small log fort on the bank of a rivulet opposite Stadacona, Cartier prepared for a voyage to see Hochelaga. This was strenuously opposed by the Indians, who were

entranced with the iron tools and bright trinkets of the French and wanted them all for themselves. Donnacona offered Cartier several Indian children if the visitors would remain with them, and when that failed to work the Frenchmen were visited by a canoe full of dancing, shrieking creatures masked as devils, who warned them against the people of Hochelaga.

Still, to the Indians' disgust, Cartier persisted in his plan. He left the two large ships and some of the crew, sailing onward in the small *Emerillon* with a few companions. The banks of the river were luxuriant in vegetation and the woodlands aflame with the autumn colors of hardwood trees among the spruce and pine. It was a gorgeous country indeed that they had found.

They reached a place where other streams joined the great river, winding about islands, one of which was crowned by a wooded mountain. While they were at anchor during the night, the wilderness was disturbed by the yelping chants of Indian warriors who built great fires on the shore and danced around them. The naked bodies, leaping in the flickering fire-light, and the din of their shrieks made more awesome the mysterious darkness surrounding them.

Next morning when Cartier and his companions set out in a small boat Indians waded into the water to carry them ashore on their shoulders. They led the visitors by a beaten path through beautiful woodland to their town of Hochelaga. It was a well-constructed village of the Iroquois type, with long bark houses surrounded by a triple palisade of tree trunks. In open glades around it fields of maize and pumpkins were growing.

The godlike strangers were brought eagerly to the chief and invited to sit on furs around the council fire. Women and children crowded around them stroking their beards, touching their clothes and muskets. The Frenchmen responded courteously to the friendly welcome and Cartier distributed presents. Trustingly the sick people of the village were brought to the white chief who seemed to the Indians to be a powerful medicine man. Cartier did his best to play the part expected of him by making the sign of the Cross over the sufferers and preaching the Gospel to them.

One of the warriors led Cartier through the woods to the top of the mountain, which the Frenchman promptly named Mont Réal or Mount Royal. Happily he looked out upon an expanse of country beautiful enough to satisfy the most hopeful explorer. The shining river wound in and out among meadows, forests extended to the distant blue of mountains. The Indian, pleased that his land made such an impression upon the white stranger, spoke of the Kingdom of Saguenay, as the Indians of Stadacona had. There was no doubt in Cartier's mind but that the kingdom existed somewhere in that beautiful wilderness and that it would prove to have treasures. He had seen pieces of copper among the Indians' belongings, and they had given him to understand, by touching a gold whistle he wore, that they were acquainted with the metal. He knew now that the great river would not lead him to the Northwest Passage, for its water had turned fresh, but his imagination fastened on the kingdom to be found.

Great was the disappointment of the Hochelaga people when the strangers possessed of such desirable trinkets insisted on leaving them. They gathered on the shore to watch the *Emerillon* spread its sails and disappear down the river.

When Cartier reached Stadacona the early Canadian winter was setting in. It was too late to return to France so the men prepared to pass the winter as best they might in their fort and on the ships. These were frozen into solid ice in the river, and deep snow and bitter cold enveloped the land. The Frenchmen

wheedled some dried corn and pumpkins from the Indians by trade and experimented with that joy of Indian life, tobacco. Smoked in Indian pipes they found it very peppery, but it helped them in their days of hunger.

Soon the dread disease of that age, scurvy, began to take its toll.   One by one the men sickened and died and were secretly buried in the snowdrifts.   When Indians approached the fort the survivors kept up a great racket of shouting and hammering to deceive the savages as to their numbers.   They were always uneasy about the trustworthiness of their Indian neighbors across the rivulet.

Cartier, courageous, staunch and cheerful, kept up the spirits of his men to the best of his ability.   He fastened a small statue of the Virgin to a tree and there, amid the snowdrifts, the little band of white men comforted themselves with prayers.   Cartier learned from a friendly Indian that an infusion of the bark and needles of the spruce would cure the scurvy and, by this means, some of the men recovered.

As spring approached, a suspicious number of strange Indians began to gather at Stadacona.   The Frenchmen were convinced the Indians were preparing to murder them for their knives, pots and other treasures at the first opportunity.

At last the ice thawed and broke up, the ships were free, and preparations were made for the return voyage.   With such reduced numbers it was not possible to man all the ships so one was left behind.   When they were ready to leave, Cartier invited the chief, Donnacona, on board for a final feast.   He kept the Indian occupied with food, wine and oratory while, by his orders, the sailors got up sail and the ships glided down the river with the kidnapped Indian on board.

If Cartier could not bring his king gold, he at least brought rumors of treasure and an exhibit in the person of the chief, Donnacona.

In 1536 Jacques Cartier was safe at home in Saint Malo once more. The Indian chief was received at Court, dressed in French finery and taught to speak French. Francis I, however, was not sufficiently impressed with the results of Cartier's explorations to send another expedition until five years had passed.

Meanwhile the homesick Indian languished for his free wilderness. Hoping to be sent back to guide Europeans to chimerical treasures, he invented stories of the Kingdom of Saguenay, embroidering his tales with childlike imagination. He had discovered how much white men valued the gold and jewels he saw at the French Court, so to Indian legends of weird people were added the glitter of gold and treasure.

Donnacona died in exile, but his romancing about the Kingdom of Saguenay finally caught the king's ear. Francis was increasingly jealous of the wealth coming to the Spanish monarch from Mexico and Peru. He realized, also, that it would be wise to establish his claim to Canada by making a settlement.

In 1541 a large expedition was prepared, with the double purpose of settling colonists and finding treasure. The Sieur de Roberval was appointed viceroy of the colony he was to found, while Cartier was to be the explorer of the expedition. The two leaders clashed from the start, the ships were separated and each man went his own way. The Sieur de Roberval did settle an unfortunate band of colonists on the shore where they suffered such hardships that Cartier was sent, two years later, to bring the survivors home.

The discoverer of Canada, meanwhile, pursued the will-o'-the-wisp of Indian tales up the Saguenay and the St. Lawrence, still believing firmly in the existence of the mythical Kingdom of Saguenay. He found nothing more valuable than a small amount of gold and some glittering stones which he thought were diamonds.

The costly expedition had been a failure and the king was too much involved in war with Spain to pay further attention to Canada. Jacques Cartier never saw again the glorious land he had found for France. For fifty years New World empire was forgotten while France was torn by devastating wars of religion between Huguenots and Catholics.

Save for visits from fishermen and individual fur traders, the Indians of the St. Lawrence pursued their usual savage life of fishing, hunting and warfare. The wilderness waited, serene and undisturbed, for the next invasion of empire seekers.

CHAPTER II

The French Seek Empire in North America
[Seventeenth Century]

FURS and fisheries kept alive in France the memory of Canada and the great river. Every summer Basque and Breton fishing fleets came to the Gulf of St. Lawrence and the lower river to catch seals and the whales and walruses from which they obtained the oil called "train" used for lighting.

The little cove of Tadoussac beside the mouth of the Saguenay River made a convenient place for the fishermen to boil the blubber and barrel the oil for return voyages. On the shore, before the dark ranks of forest trees, Indians set up their wigwams in the summer and their canoes swarmed around the French vessels lying at anchor. Cartier's visits had introduced to the natives the knives, hatchets and iron kettles that lightened so much the labors of their primitive existence. They would trade anything they had — fish, meat, tobacco, furs — for these precious articles. The fishermen found it profitable to do a lively trade in furs while they were at Tadoussac and skins of bears, foxes, wolverene and beaver found their way to France every year. When hatmakers discovered that the soft inner fur of the beaver was the perfect material for the swaggering wide-brimmed hats then fashionable, the Indians had a market for all the beaver they could trap, and the fur trade was well under way.

At the beginning of the seventeenth century this trading was brought under the control of the French Crown by Henry of Navarre who had come to the throne as Henry IV. He was engaged in making France a great nation after the destructive years of religious warfare and believed in the value of overseas empire. Henry IV devised the scheme of accomplishing settlement without cost to the Crown by giving the monopoly of the fur trade to ambitious gentlemen on condition that they bring settlers to people the country. For exploration he chose young Samuel de Champlain who had served in his army during the recent wars and who was sailor as well as soldier, passionately devoted to navigation. Champlain had spent much of his youth at sea and, after the wars, King Henry sent him in command of a fleet to visit the West Indies and Mexico.

On that voyage the wide-awake young Frenchman had his first taste of exploration among strange lands and their people, a pursuit which was to become the passion of his life. He wrote a vivid story of his experiences illustrated with naïve drawings of scenery, natives and animals. His romantic spirit was captivated by colorful natives and credulously convinced by tales of monsters. After going ashore on the Isthmus of Panama he noted that if a canal were built across the narrow strip of land it would shorten the voyage to Asia and make it unnecessary to find a Northwest Passage.

In 1603 Samuel de Champlain made his first voyage to Canada for King Henry. He accompanied the Sieur de Pontgravé, a Huguenot gentleman who was to engage in the fur trade at Tadoussac, on a voyage to the St. Lawrence River. While Pontgravé dealt with the Indians Champlain explored the Saguenay, marveling at the depth of its dark waters and the imposing headlands which were later named Cape Trinity and Cape Eternity.

The next year he was at sea again, accompanying another group of gentlemen traders, this time with the commission to explore the Atlantic coast. A Huguenot gentleman, the Sieur de Monts, had received from the king the monopoly of the fur trade, with the command to colonize as well as trade. The Sieur de Pontgravé was also a member of the expedition.

The explorers skirted the coast of Nova Scotia and sailed southward to a river they named St. Croix, now the boundary between Maine and New Brunswick. There, on an island, Champlain decided to build a fort and spend the winter. It was an unfortunate choice, for floating ice cut them off from the mainland and from hunting during the freezing weather. They nearly starved and their supplies froze. Good Normandy cider was issued to the men in chunks. Many of the company died of scurvy before spring released them from their sufferings.

De Monts returned to France for supplies and more colonists while Champlain and Pontgravé sailed in search of a better site. The navigator explored the Bay of Fundy, noting its tremendous tides, and discovered the Saint John River with its remarkable reversing falls. Then he sailed through a narrow gap between cliffs, now called Digby Gut, and found himself in a great protected basin where, he wrote enthusiastically, "two thousand ships could shelter in safety." He named the bay Port Royal.

The log huts on St. Croix Island were pulled down and transported to a site on the shore of this bay near the mouth of a small river. It was 1605 when Champlain and his men started to build the first little French Habitation in North America.

That was Champlain's name for the combination of fort and dwelling place which he designed and built at Port Royal, and later at Quebec. He set the men to cutting down trees and hewing them into timbers for the hollow square of small buildings with steep wooden roofs. Two bastions were built, one on either side of the gateway, with platforms for cannon. The plans were preserved with Champlain's narratives of his voyages, and the Habitation has been accurately rebuilt on the site of the original settlement that visitors today may see how Frenchmen lived in their first North American home.

Soon De Monts returned from France with a fine shipload of colonists. He had with him the Baron de Poutrincourt, a patriotic Frenchman whose chief aim was to colonize for France, not to make profit from furs, and the witty, learned Marc Lescarbot, a lawyer and man of letters. We owe to his lively, entertaining narrative, *History of New France,* the human story of Port Royal in its first years. Frenchmen at home had heard the sad tale of the winter on St. Croix Island. "That country was so cried down that everyone commiserated us on the misfortunes of those who had already been there," says Lescarbot.

Nevertheless the newcomers were delighted with the situation on the brink of the long bay, sheltered by two lines of hills. Salt hay meadows fringed the shores and the fields behind them sloped up to dense woodland.

The colonists set to work to clear the fields and plant wheat, rye and barley. Champlain constructed ditches from brooks to his meadows and stocked them with fish, so that seafood would be always ready at hand. He built in the meadows a little summer house for the pleasure of the company and writes of its charm, how the little birds gathered there, "warbling and chirping so pleasantly that I think I never heard the like."

Leaving Marc Lescarbot in charge, the other leaders accompanied Champlain of the itching foot on a voyage of exploration along the coast. As Royal Geographer he charted shores and bays, and as wide-awake traveler he made friends with the natives, noting their villages and their fields of maize and squash.

Meanwhile Marc Lescarbot directed the work of the farmers, for he was a firm believer in cultivating the earth rather than searching for metals. He employed his time also in composing a pageant to welcome the voyagers on their return, and trained the soldiers to play parts in it.

When the ship of the explorers anchored before Port Royal, Champlain and his company were astounded to behold the *Theatre of Neptune* performed on the water front in the classic style of the period, the first theatrical show in North America. Wreaths of laurel had been twined around the shield of France above the gateway to welcome them back to Port Royal.

As winter approached, Champlain devised a scheme to keep the colonists healthy and happy during the months of cold and snow. He instituted the Order of Good Cheer, accepted enthusiastically by officers and men alike. Each day a member of the Order was appointed chief steward, charged with the responsibility of providing fish or game for their meals. The hunters, Indian and French, brought in ducks, geese, partridges, moose, beaver, rabbits and other game. The chief steward directed the cooks as they prepared the game into savory French dishes.

At night, when the officers gathered in their common room before a blazing log fire in a huge stone fireplace, friendly Micmac Indians crowded into the room to see the show and receive their dole of bread. The chief steward, wearing around his neck the collar of the Order, carrying a wand and with a napkin over his shoulder, marched in from the kitchen. After him came the other members, each bearing a smoking dish.

Indian families squatted against the walls, solemnly watching this scene of feasting and merriment as the wine cups were passed around, and Frenchmen entertained themselves with good food and lively talk. Their chief, Membertou, and some of his warriors ate at the table with the officers.

Marc Lescarbot says their food equaled that of their favorite cook shop in Paris in the Rue aux Ours. He speaks of the excellent pasties of moose meat and remarks that nothing is so delicate as beaver's tail.

For two years these gallant Frenchmen raised their crops and brought Gallic wit and French manners to their home in a primitive land. Until 1607 they were the only Europeans on the whole Atlantic coast north of Florida. Then the English founded a colony at Jamestown in Virginia and the rivalry between French and English on the coast soon began.

If Port Royal had been supported by the home government the French might have developed a thriving agricultural colony in Acadie as they named the country, from the Micmac word *akade,* meaning region. But the king left his American possessions to the fur traders and there was rivalry between Catholic and Huguenot gentlemen for the profits in fur. Even on the voyages across the ocean men of differing religious beliefs were always quarreling. The Catholics objected to the psalm-singing of the Protestants and they in turn resented the preaching of the Catholic priests. De Monts was a Huguenot and his claim to the fur trade was opposed by ambitious Catholic gentlemen.

In 1607 a ship from France brought sad news to the industrious Frenchmen in Acadie. De Monts had lost his monopoly of the fur trade and Port Royal must be abandoned. Regretfully the colonists left their fine fields and cosy Habitation, taking with them samples of grain to show the king what they had accomplished. Membertou and his tribe, devoted friends of the French, mourned their departure and promised to take care of the buildings until they could return. The first sojourn at Port Royal was a delightful, cheerful episode, unlike the struggles with cold, hunger and Indians which were to be the lot of Frenchmen on the St. Lawrence.

Baron de Poutrincourt and his son Biencourt, still set on colonizing, returned before long to be welcomed by the aged Membertou and his people. Then in 1613, while the men were at work in distant fields, English ships appeared in the basin. Samuel Argall of Virginia had been exploring the coast and was determined to wipe out the French foothold. The buildings were burned and the people scattered to live among the Indians.

Port Royal was rebuilt after a while at the head of Annapolis Basin, where the ruins of the English Fort Anne stand today, and there were a few other forts in Acadie. Acadian farmers cultivated their fields and fruit orchards around Minas Basin. But for a hundred years Port Royal changed hands frequently, as England and France made war or peace in Europe, or as Acadians and New Englanders clashed over fisheries and farmlands.

Meanwhile, Champlain, after starting Port Royal, set out on his life work of exploration and empire building for France.

In 1608 he was once more on the St. Lawrence, accompanied by Pontgravé and De Monts who had obtained a new monopoly for trade on the St. Lawrence. Tadoussac was rejected as a site for settlement because of its poor soil and wild winter storms.

Leaving the traders to gather furs at this accustomed meeting place with the Indians, Champlain sailed on up the river Cartier called "the ready way to Canada." The mighty stream and its shores were as magnificent in their solitude and grandeur as they had been when Cartier, the discoverer, passed that way more than half a century before. There was no trace of Stadacona below the promontory. The village had been destroyed in Indian warfare and its Huron-Iroquois people driven away by tribes of the Algonquian nation who inhabited the shores in their stead.

Champlain chose the shore at the foot of the cliffs for his Habitation, a more elaborate structure than the one he had designed for Port Royal. He describes how he went about it: "I at once employed a part of our workmen in cutting down trees that we might construct our Habitation there: one I set to sawing boards, another to making a cellar and digging ditches, another I sent to Tadoussac with the barque for supplies. The first thing we made was the storehouse for keeping under cover our supplies, which was promptly accomplished through the zeal of all and my attention to the work. . . I had a gallery made all around our buildings, on the outside at the second storey, also ditches fifteen feet wide and six feet deep. On the outer side of the ditches spurs with places for cannon, and good gardens around the Habitation."

Thus did this wise and steadfast Frenchman lay the foundations for king and country of Kebec — "the place where the waters narrow" — in the Algonquian Indian language. In their small wooden fort below the towering cliff the little band of Frenchmen were surrounded by silent wilderness; their only neighbors were unstable savages who vanished and reappeared like birds according to the season.

The Indians camped in bark huts outside the Habitation during the autumn while they were fishing for eels, drying and smoking them for winter food. Then they disappeared in the forests for their winter hunt of moose, deer and beaver. Champlain notes that in cold weather the savages were completely clothed in skins of the animals they hunted and that they wore large oval snowshoes for traveling. Frenchmen adopted these as soon as they began getting about in winter woods.

Only eight out of one hundred and twenty-eight men survived the cold, hunger and scurvy of that first winter at Quebec, but Champlain was undismayed. When ships came in the spring to reinforce the garrison and bring supplies, he organized life at the fort and then set off with friendly Indians to discover more of the country.

He had an inveterate love of exploring untrodden wilderness and great interest in the natives. From his first meeting with the Indians Champlain took a fatherly interest in them, studied their manners, customs and superstitions, learned their language and made them his friends. He was a man of sincere piety whose concern for the conversion of the savages was as keen as his dream of a great New France in America.

From the natives Champlain learned of the enmity existing between the Iroquois nations to the south and the Algonquian people who had gained possession of the St. Lawrence shores. They begged their powerful French friend to help them make war on the Iroquois. Irresistibly drawn by the unknown interior where, he was convinced, a great empire for France could be attained, Champlain decided that it was necessary for the French to ally themselves with the tribes of Canada. Otherwise, exploration of their country would be impossible. By becoming the friend of the Hurons and Algonquins Champlain paved the way for a century of war with the implacable Iroquois, but he also opened the path into the continent to the French.

With a few companions the explorer set out in the canoes of his Indian friends, paddling slowly up the St. Lawrence. He saw Cartier's Mont Réal, but found that Hochelaga, like Stadacona, had disappeared. A fort for fur trading could be built on the shore of the island, he decided.

The Indian canoes went on through the Richelieu River into the great lake which was Iroquois territory and which was to

bear Champlain's name. When they sighted an Iroquois encampment on the shore the Algonquins camped near by. The
two bands of warriors danced and yelled all night around their
fires, shouting insults at one another in preparation for the battle next morning. When the Iroquois saw white men in armor
emerge from the woods, with fire-spitting weapons which killed
several of their chief warriors, they were so startled they ran
away. The Algonquins were pleased with the easy victory and
quite ready to return with Champlain to Quebec.

His first trip into the wilderness increased Champlain's interest and curiosity. For the next twenty-five years, whenever
he could break away from the cares of Quebec or was not in
France stirring up royal interest in New France, the explorer
made off into the woods and waterways with the Indians. He
was the first of many adventurous Frenchmen to endure the
smoke and filth of Indian lodges and to eat unappetizing con-
coctions ladled out of the cooking pots, while he smoked and
held council with copper-skinned warriors.

In his first confabs with them Indians had told him that tribes
of the north, who came down the Saguenay with their furs, saw
the salt sea in their home territory. They were speaking of
Hudson Bay, but Champlain believed that this sea must be the
way around the continent to Asia. He followed the dream of
finding that route through many a wild-goose chase in the forests. On one of these quests he went with Indian friends up
the Ottawa River and explored the country of the Hurons around
Georgian Bay.

Even while Champlain speculated about this northern sea
an explorer for England had discovered it. In 1610 Henry Hudson, in his ship the *Discovery,* sailed through Hudson Straits and
wintered on the shore of the great bay. He too was searching
for the Northwest Passage but his life came to an end in the

frozen solitudes. His mutinous crew set him adrift in the summer and returned home without him. His discovery led various other English sea captains to seek the Passage in the ice-clogged waters of Hudson Bay, without success. So the dream of the route around the continent in the north continued to occupy the minds of explorers.

Meanwhile Quebec grew but slowly. France had two outposts in North America, Quebec and Port Royal, but they were separated by thousands of miles of trackless wilderness. Indians followed the Saint John River through the interior to reach Tadoussac on the St. Lawrence, but that was an almost impossible route. The only other way the colonies could communicate was by a long dangerous sea voyage.

The monarchs and gentlemen traders did little to develop Acadie, or Acadia as it came to be called, for their interest was only in the furs to be obtained. Port Royal changed hands so frequently, the settlers were so harassed by local wars, that the land could not become a strong colony.

At one time, while the English were in control, King James I gave Acadia to a Scotch nobleman, Sir William Alexander, to be colonized. The land was named Nova Scotia and given a flag and coat-of-arms which, by the way, Nova Scotia retains to this day. The Baronets of Nova Scotia were supposed to send settlers to their lands, but Scottish colonizing did not succeed. Before long Acadia was in French hands once more.

The St. Lawrence, however, was the route to the fur trade of a continent and Champlain had some success in getting help for Quebec. He never lost courage or faith, although the trading companies who controlled the colony gave him no assistance. Their object was to trade in furs with the Indians, not to found a settlement. The obligation to colonize was never fulfilled and the few people who came to the wilds of the St. Lawrence were not good colonists. The inhabitants of the cluster of wooden houses below the cliff were soldiers and adventurers, rather than people in search of new homes. They had no interest in cultivating the earth and many preferred the life of the forests, hunting and trapping with the Indians. The colony was dependent on the yearly ships from France for supplies, since they grew so little of their food. Often they went hungry, living on dried eels or the game they could kill.

There was, however, one good farmer at Quebec in those early years, a friend of Champlain's from the days of the Order of Good Cheer at Port Royal. Louis Hébert was a Parisian apothecary who had come with De Monts to that short-lived settlement. He returned to Paris and later, when Champlain urged him to come to Quebec, Louis Hébert closed up his Paris business and, with his wife and children, embarked once more to be a pioneer. He was to serve the settlers with his herbs and drugs, but was also to be allotted land for the farming he loved.

While the other colonists remained in the cramped settlement below the cliffs, Louis Hébert climbed up to the top and there, with prodigious labor, he cleared the trees from his land and planted crops. Before long his farm on the heights was the only thriving, cosy place in the rough settlement. He had a stout stone farmhouse surrounded with fields of grain and pastures for his cattle. There were few women in early Quebec so that it must have been a lonely life for Madame Hébert and her daughters. They were good pioneers, however, who made the farmhouse a warm little center of civilization.

Champlain built a fort and governor's house on the cliff-top and there he brought his young wife Hélène from France. It was a rough life for a delicately reared lady but she occupied herself in teaching little Indian girls and probably found companionship with Madame Hébert and her daughters.

While the English colonies on the Atlantic coast grew rapidly because the settlers were people who came to build homes and remain in the land, Quebec was small and poor, with scarcely a hundred inhabitants. The post was defenseless when the English, with an eye to the fur trade, sent a fleet up the river in 1629 during a war between France and England.

Champlain had to see the lilies of France hauled down and was himself taken prisoner. When peace was made a year later, however, Quebec was returned to France. Charles I of England traded it for the dowry of his French wife which had not been paid.

Cardinal Richelieu, the shrewd minister of Louis XIII, realized the importance of New France. He organized a trading company, called the One Hundred Associates, which was to have control of the fur trade and fisheries on condition that settlers were sent out and given grants of land to cultivate. Champlain returned to Quebec in 1633 as governor of reorganized New France. This courageous and devoted leader, who had served France without thought of profit for himself, had only two years left in which to guide the destinies of the colony. He died on Christmas Day, 1635, in the town he had founded on the promontory.

After Champlain passed from the scene other French explorers, throughout the seventeenth century, carried the banner of France farther and farther into the interior. Not the least among them were valiant missionaries who combined their desire to save the souls of savages with a love of exploration. They learned to travel with the Indians on foot over forest trails and by canoe on waterways. Not only did they explore rivers, but they were the first white men to see some of the Great Lakes.

Father Allouez traversed the lakes to the shores of Lake Superior, where he and other priests built their mission near the rushing rapids which they called Sault Sainte Marie.   After the missionaries had led the way King Louis XIV, in 1671, sent a French officer, St. Lusson, to establish French claim to the north-west.   Children of the wilderness, barbarically painted and clad in skins, joined with French soldiers and missionaries in a vivid pageant staged on the heights above Sault Sainte Marie.   After raising a great cross with the shield of the lilies of France, St. Lusson announced the claim of Louis XIV to practically the whole continent, so far as they could conceive of it.   After the priests had celebrated Mass the whole company took part in a great Indian feast and dance.

The Sulpician priest, Dollier de Casson, with a young deacon, Galinée, explored Lake Ontario and wintered on the shore of Lake Erie.   Snug in their bark hut, they survived the cold successfully and, before they left, another cross was raised to claim the lakes for France.   In the spring they crossed Lake Erie, reached Sault Sainte Marie, and returned by way of Lake Huron and Georgian Bay.   Writing the story of their adventures Dollier de Casson spoke enthusiastically of "this earthly Paradise of Canada."

Father Marquette, one of the gentlest and most spiritual of these intrepid men, spent years of missionary work and exploration on the shores of the lakes.   Then, with the trader Louis Joliet, he went on a long journey of exploration which led them to the Indians' Great Water, the Mississippi.   They paddled down its broad stream to its junction with the Arkansas.

The man who was to extend France's claim to the Father of Waters was in New France in 1667.   René Robert Cavelier de La Salle came to Canada as one of the seigneurs who were given large grants of land.   For a year or two he was busy on his estate, La Chine, above Montreal.

Urged on by love of exploration and great schemes for the

fur trade, La Salle was soon following forest trails and rivers with the Indians. He was one of the greatest of explorers, undaunted by the hardships of the wilderness, and courageous enough to surmount the disappointments and misfortunes which beset him. La Salle was an empire builder for France although his patriotism was not so unselfish as that of Champlain. He was a man driven by the spirit of adventure and by desire for wealth and power.

Eventually he accomplished the feat of following the Mississippi to its mouth. Some of the forts he built along the route to obtain the furs of the interior became important outposts for the French, such as Cataraqui which soon became Fort Frontenac, on the site of Kingston, and Saint Louis at the junction of the Missouri and the Mississippi.

His last and greatest adventure, the attempt to found a colony at the mouth of the Mississippi, ended in disaster. He brought colonists by ship from France, but missed the delta of the river and finally landed on the coast of Texas. Wandering hopelessly in the wilderness, most of the men died and mutinous survivors turned against La Salle, shooting him from ambush. The bones of the explorer rested in the country of his ambitious dreams.

France was served by men of courage and high resolve during that century of exploration. Many of them were inspired by devotion to France as well as the lure of the unknown. They had a greater vision of French empire in America than the monarchs who often failed to support them. Due to their far-flung journeyings France could claim the interior of the continent as well as its gateway, the St. Lawrence River.

CHAPTER III

Missionaries and Nuns
[Seventeenth Century]

MEN OF the Church followed Champlain to Quebec soon after its founding, and intrepid missionaries, as we have seen, often preceded other explorers into the unknown continent. The Recollet friars, a Franciscan order, were the first to come. By the year 1639 they, as well as the Jesuits, had their establishments at Quebec. Jesuit fathers were missionaries who came to Canada filled with a burning zeal to convert the Indians. Every year some came out with the fleet from France to undertake a life of hardship and loneliness in a primitive land.

A yearly report of their work was sent by the superior at Quebec to the headquarters of the Order in France. These *Relations,* written by men of intelligence and keen observation, were read with eagerness by nuns and priests and the pious nobility. In those narratives, which make fascinating reading even today, people in France learned of life in the outpost of Quebec and among a people of strange customs in the wilderness. They thrilled to tales of suffering and indignities nobly borne and of triumphs in winning souls for the Faith.

During the early seventeenth century a wave of religious exaltation was sweeping France, affecting not only men and women of the religious orders but devout nobles and aristocratic ladies who burned to advance the glory of God by founding missions and hospitals in New France. Mysterious Canada, with its mountains and rivers, its forests inhabited by heathen savages, haunted their imaginations as a world to be won for Christ and

His Church. Jesuit fathers longed for the order to go to Canada and nuns besieged the saints with prayers to be chosen for the work.

So it came about on a May day, in 1639, loungers on the quayside of Dieppe watched with curiosity the embarkation of a most unusual company, with the annual fleet for New France. Dignitaries of the town with their wives were there to wish Godspeed to the first nuns to undertake missionary work in Canada. Shepherded by Father Vimont, Superior of the Jesuits in Quebec, three Ursuline nuns were setting forth to found a convent of their Order, and three nursing nuns, under the patronage of the Duchesse d'Aiguillon, were to found a hospital in Quebec. Vivid silks and plumes of their aristocratic friends contrasted sharply with the severe black and white of religious habits as farewells were said.

In the harbor lay the small clumsy wooden ships of the seventeenth century, with high poop and stern. Sailors were at work in the rigging, preparing for departure, when the company of gentle ladies and their priestly guardian went aboard the ship *Saint Joseph,* rejoicing that their voyage would be under the special care of the patron of New France.

Anchors were raised, and under swelling sails the ships glided out of the harbor, followed by the prayers of nuns and priests in their cloisters and the hopes of pious benefactors.

For Mère Marie de l'Incarnation, Superior of the Ursuline nuns, that voyage meant the fulfillment of her greatest desire, that of founding a convent in Quebec for the teaching of Indian girls. Born Marie Guyart, she had joined the cloistered Order of the Ursulines after the death of her husband, separating herself from her beloved little boy, Claude, to give herself to God.

In her convent life the visions and prayers of the nun were concentrated on missionary work in Canada. Mère Marie de l'Incarnation was a mystic, but visionary contemplation was balanced by good sense and great practical ability.

While the nun prayed to be chosen for work in Canada, an emotional, impetuous young noblewoman, Madame de la Peltrie, was also consumed with the desire to devote herself and her wealth to founding a convent for work among the Indians at Quebec. Eventually she overcame the obstacles put in her way by her family and arrived at the convent of the Ursulines at Tours to choose nuns for her enterprise.

There she found Mère de l'Incarnation, and the meeting of the two women was a joyous recognition by each of the inspired partner for work they both wanted to do.

Two young and charming nuns, Cécile de Sainte Croix and Marie de Saint Joseph, were selected to accompany Mère Marie. They were as eager as their superior to leave their peaceful convents for a life of adversity about which they had no illusions. Indeed, they welcomed this mission to Canada as a great opportunity for achievement and sacrifice. Their patroness, Madame de la Peltrie, accompanied them on the journey across the sea.

When the little band of high-hearted women set sail from Dieppe on that May day, they looked forward with exaltation to their life of service in a primitive land. It took three months for the fleet of small ships to make the rough crossing of the Atlantic. The nuns were cramped in small quarters, seasick and sleepless, but they never complained. Father Vimont comforted them each day with the service of the Mass. As they drew near the coast, a huge iceberg loomed through the fog, looking to the voyagers like a terrifying castle of ice. It seemed as though the *Saint Joseph* was about to be crushed, but, by a quick change of course, all the ships escaped. The nuns were convinced that Saint Joseph himself had saved them.

At Tadoussac the ships lingered for trade, and the passengers were put aboard a small craft to continue their voyage to Quebec. The boat was piled high with dried, salted cod for the town, so the nuns and their patroness, after their long wearisome sea voyage, were submitted to another trial. For two weeks they had to live in close proximity to the odoriferous cargo and to subsist on the cod soaked in vinegar, while the boat beat its way up the river to Quebec. Their courage was still high, however, and they watched with wonder the mountainous forested shores and vast green river which tossed their little craft on its powerful current.

When the boat was sighted from the fort on the Rock a salvo of cannon greeted the wanderers. Pious Governor Montmagny marched to the wharf to welcome the nuns, accompanied by black-robed Jesuits, soldiers, traders and wild-looking Indians.

As soon as they set foot on shore the nuns fell on their knees, joyfully kissing the soil of Canada. They were led in procession up the steep winding trail to the top of the cliffs to hear Mass and sing a *Te Deum* of thanksgiving in the Jesuit chapel. Madame de la Peltrie and the nuns, rather self-conscious about their travel-stained robes, were entertained at dinner by the governor, to meet the few important personages of small Quebec.

The day ended with a thrilling celebration, for the ships had brought news of the birth of an heir to Louis XIII, the Dauphin who was to become Louis XIV, the first king to take a personal interest in New France. While the boom of cannon roused echoes in the cliffs across the river, a display of fireworks — stars, serpentines and candles — spangled the dark sky, to the wonder of the Hurons who hovered on the outskirts of the show.

From the peaceful dignity of their convent in France, the Ursulines came to a small log dwelling of two rooms on the shore near the cluster of wooden buildings which still composed most of Quebec. They accepted the rough quarters as good pioneers, wittily christening their log hut "the Louvre." Sister Cécile de Sainte Croix wrote to friends in France, "We have the most beautiful view in the world. Without leaving our room we see the ships come in. They anchor in front of our house all the time they remain." The nursing nuns were sheltered in the Jesuit mission house at Sillery, above Quebec, until a hospital could be built.

On the day after their arrival the Ursuline sisters and Madame de la Peltrie were taken to Sillery to hear the Huron converts chant and pray in their own language in the Jesuit chapel. These warm-hearted women were overjoyed by the first sight of the wild, dark little girls who were to be their charges. Madame de la Peltrie, always emotional, embraced and kissed every one, no matter how dirty they were, says the chronicle, and the nuns followed her example.

The Ursuline sisters set to work to make convent and school of their two-room hut. There was no privacy for these women used to the seclusion of convent cells. The little place was soon crowded with Indian girls, sleeping in bunks or on the floor. All the nuns had their courage and strength taxed to the utmost in the months following their arrival, for one of the frequent plagues broke out among the Indians. The hospital nuns and the Ursulines wore themselves to exhaustion, tending the sick and dying, thereby winning the affection and trust of the Indians.

It is a charming picture given by the chroniclers of these devoted women, gently nurtured and accustomed to the amenities of seventeenth-century French civilization at home. Madame de la Peltrie bathed dirty little savages, combed their tangled hair, and made dresses for them. Sister Marie de Saint Joseph, young and gay, could sing and play the viol. Music made a strong

appeal to the wild hearts of the forest children, so that she soon
had them singing sweetly with her to the music of the viol.

Not only did the nuns tend and teach the girls entrusted to
them, but the doors of the Louvre stood open all day to welcome any Indian, man, woman or child. The iron kettle
swung over the fire, filled with sagamité, the Indian porridge
made from pounded corn, boiled with scraps of meat or fish
when they had it. Their food supplies were limited but the
sagamité would be ladled out to any Indian who asked for it
as long as it lasted, even if the nuns themselves went hungry.

Within six years after their arrival Mère Marie and her companions, reinforced by sisters from France, were at home in a
small stone convent on the heights. They nearly froze during
the bitter winters, sleeping in beds closed in like cupboards,
and thawing their stiff fingers at intervals before the log fire in
one stone fireplace.

Ensconced in a small Hôtel-Dieu, forerunner of the splendid
hospital of today, the nursing nuns ministered with equally unselfish benevolence to sick Indians and settlers. They had little
to work with and must wait for the yearly ships from France
to bring them supplies and drugs. All the nuns lived in poverty, cheerfully performing the menial tasks of their households
as well as their endless work of teaching and nursing.

Mère Marie de l'Incarnation found time, despite her endless
duties, to learn the Indian languages and teach them to the
younger nuns. During her long life of service in Quebec, she
wrote a catechism and made dictionaries of the Huron and Algonquian tongues.

This accomplished woman came of a famous family of tap-
estry weavers, and in their convents Ursuline nuns were trained
in exquisite needlework. They missed the fine stuffs and embroidery silks of the art in their pioneer life, but made ingenious

use of native materials to teach needlework to their girls. Indian belts, adorned with dyed and flattened porcupine quills
worked into patterns, were an inspiration to these clever women
who developed an interesting art from a primitive craft. They
discovered that charming embroidery could be done with dyed
moose hair and with colored beads brought to Canada by the
traders. Indian materials and European beads, worked into
the fine flower of French design, created a unique art. Nimble-
fingered Indian girls of the school learned to embroider buckskin, wool or silk with graceful floral design, done with porcupine quills, moose hair or beads. When these girls returned to
their tribal homes the older women learned from them to ornament buckskin garments, moccasins and belts with this colorful embroidery. In the course of time a convent-bred French
art traveled, far ahead of white settlement, by trade from tribe
to tribe into the western wilderness.

Docile young Indian girls, who became Christians during their
sojourn with the Ursulines, brought their families into contact
with the gentle nuns and often converted their parents, so that
the civilizing influence of the convents spread far.

All the nuns were friendly, affectionate teachers, but Mère
Marie, moving among her nuns and flock of pupils, stately, calm
and serene, was adored by the small savages as their Mother.
Dignified though she was, they felt her maternal warmth.

The Jesuits, also, realized the importance of reaching the
primitive people through the young. As early as 1637 they had
begun a seminary for Huron boys. They had their troubles
with the wild young things of the forests, who tired very soon
of the disciplined life of study, work and prayer. The boys
took every opportunity to escape to the woods and the smoky
lodges of their families. Both the fathers and the nuns tried
to bring their converts into the French life of the settlement by

marriages beween their pupils, but it was a discouraging task. Before the end of her missionary work Mère Marie made the wise observation that it was easier for a Frenchman to become a savage than for an Indian to become a Frenchman.

While the Ursuline nuns were still in the first hard years of their work, religious fervor in France was leading to another missionary enterprise.

In Paris a young priest, Jacques Olier, while praying in the old church of Saint Germain des Près, heard voices from Heaven telling him that he was destined to found an order of priests on the island of Montreal in Canada. At the same time, in Anjou, a similar inspiration came to a good gentleman named Dauversière, while he was absorbed in prayer. Voices commanded him to found an order of nursing nuns on the faraway island. Both men were convinced that the commands to undertake missionary work in Canada came straight from Heaven. It was not strange, however, that the island of Montreal should have come into their minds, for the people in France had learned a good deal about Canada from the narratives of Samuel de Champlain, who had mentioned the island as a good site for settlement. All religiously inclined people were also reading the *Jesuit Relations*.

The two enthusiasts, set on missionary work, finally met and joined forces. With other devout people who had money to put into the enterprise, they organized the Société de Notre Dame de Montréal. They intended to found a mission, a hospital and a school. A wealthy lady, Madame de Bullion, was eager to finance the hospital and for the director of it the Société found a lovely and devout young woman, Jeanne Mance. She had been inspired by the story of Madame de la Peltrie and the Ursulines with a great longing to serve God in Canada. Without hesitation she accepted the invitation to set out on a mission

of mercy.   For the military leader of their colony, the Société
chose a valiant soldier, imbued with faith as strong as their own.
He was Paul de Chomedey, Sieur de Maisonneuve.

It was a company of crusaders, upheld by faith in an im-
practical enterprise, who set sail from La Rochelle late in the
year 1641.   The two founders, Jacques Olier and Dauversière,
did not accompany their colonizers.   When the ships reached
Quebec the pious company was not received with the enthusiasm
which greeted the Ursulines and hospital nuns.   The governor
and the religious orders would have preferred to have Quebec
strengthened by the newcomers.   Governor Montmagny offered them land on the Île d'Orléans, saying that their site
would be too exposed to attacks of the Iroquois who were
always on the warpath.   Maisonneuve, however, insisted on the
island chosen by the visionary founders of the Société de Notre
Dame.   He would go to Montreal, he said, even though every
tree were an Iroquois.

After wintering in Quebec, the company embarked joyously
to found the mission of their dreams.   Madame de la Peltrie
accompanied Jeanne Mance.   She was so inspired by the prospect of a new field for her sacrifice and money, even more difficult than the beginning of the nuns' work in Quebec, that she
deserted, temporarily, her dear friends the Ursulines.

It was a bright spring day in May, 1642, when the crusaders
sighted their island.   They were entranced with the gorgeous
spring flowers in the meadow lands, with the songs of birds,
and the woodlands rising in terraces toward Mount Royal.   As
soon as they had disembarked, an outdoor altar was set up,
decorated with spring flowers by the ladies.   Kneeling about it
the little company received Holy Communion from Father
Vimont in a spirit of exaltation.   He exhorted them in prophetic
words: "Look, gentlemen, what you see is but a grain of mus-

tard seed, but it is sown by such pious hands, and so moved by faith, that this seed will grow into a great tree, be multiplied and spread to all parts."

The Host was exposed on the altar all day, while soldiers set up tents. When darkness fell, fireflies were caught and hung on wires on the altar to serve as candles. In such romantically pious spirit was founded the town dedicated to the Virgin, called Ville Marie de Montréal.

Maisonneuve directed the building of log houses and a small fort on the shore, and for a year the tiny settlement lived in peace and harmony. It was the last quiet period that Ville Marie was to know for a long time.

The houses were nearly swept away by a flood during the first winter, and in the spring came the Iroquois, pursuing a frightened band of Algonquins who took refuge in the fort. The enemy savages discovered a new settlement of the hated French to harass so that Ville Marie knew no peace.

The settlers clung to their lonely island, however, and the place grew in spite of Indian attacks. Maisonneuve was a great leader, able by sincere faith to direct the morals of his people and by his bravery to organize their defence against Indian ene-mies. Jacques Olier founded the Seminary of Saint Sulpice in Paris, sending priests of this Order to be the spiritual fathers of Ville Marie. Nursing nuns came to live with Jeanne Mance in her little log hospital. They had their hands full tending settlers wounded in Iroquois attacks as well as sick Indians who came to them. The chapel and hospital, in one building, be-came the refuge and solace of all the inhabitants.

Every year colonists were sent to Ville Marie, so that presently the little outpost was a town of growing families. Then came the pioneer school mistress, Marguerite Bourgeoys, who was a woman of great ability and splendid character, attached to the

Sisters of the Congregation at Troyes. She came to find her life work in primitive Montreal. In her log hut she gathered little Indian and French girls for instruction, and, as her work increased, other teachers joined her. She founded the Sisters of the Congregation of Notre Dame, an order of teaching nuns which carries on the work of the founder in modern Montreal.

New France owed a great deal to the warmhearted, unselfish women who left everything they loved in France to give themselves to work for their countrymen and the Indians in a savage land. They brought civilization to the rough settlements, reaching the Indians through the girls they trained and through their charity to the childlike natives who came to them in sickness and trouble. Their hospitals and convents were islands of peace and order in towns of traders and soldiers, and were refuges for the wives of the inhabitants. They trained the French girls, also, who were to be the mothers of Canadians.

The leaders among these splendid women — Mère Marie de l'Incarnation, Jeanne Mance and Marguerite Bourgeoys — came to Canada to stay, devoting their lives to the work. The institutions these brave women founded in Canada — the Ursuline convent, the Hôtel-Dieu in Quebec and in Montreal, and the convent of the Sisters of the Congregation — have never ceased their ministrations to French Canadians from the seventeenth century to the present day.

The missionary fathers were also a civilizing influence. After the arrival of the Jesuits, the Recollet fathers devoted themselves to work in the settlements. The Jesuits were primarily missionaries, whose chief aim was to convert the savages and glorify God by their sacrifices. They were men of education and keen intelligence, many of them of rare spiritual quality. They loved books and music, the devotional quiet of monasteries, the ritual and beauty of great churches. All this they gave up for a life of adversity and loneliness in Indian villages. Often health and even life, itself, were sacrificed.

As soon as they had established a simple residence at Notre Dame des Anges outside Quebec the fathers set themselves to the task of learning the Huron and Algonquian languages so that they might follow the Indians to their villages and live among them, preaching and baptizing.

The Indians at first regarded these "black-robes" with amused curiosity. They were interested in the service of the Mass with its chanting and incense. It seemed to them a powerful "medicine" like the incantations of their own medicine men. They liked the bright-colored pictures of saints and the few cherished statues with which the fathers adorned their altars. Indolent and changeable as they were, however, it was as difficult to hold their attention as though they were children in years as well as character. Indeed, the Indians often acted like impish children, tormenting the fathers and making sport of them.

Every gleam of response to their explanation of Christian doctrine was hailed with joy by the good fathers. The Indians were willing to squat in the chapels, listening to services and preaching, they would learn to chant and pray in their own language, but it was difficult to make converts. Some of the Huron elders with whom the Jesuits had been laboring for a long time replied to their urging to accept the Faith: "It is good for the French, but we are another people with different customs."

Nevertheless the missionaries never lost heart. As soon as Father Jean de Brebeuf had learned the Huron language and made friends with the Indians who came to the settlement to trade, he persuaded them to take him to their distant country near Georgian Bay and Lake Huron. Father Jean de Brebeuf was a man of physical vigor, forceful personality and unquenchable courage. These qualities, admired by the Indians above all others, won him their respect and love.

When bands of Hurons set out for their distant villages the fathers went with them, sometimes two together, at other times, one lone missionary depended on the good will of the savages. The fathers learned to take their share of work on the wearisome journey by the Ottawa and French Rivers to Georgian Bay. They paddled long hours on lake and river, carried canoes over portages, slept on wet ground or on rocks in the forests. Often they were close to exhaustion from hardship, hunger and exposure. They might be reduced to a handful of dried corn for food, but they always carried books and writing materials and small altar services, in packs on their backs.

After the missions had been established a paper of instructions was printed in France for the fathers who were to go to the Hurons. It is very revealing. "You should love the Indians like brothers, among whom you are to spend the rest of your life. Never make them wait for you in embarking. Take a flint and steel to light their pipes and kindle their fire at night; for these little services win their hearts. Try to eat their sagamité as they cook it, bad and dirty as it is. Fasten up the skirts of your cassock, that you may not carry water or sand into the canoe. Wear no stockings or shoes in the canoe; but you may put them on in crossing the portages. Do not make yourself troublesome, even to a single Indian. Do not ask them too many questions. Bear their faults in silence and appear always cheerful. Buy fish for them from the tribes you pass; and for this purpose take with you some awls, beads, knives and fishhooks. Remember that it is Christ and His Cross that you are seeking and if you aim at anything else, you will find nothing but affliction for body and mind."

These instructions explain the skill and discipline with which the Jesuits won their way among fickle, childlike natives. When they reached the Huron villages they endured everything that was revolting in Indian life without a murmur, as they proceeded by kindness and patience to win the trust of the people. There were times when the black-robes were suspected of being sorcerers because of the ceremony of baptism, but eventually the people came to regard that as good medicine.

The Huron villages were large, with long bark houses surrounded by a triple row of tree-trunk palisades, effective protection against enemies equipped with bows and arrows. When the people had accepted the black-robes, they helped to build them bark mission houses in Indian style.

Indefatigable work over a course of years won most of the Huron natives. Bells rang from bark chapels in missions called Saint Ignace, Sainte Marie, Saint Joseph. Indians gathered to hear Mass before rude altars adorned with colored pictures of saints. The fathers allowed any number of Indians to squat around the fire in their mission house all day, while they taught, preached, and increased their knowledge of the language.

The Indians were captivated by magical possessions of their instructors such as a magnifying glass, a magnet, a prism and a handmill. They were so impressed with the power of the fathers over these mysterious objects that it helped the missionaries in their teaching of equally mysterious doctrines. The greatest wonder of all was a clock which the Indians believed was alive. They would sit expectantly waiting for it to speak. "What does the captain say?" they would enquire. The father would reply, "When he strikes twelve he says, 'Hang on the kettle,' and when he strikes four he says, 'Get up and go home.'"

So the Indians learned the time of day when they would be allowed to share the fathers' midday meal from the copper kettle hanging over the fire, and the hour in the afternoon when they would be gently urged out of the house and the bark door closed. Then, for a while, the weary teachers might be alone, to read their breviaries by smoky, flickering firelight, to discuss the problems of the mission and to work on a grammar for the Huron language.

The Sulpician priests of Ville Marie de Montréal were also towers of strength to the inhabitants and a refuge in sickness and terror for the friendly Huron and Algonquian Indians who haunted the settlement. The priests were bold men who would snatch up muskets to help soldiers and settlers ward off Iroquois attacks. One of the fathers went to the rescue of men who were attacked while working in the fields without their guns. Swinging a broadsword in both hands the priest exhorted the savages while at the same time he laid low his assailants. They made an end of him with arrows and gunfire and cut off his head. It was a legend firmly believed, and related by Dollier de Casson in his history, that the severed head spoke to the Indians, reproaching them for their evil deeds.

Dollier de Casson, who was Superior of the Seminary of Saint Sulpice at Montreal during the turbulent years when the town was an outpost of French settlement in the wilderness, was a marvelous man. He had been a soldier of the king in his youth and became one of the most stalwart soldiers of the Cross; priest and warrior, explorer and historian. He it was who led and comforted his flock in their times of hardship and Indian attack; he who planned the layout of the larger town of stone buildings which was built within strong walls. When he could leave his work he explored the Great Lakes and, in the midst of diverse activities, he found time to write the heroic history of Montreal as it was during his lifetime.

Both Montreal and the Huron villages lived in constant terror of the Iroquois, their implacable enemies. These people of the

Five Nations — the Senecas, Onondagas, Oneidas, Cayugas and Mohawks — were determined to dominate the forest world in spite of red man or white. Hurons and Algonquins had been their enemies before the French arrived, and the Iroquois hated the French because they gave their trade and armed strength to the enemy tribes. The Iroquois made friends with English colonists of Albany and Schenectady, trading furs for guns and hatchets, but they would make alliances with them only when it suited their purposes.

With success the Iroquois clans became increasingly bold and arrogant. Lurking in the forests they fell upon Huron hunters and exterminated whole bands of them or attacked them on their way to trade with the French. Villages were burned and women and children murdered while the men were away. Hundreds of prisoners were carried off to be tortured with fiendish cruelty, burnt alive, or served up in the cooking pots at warrior feasts.

The Huron people were completely demoralized with terror. They abandoned one village after another to hide in the depths of the forest. Never did the heroic missionaries prove more clearly their strength and devotion than in these times of terror. The Hurons turned to the trusted black-robes for help and the fathers urged them to fight for their homes and faith. In the midst of flaming villages and yelling murderers they baptized the dying and spoke of Heaven to their terrified people. Many of the Jesuits won the martyrdom which was to them the crowning glory of their work.

Father Daniel was butchered before the eyes of his flock who were gathered about him in the chapel when the whooping devils descended on their village. The two fathers, Jean de Brebeuf and Gabriel Lalemant, were captured with their people and carried off to the tortures of an Iroquois camp. The savages were pleased to have in their power Father Brebeuf, the most beloved of the black-robes. Tied to stakes the two priests suffered hours of the most terrible tortures.

Father Brebeuf stood like a rock, uttering no sound while the savages tried every ingenious cruelty they knew to break his spirit. They tore out his nails, hung red-hot axes around his neck, poured boiling water over his head in mockery of baptism, cut off pieces of his flesh and roasted them before his eyes. Finally, in a fury, they tore out his heart and ate it, to give themselves the courage they could not help but admire in their victim.

The flourishing Huron missions, pride and joy of the Jesuits in Canada, were heaps of ashes. A remnant of the people, starving and dying of disease in the forests, was gathered together by priests and soldiers and taken down the river to Quebec.

There the Jesuits gave them land for a village on the Île d'Orléans and, for a time, the beaten Hurons tilled their fields and recovered some of their courage. Even there they were not safe, for the Iroquois attacked them under the very guns of Quebec. The survivors were brought to live in a palisaded enclosure near the fort, and from there were moved to their final dwelling place, a wooded spot called Indian Lorette, near Quebec. A chapel was built to Our Lady of Lorette and the remnant of a once-proud Indian nation settled down to a quiet Christian life.

From the time of their arrival in Canada to the destruction of the Huron missions the spirit of the Jesuits had been a clear flame of religious zeal. They had devoted themselves with heroism and dauntless determination to the spreading of the Faith. They were to go on carrying the Cross westward ahead of French settlement, and were to venture into the dangerous country of the Iroquois themselves.

The priests were a powerful influence in helping the French to deal with the Indians because they had learned so well to understand Indian mind and character. But for the sacrifice of many brave men the result, in taming and civilizing the children of the forests, was small. The Indians remained savages at heart, even when they told their beads, and went to Mass and believed in saints. In mission villages the people did not put their prisoners in the cooking pots, to be sure, but they enjoyed the game of torturing them, and the Jesuits seem to have considered that inevitable.

The Jesuit Order, firmly established at Quebec, became a political as well as religious power in New France. The priests were educators of the boys, the spiritual mentors of the inhabitants, and the critics or close partners of the governors.

CHAPTER IV

Life in New France
[Seventeenth Century to 1759]

IN THE spring when the highway of New France, the St. Lawrence, was released from ice, canoes came sliding down the mighty stream from the interior. Paddled by bronzed men who looked half Indian in their fringed buckskin shirts, the canoes came to rest on the shore beside the wharves of Montreal or Quebec, or before the small trading hamlet of Trois Rivières.

With shouts and snatches of French song the men descended upon the prim, pious towns of Quebec and Montreal. The drinking shops rang with their boasts and songs as strong French brandy was poured down their throats and French sweethearts welcomed them back from the woods. When the brandy had done its work the quiet of the streets was disturbed by the quarrels and drunken brawls of the wild fellows and their Indian companions.

These men were the coureurs de bois; adventurous, spirited Frenchmen who found irresistible the lure of the forests and the untrammeled life of the Indians. They could shoot their canoes through the rapids with the best of the natives, from whom they learned to make their own canoes; those slim strong craft, white shells of birchbark streaked with the black of spruce-gum seams, narrowed to a sweeping curve at either end.

The coureurs de bois could travel on Indian snowshoes, and make camp in the deep snow of winter forests, with beds of fir boughs to lie on around the fire. Rugged and bold, at home with Indian speech and manner of thought, the French wanderers shared the dirty, smoke-filled bark shelters of the Indians, swarming with children and dogs. They mated with the native women, producing the race of half-breeds who became so much a part of French Canadian life. Half savage they were themselves, these wanderers of the forests, often dressed like the Indians even to paint and feathers.

Loving the adventure of penetrating lands where white men had never before set foot, their explorations and search for furs planted French outposts far to the west.

When they returned to the settlements the coureurs de bois brought bales of skins, beaver, marten or mink trapped by themselves or won from the Indians by trade. These were sold to the companies which tried to keep complete control of the fur trade. With the proceeds the adventurers caroused riotously while staid townsfolk were scandalized. As they were Catholics after their fashion they also knelt in the chapels to hear Mass and confess their sins.

To boys and young men the coureurs de bois were heroes. Despite the efforts of priests and military governors to keep them at work they often escaped from dull shopkeeping or farming to take to the woods with them.

Before summer was over the fleet canoes were disappearing up the shining highway to the interior, paddles flashing, while the swarthy men in buckskin and gay red knitted caps roused the echoes with their rollicking chant. The canoes were laden with trade goods and a store of smoked eels and dried corn to eke out their diet of game and fish. The men were off to explore and live with the Indians for another year or so.

The coureurs de bois were a thorn in the flesh to the priests, and to the fur traders because their free-lance gathering of furs interfered with legitimate trade. No man was supposed to go to the woods without obtaining a license to trade, but these men often eluded the vigilance of the authorities.

Their free life contrasted sharply with puritanical existence in Quebec, which, until 1665, was little more than a trading post and mission. Religious fervor was strong in the inhabitants, but if anyone became lax in church duties he was soon taken to task by the priests. Bells rang and chants arose all day in the churches; the nuns of the Ursuline convent and the hospital sisters followed the observances of convent life as devoutly as though they were in France.

The priests did not have everything their own way, however. Feminine frivolity would creep in, as women enjoyed silken gowns and the few fineries which could be imported from France. Father confessors frowned on ribbons, fripperies and elaborate hairdressing, but the instincts of beauty-loving French women survived in the pioneer daughters of Quebec despite their priests.

In the waterfront settlement the priests labored in vain with mercenary fur traders and rough coureurs de bois, carrying on a valiant campaign against the evils of brandy which lured men to the drinking shops.

Despite rough conditions and the stern rule of the priests there was a kindly simplicity about pioneer life in Quebec. Everyone was a neighbor and all rallied to help one another when disasters came.

The religious orders rejoiced when the Church in Quebec received its first bishop, François de Laval, who arrived in 1659. He was a man of strong, autocratic character, austere in his personal life. With single-minded devotion he gave himself to the work of strengthening the Church and educating boys, both Indian and French.

Soon after his arrival he founded the Séminaire de Québec for the training of Algonquian and French boys, while the Jesuits continued to teach young Hurons. The Séminaire was also intended to be a refuge for study and prayer for the parish priests, whom the good bishop soon sent out to the settlements and seigneuries along the St. Lawrence.

Laboring with heart and soul to make New France a land of good Catholics, priests and nuns were convinced that demons of the savage world fought the true religion by overwhelming the colony with disasters. To the devastation of Indian attacks were added, in 1663, terrifying upheavals of nature. Deep rumblings were heard in the earth, the land was shaken with earthquakes, houses rocked, walls fell in on the inhabitants, church bells rang of themselves in swaying steeples. Forest trees were uprooted, mountainsides slid into the river and islands appeared where none had been before. In the sky above Quebec, awed townsfolk saw three suns in a row, spanned by a rainbow arch. The darkness of night, filled with the noise of wind and groaning earth, was made worse by wailing cries, and visions of phantoms of fire with torches in their hands. In all the settlements, terrified people prostrated themselves in the streets, crying for mercy, or crowded the churches to pray for safety. The nuns and fathers worked incessantly to lead these frightened souls to penitence, telling them that the disasters had come upon them for their sins.

It was into this atmosphere, all a-quiver with penitence, into a town where civil garb was overshadowed by the black robes of priests and the severe habits of nuns, that the new royal governor, with his retinue, and brilliantly uniformed officers of a French regiment came like a flock of bright birds in 1665.

That year marked a time of great change for the gray town on the cliffs. The young King Louis XIV had taken New France under his fatherly care, and in 1663 proclaimed it a royal province. When he came to the throne the king and his wise minister, Colbert, investigated the affairs of the colony and found them in a deplorable condition. Under the rule of the Company of New France, or One Hundred Associates, settlement had not been encouraged and even the fur trade had languished. In Quebec there were but seventy houses in 1665 and five hundred and seventy people, while in all New France there were less than twenty-five hundred inhabitants.

Louis XIV and Colbert envisaged France as a great world empire and set about creating it. At home the king was deliberately undermining the power and privileges of the nobility, to center all control of the State in himself. He intended to develop an empire overseas under the same autocratic control, and to this end organized a government for New France and appointed a royal governor.

The governing body of the province was to be the Sovereign Council of Quebec, consisting of the governor, bishop, intendant and five councillors chosen from among prominent colonials. The Council was supposed to administer the laws of France in the province, promulgate royal decrees, make and administer local ordinances. However, this body had little real control of government. To prevent concentration of power in one man the governor was checked by the bishop and by the intendant, an officer with more real power than the governor. The intendant was to watch over the finances, stores and equipment, and in practice he had a hand in all the civil affairs of the province.

In order to free New France from the menace of Iroquois attacks Louis XIV also sent out a French regiment, the Carignan-Salières, commanded by a distinguished soldier, the Marquis de Tracey. He was to have full military command while he made war on the Indians. The marquis and his regiment, accompanied by a group of young noblemen, were the first of the new officials to reach Quebec.

It was a spring day, in 1665, when ships bearing the officers and soldiers appeared in the river before Quebec. From the decks the newcomers surveyed with interest the citadel in the wilderness. Thrust out into the grand sweep of the river, the promontory of Cape Diamond dwarfed the man-made fortifications on its crest and the jumble of timber houses on the shore at the foot of the cliffs.

Bells rang from the church steeples, cannon boomed from the fort as sails rattled down and boats were lowered to take the noble company ashore. The first sight of their new post was strange to men from civilized France. Through lines of cheering townsfolk in sober homespun, mingled with tobacco-brown Indians, they were led by the governor and an escort of militia up the rough track to the upper town.

It was an austere settlement that greeted their eyes. Dark green of woodland made a background for the gray stone of monastic buildings, churches and scattered dwellings with steep-pitched roofs. Bark wigwams under the trees gave a savage touch to the scene, and the might of France was represented by the grim lines of the Château Saint Louis on the crest of the cliffs.

Mère Marie de l'Incarnation, who had shared the hardships and achievements of pioneer Quebec for so many years, was there to enjoy the occasion which inaugurated a new life for her beloved town. Her letters to her son, Dom Claude, give a living picture of those early years, and she describes the arrival of the first officers after New France had become a royal province, from the viewpoint of the townsfolk.

"Never has Quebec seen so great a display as the escort of this 'high and mighty lord,' when he reached the wharf. Twenty-four guards and six pages of honor preceded, in court costume, then came the Viceroy surrounded by officers whose gorgeous uniforms glittered with silver and gold; six footmen in livery followed; the militia closed the march and in their wake were the people whose cries of joy added to the concert of bells and cannon. Bishop Laval awaited the marquis at the door of the parish church and, offering him holy water and the cross, led him to the seat of honor prepared for him; but this truly Christian gentlemen knelt on the pavement like the least of the crew, while the sanctuary resounded to the hymn of thanksgiving accompanied by the organ."

Before the summer was over the townsfolk gathered once more to welcome their first royal governor, Sieur de Courcelle, accompanied by Jean Talon, the intendant, and various lords and ladies.

These officials and noblemen with their wives brought the pleasures of French civilization and the graces of social life to somber Quebec. In the dignified rooms of the Château Saint Louis the governors, henceforth, kept up a miniature court in imitation of Versailles. Carved furniture from France adorned the rooms, and candles glowed in silver sconces when the small aristocratic society of Quebec gathered for a ball. In the silks and furbelows, towering headdresses and powdered wigs of court fashion, the gentlefolk of New France brought the glamour of the homeland to their outpost of empire.

The great feast days of the Church were celebrated with glittering processions, rich with banners and priestly robes. Dignitaries of the government and their families, gorgeously arrayed, marched with the religious orders. Christian Indians dressed in beaver skins or Huron boys in scarlet satin were often given the honor of carrying the silver reliquaries of the churches, adding a truly Canadian touch to the processions. The Ursulines shepherded their flock of Indian girls dressed in French style. Displays of fireworks finished off the greatest festivals.

Winter was the time of gay social affairs, for then the city on the cliffs was shut off from the world, and no outdoor work could be carried on while the land was held in the grip of snow and cold.

The ships for France departed when the storms of autumn began, bearing packets of letters and documents in which Quebec people, personally and officially, communicated with friends and superiors at home. There were voluminous reports of the governor and intendant for their master, the king; the yearly *Relation* on the progress of missions and the Order from the superior of the Jesuits in Quebec to the superior of the Order in France; Mère Marie's letters to her son and to wealthy noblewomen who helped her with the finances of the convent; letters, homesick or courageous, describing life in Canada for dear ones at home.

The broad river was stilled under its thick sheath of ice, and the world the Quebec folk looked out upon was a vast silent whiteness of snow and ice, accented by the black of fir forests and the sharp blue line of mountains.

Women visited from house to house to gossip over their sewing and weaving. Sleighing parties on the ice amused lively French aristocrats and there were balls and dinner parties in cold houses warmed only by blazing fires of logs in stone fireplaces. The ladies of Quebec were fond of dancing, reported a visiting French nobleman, and he commented on their gaiety, wit and delicacy.

After the ice had gone out in the spring, people on the ramparts gazed down the river every day, straining their eyes for the first sight of white sails, bringing the ships from France with news from home, with supplies of all sorts and new settlers for the province. The whole town bustled with activity during the summer months when the ships lay at anchor in the basin. In the lower town of the merchants, goods from France were un-packed and displayed in the shops. Fleets of canoes glided down the river, bringing traders and Indians with bales of beaver skins to the storehouses of the fur merchants. French sailors made the streets and drinking shops resound with their revelry.

The ships brought sheaves of documents for the governor and the intendant from King Louis XIV. There were answers to their letters and reports sent to France six months before; new orders, instructions and edicts from the meticulous king and his minister, who insisted on managing the affairs of the colony to the smallest detail.

Under the paternalistic rule of Louis XIV the people had not the slightest chance to learn self-government. The only voice of the citizens in the Sovereign Council was that of the seigneurs who were owners of large grants of land and belonged to the privileged class. The king kept his province dependent on the home government for almost everything necessary to its progress, yet expected the inhabitants of Canada to build for him a powerful colony of well-organized towns and a farming countryside.

In France the office of intendant was an important one. The intendants were the king's men, appointed to each province to oversee the work of other officers, manage the finances and see to it that the king's orders were carried out. Louis XIV added the office of intendant to the set-up in New France for the same purpose. No officer was to have sufficient power to interfere with the supremacy of the king, so that the governor was con-stantly checked by the intendant and he in turn constantly complained that the governor interfered in his domain. Both officers sent their complaints to the king, giving him the oppor-tunity to learn both sides of the story as to what was happening in Quebec. Added to the jealousy between governor and intendant was the struggle for supremacy between civil rule in the person of the governor and Church rule in the persons of the bishop and the superior of the Jesuits. The Order had power at Court through which the Jesuits influenced the appointment of governors, trying to get men who would be easily managed by the Church. Bishop Laval was firmly convinced that the Church should be the guiding influence in the government and the Jesuits worked with him to that end.

There was no conflict of race or religion in New France, for Cardinal Richelieu had long ago established the rule that only Frenchmen and good Catholics should be permitted to live in the colony.

Conflict there was, however, between Church and State when the governor resisted the domination of the Church. Most of the governors, even when they were weak, foolish or inefficient, were pious men, amenable to the wishes of the Jesuits and the bishop. When they had to deal with arrogant Count Frontenac, however, it was a different matter.

There were constant quarrels over precedence during his regime and great antagonism between the Jesuits and Governor Frontenac. He had been sent by Louis XIV to bring order and strength to a province torn by dissensions and, although he did not bring peace, he generally managed to have his own way and to dominate the entire Sovereign Council. He was the only governor who tried to establish a sort of Commons through which the voice of the people might be heard, but he got nowhere with it. From both king and Church he met opposition to such a plan.

The intendants were, as a rule, honest hardworking men, and Jean Talon, the first to hold the office, was the finest of them all. He was the busiest man in Quebec and one of the most important. Indeed, he probably did more to set New France on

its feet than any other one man. He and Governor de Cour-
celles worked in harmony, proving what could be done when
the two chief officers co-operated instead of spending their time
in bickering.

Jean Talon ably carried out the king's plans for New France.
The most fundamental need was population, to increase the
settlements and to raise food on the good land which was still,
for the most part, unbroken wilderness. The French feudal
system of land tenure was transplanted to Canada. In France,
with the growing power and wealth of the nobility, the early
relationship between lords and vassals which at least gave protection to the peasants in return for their labors, had changed.
The suffering of the down-trodden peasantry was laying the
foundation for the hate and fury of the French Revolution.

Pioneer conditions in Canada, however, created a simple, useful relationship between the lords, or seigneurs, and their ten-
ants, and the system proved to be a successful means of developing the country. Large grants of land, seigneuries, were made
to landless noblemen or, more often, to retired army officers,
religious institutions and ambitious provincials in Canada. In
return for this land the seigneur was obligated to allot sections
of his territory to settlers, the habitants, who were to clear the
land and produce crops. Some of the seigneurs, particularly
those from France, were very remiss in settling farmers on their
lands, but the Canadians and religious orders did a good job of
building up a rural population for Canada.

The religious orders came to be the largest landowners in the
country and were among the best. They took pains to settle
industrious families on the land, helped them to get started with
implements and animals, and encouraged them in agriculture.
Bishop Laval owned land on the Côte de Beaupré along the
river, the Séminaire de Québec had a large part of the Île

d'Orléans, the Jesuits and Ursulines had large holdings, and the Sulpician Order, the Gentlemen of Saint Sulpice, became the seigneurs of the island of Montreal.

When the Carignan-Salières regiment was disbanded after accomplishing its purpose, Louis XIV gave seigneuries along the Richelieu River to officers who consented to stay in Canada, and their soldiers settled down on the officers' lands to become habitant farmers. It was part of the king's scheme to make New France a military province, able to defend itself against Indians and the English. Seigneurs and their habitants were required to serve as soldiers when necessary. Habitants were furnished with muskets which they might use for hunting when they were not required for war. It was particularly important to guard the Richelieu, between the St. Lawrence and Lake Champlain, for that was the frontier constantly in danger.

A big colonizing venture was undertaken by the king. French officers spread propaganda about Canada, and rounded up emigrants to be shipped from Dieppe or La Rochelle each year. The majority of the settlers came from northern France, Brittany, Picardy, Perche and Normandy. The last province furnished by far the largest number of settlers, so that the backbone of the Canadian population came to be peasant families and artisans of Norman stock — a staunch, bold race, light-hearted and adventurous. Some of the men came with allotments of land already arranged for. Others, when they arrived in Quebec, were met by seigneurs who offered them farms on their land. Emigrants who could claim to be gentil-hommes, not peasants, applied to the intendant for seigneuries and received land.

As the forest was cleared and log houses were built along the river, the problem of wives for the settlers came up. Jean Talon and Louis XIV realized that Canada must be populated chiefly from within. Families must be established and encouraged to produce not only grain but children. So the plan of the "King's girls" was devised.

Homeless girls were taken from charitable institutions, and peasants with too many children contributed daughters. The girls traveled in the care of nuns and were handed over to the Ursulines in Quebec while, in Montreal, Marguerite Bourgeoys and her Sisters of the Congregation gave them motherly care and religious instruction while they waited for husbands. Presently Jean Talon requested King Louis XIV to send a consignment of demoiselles to be the wives of officers. They came, were duly married, and added their French charms to the society of Montreal and Quebec.

Mère Marie, in one of her letters, admits that the consignments of girls were sometimes "mixed goods," rude and hard to handle. But they were submitted to the civilizing influence of the nuns on arrival and soon settled down to become good wives of habitants and shopkeepers.

Wife hunting added to the usual excitement attending the arrival of ships from France. The bachelors crowded the water front to watch the girls disembark. Soon after their arrival the prospective brides were assembled in a large hall for the men to take their pick. There was some freedom of choice for the girls, and thrifty peasant maidens took care to inquire whether the young men who asked for them had farms and houses to live in. Pretty or plain, they all found husbands within a few weeks. Marriages were speedily performed and each couple was presented by the governor with an ox, a cow, a pair of swine and of fowls, two barrels of salted meat and eleven crowns in money. The king also gave a dowry in goods to the girls he sent over.

Jean Talon made ordinances to entice or force young people

into marriage. Recalcitrant bachelors were heavily fined and were forbidden to hunt, fish, trade with the Indians or live in the woods. Twenty livres were given to every youth married by the age of twenty and to every girl who was married by the time she was sixteen. Bounties were given to parents with many children. So did the industrious intendant and his master the king succeed in peopling Canada.

The land along the north shore of the St. Lawrence, from the Côte de Beaupré to Montreal, was the first to be taken up by seigneurs. Everyone wanted a frontage on the river, for that was the highway of New France, on the ice in winter, by boat in summer. It was some time before a road was built and then it followed the shore line closely. The habitants also wanted access to the river, so that the plots allotted to settlers were long and narrow. Each farmer had a frontage on the river, while his land extended back a mile or more toward the hills. When these plots were all taken settlers had to be content with land back from the river.

To the habitants the river was the Chemin du Bon Dieu, the highway past their doors which led to the outside world. Their sturdy houses, generally built of stone, were strung along the water highway, close together for companionship and safety. With whitewashed walls and great roofs ending in curled-up eaves, they were reminiscent of Norman farmhouses, but had a Canadian character all their own. In the flourishing days of the seigneuries a traveler coming up the St. Lawrence to Montreal might have seen most of New France in that straggling row of whitewashed, companionable houses.

The manor houses of the seigneurs were not much more elaborate than those of the habitants unless the lord of the manor was wealthy and of the noblesse. They were simple dignified dwellings of thick stone walls, whitewashed under the pitch of great dark roofs from which dormer windows peered out. Furniture, hangings and silver from France gave charm to the seigneur's rooms.

It was necessary for the habitants to become self-sufficient, for ships came from France only once a year and the goods they brought were expensive. Jean Talon soon requested the king to send out artisans — carpenters, masons, blacksmiths, weavers — to teach the habitant to take care of himself. He became a very handy man indeed, able to build his house, his two-wheeled cart and carriole sleigh, to forge the iron for hinges, locks and tools, and to make the simple peasant furniture for his home.

Habitant women spent the long winters weaving wool from their sheep into homespun cloth from which the whole family was clothed, as well as blankets and rag rugs for the floors. Jean Talon wrote the king proudly one year that he was clothed from head to foot in materials made in the province. This training in craftsmanship was one of the greatest benefits that the far-sighted intendant brought to the province.

There was a simple, sturdy charm about the life of seigneur and habitant in old French Canada, and a friendly relationship between the lord of the manor and his people. Occasionally the owner was a man who had won his way to a seigneury after years of industrious work as a habitant, so that he and his family were not above working in the fields to help harvest the crops when necessary. The manor house was a social center in the great lonely countryside.

There, on May Day, the habitants gathered to plant a tall, stripped fir tree in honor of the seigneur. While youths and girls danced around the maypole the men saluted it with a volley of shots, and the seigneur's family looked on with pleasure. There were shouts of "Long live the king!" and "Long live our seigneur!" The people trooped into the house to be served with brandy and cakes, drinking the health of the seigneur and all his kin so enthusiastically that they departed in exceeding merry mood.

On Saint Martin's Day in November, after the harvest was over, the habitant families gathered again at the manor house to pay the annual dues, called *cens et rentes,* for their farms. It was not a very heavy payment for their good acres, since it consisted of ten or twelve sous, a bushel of grain, a pig or a few chickens from each farmer. It was the biggest neighborhood day of the year for the entire population of the seigneury. Men and women gossiped, children played, while the seigneur's flagon of brandy passed from man to man. Everyone smoked pipes of strong *tabac canadien,* home-grown on each farm. Amidst the hubbub of chatter and squawking of fowls the seigneur checked over his *rentes,* talked to the people and shook hands all round before they piled into their carrioles and drove away over the snowy country.

In addition to the dues, the habitants were required to bring their grain to be ground in the seigneur's stone gristmill. They might do their baking at home, however, in outdoor stone ovens of the same type as those which dot the Laurentian countryside today. When they caught fish, one eleventh of the haul belonged to the seigneur and he had the right to take timber or stone from their land, as well; however, he generally gave something of equal value in return. The habitants were required to give some days during the year to work in the seigneur's fields at the seasons of plowing, planting and harvesting. These tenant farmers of Canada were far better off than the peasants of France in their circumstances and position.

The habitants also paid a tithe of their grain to the parish priest for the support of the church. Sometimes the curé lived with the seigneur and services were held in the family chapel of the manor house. But, as time went on, parishes were established up and down the river. The narrow stone churches with their slim arrowlike spires became, with the white farmhouses, a Canadian type of architecture as much a part of the Laurentian country as the forest-crowned hills and the splendid river.

Seigneur and priest, manor house and church, these were the guiding lights of the habitants' lives. The curé was their spiritual father, their counsellor and friend. Every family, with a cart or a sleigh full of children, went to the village church for Mass on Sunday. After the service the *capitaine de milice,* who represented civil government, made announcements of local interest on the steps, and the rest of the day was given over to visiting and festivity.

Feasts of the Church, and winter-night gatherings in the houses along the river, constituted the social life of the habitants. They were lively, sociable, spirited people who loved dance and song. Every parish had its fiddler with a home-made violin who furnished music for winter gatherings called *veillées.* French folksongs and legends came from France with the first people and were cherished from one generation to another. No gathering of neighbors was complete without singing of the old songs in which men and women both excelled. Gradually a Canadian lore of legends and folksongs was accumulated in habitant homes, a precious heritage for French Canadians today.

Such was the life of seigneur and habitant along that magnificent river in the flourishing days of New France, early in the eighteenth century. Back from the whitewashed houses stretched the long narrow fields of grain, cabbages, peas and beans. On the hill slopes were wood lots where timber was cut, melting into the dark of spruce and pine forests. French customs and character were rooted deep in the soil of Canada, producing a life that had in it elements of the Old World and the New. It was seventeenth-century France molded to its setting among primeval forests and great waters.

Quebec was the center of Church and State, a dignified place even in the social life of the noblesse and gentilhommes with their Court etiquette. Count Frontenac had built a citadel on the crest of the promontory, and the city was surrounded with walls and gates. Around the Place d'Armes before the Château Saint Louis, and on the slopes of Mountain Street, were the tall narrow houses of the gentlefolk. Monasteries and churches were larger and more imposing than the early buildings and in addition there were the Hôtel Dieu, the Séminaire de Québec, the Cathedral and the Bishop's Palace.

The churches were enriched with rare gifts from France, such as silver sanctuary lamps, altar services, reliquaries, as well as hangings of brocade. The beautiful silver pieces, later on, were to be the inspiration for a Quebec school of silversmiths.

In their convent the industrious Ursulines found time, despite their varied duties, to work at their exquisite embroideries. Gifts from their hands adorned the sanctuaries of churches. The nuns were also skilled in the art of gilding and painting wood sculpture. Carved statues of saints came to them to be finished before being placed in chapels and churches.

From their early experiences in working with native materials the nuns developed a lucrative business. Articles of deerskin were beautifully embroidered and birchbark boxes with appliquéd designs of porcupine quills found favor with visiting noblemen, the first tourists of Quebec. This New World art became very popular in France and the proceeds of their ingenious work helped out the finances of both the Ursulines and the hospital sisters.

In the early years of his work Bishop Laval had founded a

school of arts and crafts for French and Indian boys at Cap Tourmente. Master wood carvers who came from France to teach there remained to become heads of families who passed on the art from father to son. These fine craftsmen brought to Canada the traditions of their guilds and the graceful art of the French Renaissance. Young Canadians trained in the bishop's school went out to establish wood-carving shops in the villages, and from those shops came the exquisite wood sculpture which graced parish churches.

And what of Ville Marie, the frontier town of crusaders and fur traders? In the latter days of New France it was a strong walled town, busy and industrious. Fur merchants still flourished, but in addition to this business there was a trade in woven cloth from weavers' shops and in food products from the prosperous farm lands on the fertile island. In the lower part of the town the merchants congregated in Saint Paul Street, while farther up the hill the solid stone dwellings of the gentlefolk gathered near the fine parish church of Notre Dame and the stone-walled Seminary of Saint Sulpice. Jeanne Mance's little hospital had become a large institution. There were schools, those of the Jesuits and Sulpicians for boys, while the Sisters of the Congregation cared for the girls of the town. Forest-crowned Mount Royal looked down on the walled town and its surrounding villages.

New France in the latter years of the French regime was no longer a colony of fur traders and missionaries. Along the St. Lawrence there was a population of native-born French Canadians, sturdy people who loved the space and freshness of their land and knew how to cope with the wilderness. In the towns French civilization brought grace to the lives of gentlefolk. Seventeenth-century French art came to Canada for the ornamentation of churches, and the architecture of the province had a distinctive character because of French influence. Men and women of the Church, by their encouragement of wood carving and embroidery, brought the leaven of cultured beauty to pioneer life and laid the foundations for a native school of craftsmanship.

Charlevoix, a Jesuit writer who visited Canada, wrote of the people: "The Canadians breathe from their birth an air of liberty which makes them very pleasant in the intercourse of life, and our language is nowhere more purely spoken. One finds here no rich people at all. In New France poverty is hidden under an air of ease which appears entirely natural."

CHAPTER V

The Struggle for a Continent
[1642–1760]

DURING more than a century in New France success or failure in winning the furs of the Indians affected the lives of the inhabitants, and rivalry with the vigorous English colonists could never be forgotten.

In dealing with the Indians, adventurous leaders among the coureurs de bois were invaluable. They had great influence with the western tribes. Often their persuasions brought the furs of these tribes to the French instead of to the English and Iroquois. They rounded up the Indians for conferences with the French during the long contest between New France and the English colonies for control of the natives and their furs.

These men and the traders ranged over a vast western territory, building small log forts where Indians were tempted by trade goods to bring their furs. Not only trade but the lure of the unknown led them on.

Trade with the western tribes was interfered with by the Adventurers of England when they built their first fort at Hudson Bay in 1670. Their story will be told in another chapter. This challenge was met by the French traders who built forts in the Indians' own country to win the furs before they could be taken to the English at the Bay.

In the south there was continual conflict between French traders and the Iroquois who lived south of Lake Ontario, over the furs of tribes farther west in the Great Lakes country. Iroquois territory was not abundantly supplied with beaver, so that they needed the furs of the western Indians to trade with the English for the rum, guns and hatchets they craved. Both the French and the English made use of liquor in their fur trade, a pernicious practice since it turned the Indians into irresponsible demons.

These western Indians were in the habit of bringing their furs to Montreal to trade with the French. In the early summer great fleets of canoes came down the waterways from the distant Great Lakes; by the Ottawa and the St. Lawrence, through Lake Saint Louis, and past the roaring rapids of Sault Saint Louis to the water front of Montreal.

Canoes were drawn up in shoals and Indian lodges crowded the shore. Savages in paint and feathers, in fringed hide leggings and moccasins, brought their bales of beaver pelts to the booths where traders set out the coveted articles with which they bought valuable furs. Indians paid many beaver skins for a musket, and bartered more of them for red cloth, knives and hatchets. The hubbub was tremendous as barter went on in a dozen different Indian dialects. Some traders eluded the watchfulness of the authorities to add brandy to their trade stock. Then the liquor-crazed Indians added to the uproar with street brawls.

The furs of the interior were pouring into Montreal for the French so that it is not surprising that the Iroquois determined to stop it. Every spring large bands of warriors hid in the forests beside the waterways to fall upon the canoes coming down to trade. The western tribes were so terrified by these attacks that there were some years when none came to Montreal. New France, dependent for its life on the fur trade, was then in desperate condition.

The people of Montreal lived in constant dread and danger. Farmers went to their fields with guns or with soldiers to guard them while they worked. The good sisters of the hospital kept watch from the belfry of their chapel and, when the distant sound of war whoops and gunshots reached them, they rang the tocsin to call the soldiers to the rescue of the farmers. Rumor flew among the frightened people that thousands of warriors were preparing to wipe out the French settlements.

If Montreal were destroyed the way would be open to the settlements on the St. Lawrence. In that time of crisis, the spring of 1660, the French were saved by a gallant group of Montreal soldiers. A young officer of the garrison, Dollard des Ormeaux, determined to go out to find the Iroquois and prevent them from reaching Montreal. Volunteers joined him in a venture which they knew very well meant death. Before leaving, the sixteen young men made their confessions and received Holy Communion. It was with the blessing of priests and townsfolk that they set out.

The men hid themselves within an old Indian stockade beside the Long Sault of the Ottawa River, waiting for the Iroquois to pass the rapids. The first band of warriors was surprised and slaughtered but after them came five hundred savages who attacked the stockade in a body. Behind their palisades the sixteen Frenchmen and a group of Hurons who had joined them fought so furiously that the Iroquois dead lay in heaps. Frenchmen were wounded, too, and were cut off from food and water. Presently the cowardly Hurons deserted to the Iroquois so that they knew how few Frenchmen opposed them. Protected by wooden shields they attacked in a solid mass, climbing over their own dead to reach the stockade and break through it. Every Frenchman died, sword in hand.

Their sacrifice was not in vain, for the Iroquois, startled to find that sixteen men in such a poor shelter could slaughter hundreds of their warriors, questioned what would happen to them if they attacked a fortified place like Montreal. For the time being they went home and the French breathed freely, encouraged by the bravery of that little band to fight, not fear, the pests of the forest.

The savages met their match for once when the Marquis de Tracey and his regiment, the Carignan-Salières, arrived in Canada. A great expedition invaded the Iroquois' own territory, punishing them so thoroughly that the settlements were safe for some years.

Then again, through the weakness of French governors and doubtless backed by the English of New York, the Indians went on the warpath. Once more the furs of the west were lost, farms were raided and crops burned. New France needed a strong hand to deal with the dangers. For this, King Louis XIV chose the Count de Frontenac, an arrogant, tempestuous nobleman. He was too hot-headed and blunt to get on very well at Court, but he was the man for the time in Quebec.

Although he was fifty years old when he reached Quebec in 1672, Frontenac set to work with youthful vigor to build up New France. His ungovernable temper and lordly insistence on being supreme in the colonial government brought him the enmity of councillors and the Jesuits. But to the Indians, he became the Great Father, the Onontio, as they called the governors, whom they loved and respected.

There was a bit of the savage in this man who had spent most of his life among elegant courtiers. He loved the wilderness and the wild drama of Indian councils. When he visited their camps he would smear his face with war paint and dance and whoop around the fires with the warriors. But he understood, also, how to awe them as the powerful representative of the great king across the water. When the chiefs were called to confer with him at Quebec or Montreal, Frontenac appeared in Court finery of silks, ruffles and plumed hat. He could always win the primitive men by his dramatic harangues, couched in the picturesque metaphor of Indian speech.

Even the proud Iroquois found their match in this fearless governor who never gave in to them, and who could outwit them at their own wily Indian game of diplomacy.

Frontenac had these impudent tribes so well tamed and bound by treaties that the Canadians were free from their attacks. Then the complaints of his enemies and the constant dissensions which disrupted the government at Quebec caused Louis XIV to recall him.

The timid incompetents who followed him as governors lost for the French both trade in furs and prestige among the Indians. The friendly tribes, begging French help against their ferocious enemies, were disgusted with Onontios who would neither make effective war on the Iroquois nor win them to real peace. Treaties were made and broken on both sides. The powerful Iroquois found that threats could make timid governors give in to them, so they were convinced that they could dominate the French and the tribes allied with them.

Then began a new time of terror for the Canadian settlers whose farms were strung along the St. Lawrence and Richelieu Rivers. Lachine, a village above Montreal, was attacked in the dead of night and most of its helpless inhabitants murdered. Terrified survivors fled to Montreal and from all the country round settlers hurried to take refuge within the walls of the frontier town. The Indians did not dare to attack Montreal itself, but they laid waste the countryside. Refugees in the town saw clouds of smoke rising in all directions from burning wheat fields and farmhouses.

The stream of furs from the interior was going to the English by way of the Iroquois, for the western tribes had been cowed by their enemies. Thereby the province lost its chief means of support. Worse yet, as the people were afraid to leave the towns, fields went untilled and the inhabitants were in danger of starvation. New France had fallen to a low estate indeed, and it seemed as though the flourishing English colonies might gain French territory.

In this desperate situation Louis XIV turned to the only man he knew who could save New France and in 1689 sent Count Frontenac once more to Quebec. He was an old man in years but his fighting spirit was as strong as ever. The Canadians took hope and rallied around him, while he prepared to deal with the menace of English and Iroquois enemies. With French troops, Canadian militia and Indian warriors, Frontenac invaded the Iroquois country, first attacking and burning the English settlement of Schenectady, then continuing to Iroquois towns in New York. Most of the warriors saved themselves by flight into distant forests, but their villages were destroyed, their fields laid waste, and their proud spirit so humbled that they ceased their attacks on French settlements.

Frontenac was the leader, also, in the increasing conflicts with English colonials. Wars between England and France in Europe were reflected in colonial wars for possession of the continent. Bloody and brutal fights raged along the vague boundaries between New France, New England and New York, while white men adopted Indian savagery in a war of extermination. Indian bands were encouraged in massacres of helpless settlers in undefended villages, and rewarded for their work. In the distant interior, around trading posts of the French and English, battle went now to one side, now to the other.

Behind this forest warfare French and English colonials of Quebec and Montreal, New York and Boston, formed audacious plans for conquest. The French scheme was to assemble militia and Indians to raid English posts in New York, reach the Hudson and capture Albany. Then Frontenac planned to seize the river craft and go down the river to New York. The French fully expected to capture that town, thus gaining control of New England and possessing themselves of the Hudson. The scheme had the consent of the king, but due to inefficiency, quarrels and various other disasters, the ambitious plan never got farther than attacks on settlements and destruction of Iroquois villages.

Meanwhile, on their side, New Englanders and New Yorkers, who were enraged by the border warfare, determined to invade Canada by land and sea to make an end of French power on the continent. Colonial militia from the various towns were to march on Montreal by way of Lake Champlain. Massachusetts was to assemble a fleet for the capture of Port Royal and Quebec.

Seafaring New Englanders had their commerce interfered with by privateers that found shelter at Port Royal, and they had long had their eyes on the fisheries of Acadia, so near their own territory. The people of New England though merchants, farmers and fishermen had fought boldly to protect their homes from Indian and French attack and they were quite ready to try for the conquest of Acadia.

Port Royal, the outpost in Acadia, had little help from an indifferent government so that the fort was poorly equipped. When in the spring of 1690 a small fleet from Boston, commanded by Sir William Phips, sailed up the basin, Port Royal was captured without difficulty. The small garrison left by Phips to hold the place had to exist in a hostile land, harassed by guerrilla attacks from unreconciled Acadians and their Micmac Indian friends.

Massachusetts folk were overjoyed at the easy victory. Boston went to work vigorously to raise militia and prepare a fleet for the capture of Quebec. Although they had no naval vessels among their merchant ships and fishing schooners, no regulars or naval men among their companies of recruits, they were quite confident. Sir William Phips, who was in command, was a bold seaman but he had no experience whatever in naval warfare or soldiering. Nevertheless, in the late summer of 1690, the fleet set sail in high spirits to attempt the treacherous navigation of the unknown St. Lawrence and to attack the citadel of Quebec.

Governor Frontenac knew of the New England plans and did his best to strengthen the feeble fortifications of Quebec and to raise militia for the defense of Montreal.

News came to him at Montreal that the Massachusetts fleet was in the river, and taking a canoe the old governor was paddled hastily to Quebec, arriving in time to hearten the alarmed inhabitants. Militia poured into the town from the countryside while armed farmers prepared to drive off any invaders who tried to land on the shore of the river. Beating drums and wild whoops announced the arrival of militia from Montreal. The stout Canadians rallied to save their river and citadel from the enemy.

Soon sails appeared down the river and ships rounded the point of the Île d'Orléans to range themselves in the basin before Cape Diamond. Anxious watchers on the heights counted thirty-four ships and knew that they were greatly outnumbered.

That natural fortress of solid rock, towering above the river with its crown of walls and steeples, was a staggering sight to inexperienced Sir William Phips. Still he held to his conviction that these Canadians, like the Acadians, would not fight and that he would win the coveted fortress without a battle.

When a young officer was sent ashore with a summons to surrender, Count Frontenac staged a reception in keeping with his audacious character. He did not intend to have the invaders learn how inadequate were his defenses or how small his forces. The messenger was blindfolded on the wharf and led by soldiers to the upper town, around corners and over barricades. People tramped by, shouting and jostling him, to give the impression of great martial stir.

In the Château Saint Louis the bandage was removed from the messenger's eyes and he found himself facing the haughty governor and his officers dressed in the powdered wigs and finery of French nobility.

Count Frontenac read the summons delivered apologetically by the dazed officer and made his classic reply: "I will answer your general only by the mouths of my cannon, that he may know that a man like me is not to be summoned in this fashion. Let him do his best and I will do mine."

The crestfallen messenger was then blindfolded once more and returned to his boat without further ceremony. The siege which began with such a well-staged comedy was a fantastic affair.

The attempts of the New England militia to win the town by land, from the rear, were thwarted by hard-fighting Canadians, while for two days the ships and the fortress exchanged a furious cannonading which accomplished little beyond tremendous din and smoke. The French gunners did manage to damage some of the ships, by good luck rather than good management.

Winds and waves hindered the movements of the ships and presently, to the astonishment of the defenders, they saw them creep away one by one to disappear behind the Île d'Orléans. The people could scarcely believe their good fortune. Bells rang and drums beat while the townsfolk gathered in the churches to give thanks for their deliverance.

Quebec was saved and so, too, was Montreal, for the overland expedition from the English colonies never got that far. Companies quarreled and became separated, while disease and hardship finished their disintegration.

For the time being, New France on the St. Lawrence was at peace. The people of towns and farms could go about their work without fear, even of the Iroquois, for those proud tribes had at last agreed to make peace with their Indian enemies and the French. The devastation of their own villages and the forceful attitude of the French brought them to terms. That was Frontenac's work, although the fighting governor did not live to take part in the great peace council. In 1698 the fiery old aristocrat died in the Château Saint Louis, mourned by the people and praised even by his enemies.

Through the patient work of French officers and Jesuit priests who understood the Indians and were trusted by them, the Iroquois and distant tribes of the interior were persuaded to meet the French at Montreal and bury the hatchet.

In the summer of 1701 great flotillas of canoes came down the river, bringing deputations from all the important tribes, each flotilla greeted by a salvo of cannon from the fort. On the day set for the momentous peace council a barbarically colorful throng gathered in a large field outside the walls, fenced with evergreens, and with a canopy of green boughs to shelter the seats of the government dignitaries.

In a ring around the grassy space sat the deputies of the tribes, more than thirteen hundred warriors. Impassive coppery faces, fiercely painted, stared from under headdresses of feathers, horns of beasts or buffalo heads. Facing them, haughty and aloof, sat the deputies of the Five Nations, their common enemy.

Opening the assembly Governor Callières made a speech, saying that he now threw his hatchet and theirs into a pit so deep that no one could find them; henceforth they must all live like brothers and bring their quarrels to him, Onontio, the father of them all.

One by one the chiefs of deputations, trailing fur robes from their shoulders, their heads held high, marched up to the governor and spoke for their tribes, promising to keep the peace.

Then the hawk-faced Iroquois chief, a bronzed figure of savage pride, strode forward, surveying them all with dignity while he made his oration. "Onontio, we are pleased with all you have done and we have listened to all you have said. We assure you by these four belts of wampum that we will stand fast in our obedience." He threw down before the governor the gorgeous belts, Indian symbol of treaty making. The governor, for his part, distributed handsome wampum belts to all the tribes.

The final ceremony was the smoking of the calumet of peace. It was passed first to the governor and officials, then to each deputation until all were united by the sacred smoke. Each chief signed his totem mark — bird, beast or other creature — to the treaty, signifying that the hatchet was buried among the Indians, tribe with tribe, and between them and their father, Onontio. Governor Callières stood up and proclaimed: *"Voici la paix; oublions le passé."*

The French were free from fear of the Iroquois, but were still engaged in border warfare with English colonists while the mother countries continued their struggle for the possession of North America. In 1710 Port Royal passed for the last time from French to English hands, captured by Colonel Nicholson of Boston with colonial soldiers and an English fleet. The great bay was renamed Annapolis Basin and the town and fort became Annapolis Royal and Fort Anne, named in honor of the reigning English queen.

The war between France and England which ended with the

Treaty of Utrecht in 1713 went badly for Louis XIV. In the peace terms Newfoundland and all of Acadia, or Nova Scotia, except Cape Breton and Île Saint Jean, now Prince Edward Island, were ceded to England.

The Acadian farmers, deserted by the motherland, were encouraged by their priests and by influence from Quebec, to resist English rule. Few of them were willing to take the oath of allegiance, nor would they move from their good lands to settle in less fertile Cape Breton under a French governor. After years of trouble, in 1755, the governor of Nova Scotia, pressed by New Englanders, determined to anglicize the province by decreeing the exile of the Acadians. It was a tragic exodus of the peasant people who loved their meadows and orchards above all else. Shiploads of the exiles were deposited in the other English colonies and many New Englanders moved in on their farms.

After the loss of Nova Scotia France set about protecting the St. Lawrence, the "ready way to Canada" by building a fortress on the tip of Cape Breton. Louisbourg was to be the Gibraltar of North America, a threat to the English and a bulwark for Canada on the St. Lawrence. The fortress was designed by the best military engineers of France but, owing to the profiteering of corrupt local officials, poor materials went into the building of the great bastions and they were never supplied with their full complement of cannon. Officers and soldiers alike hated their term of duty in dull, foggy Louisbourg. Aside from the garrison the inhabitants were poverty-stricken fishermen, small shopkeepers and men who profited from the lively smuggling trade with New England. The main idea of governors and officers was to make money from their jobs and get home again to France.

New Englanders were more interested than the British government in destroying Louisbourg, for the harbor was a base in war for the privateers that harassed their merchant ships. They were also angered because, in 1744, an expedition from Louisbourg had burned the little fort at Canseau and made a futile attack on Annapolis Royal. These attacks were the first colonial moves in a new war between France and England.

In Boston the governor of Massachusetts held council with New England merchants and officials, secretly planning a great colonial expedition against Louisbourg. They were aided by Puritan divines who roused their flocks to a crusade against the hated Papists. A fleet of merchant ships was assembled to be commanded by Commodore Warren, an English Navy officer who had married a colonial lady. The militia was to be commanded by William Pepperell, a prominent citizen but not a professional soldier.

By all rights Louisbourg should have been safe against such an expedition, for it was the strongest fortress in North America. It was further protected by a dangerous rocky coast and the narrow entrance to its inner harbor.

The fortress was weak, however, because of its defenders. It was a town of thievery in high places and resentful, impoverished inhabitants. The people had no confidence in their officers or in the garrison. Many of the soldiers were Swiss mercenaries who had just staged a revolt because of unpaid wages and poor rations. The governor and garrison officers refused to believe in their danger until the sails of the invading ships appeared in the outer bay.

Then all was confusion and panic within Louisbourg. They had not enough cannon, munitions were low, and what they had was badly used. The governor and his officers made stupid blunders when they managed to act at all. An important outwork, the Royal Battery, which protected the harbor, was aban-

doned without even spiking the guns. Thirteen New Englanders walked into it to turn the Frenchmen's own guns against
them.

The whole siege on both sides was a comedy of blundering
inefficiency, but luck was with the untrained New Englanders
because of the disintegration of the French defenses. The New
England gunners were far from expert but, having captured
batteries or got their cannon into advantageous positions, they
bombarded the fortress from all sides. Breaches were torn in
the walls, the houses tumbled into heaps of rubble.

Anguished people on the ramparts saw French ships, coming
to their relief, captured by Commodore Warren's ships. Food
was giving out, the cellars were crowded with wounded and
dying men, and the miserable people clamored for surrender.
The governor knew that the ammunition was almost gone, so
there was nothing to do but to send a flag of truce with a request
for terms of surrender.

With a great deal of pomp the colonial commanders, Warren
and Pepperell, marched with their officers into humbled Louisbourg to receive the surrender of the governor and garrison.
The soldiers and any of the inhabitants who wished to go were
to be sent to France. The rough militiamen who had hoped
for rich booty found a ruined, starving town and, to their disgust, were set to guard the houses they had hoped to loot. A
fanatical Puritan parson took pleasure in smashing the images
in the church with the hatchet he had brought along for the
purpose.

Thus ignominiously did the Gibraltar of North America fall
to a colonial expedition in the year 1745. It was a terrible blow
to French prestige and to the safety of Canada. In Boston rejoicing knew no bounds when the triumphant fleet returned.
Proud indeed were those bold colonials that by their own

initiative and with very little help from England, they had captured the stronghold which was the only sea link between New France and the mother country.

Louisbourg was held by the English for three years. Then, to the disgust of the New Englanders, a new peace treaty gave the fortress back to France. The English, in 1749, built Halifax, on the splendid Nova Scotia harbor which the Indians called Chebucto, to keep watch on Louisbourg and the French. From the day of its foundation Halifax has been a bastion for England's sea power on the Atlantic coast, a town of military tradition.

Outwardly it seemed that French empire in North America was stronger than that of England. New France had lost Acadia, to be sure, but there remained Canada on the St. Lawrence as well as Louisiana, extending from the Great Lakes to the mouth of the Mississippi. French possessions made a long thin line, four thousand miles in extent, held only by the few settlements of Canada and the chain of forts along the interior rivers. It was a difficult empire to defend.

The magnificent France of Louis XIV was no more. A bored king, Louis XV, took refuge in extravagant pleasures, allowing the fate of France to rest in the pretty hands of his ambitious mistress, Madame de Pompadour. The country was weakened by the corruption and luxury of the Court.

In England, the far-seeing William Pitt was creating empire through sea power. On the ocean England's fleets were supreme, and New France depended for life on the free passage of ships from France to Canada.

The vigorous English colonies, much larger in population than New France, extended along the Atlantic coast from Nova Scotia to Florida, and forest warfare was going on around forts of the Ohio Valley between colonials of both countries with Indian allies. Then, in 1756, England and France became involved in the Seven Years' War in Europe and both nations entered the final contest for the possession of North America.

That great and honorable soldier of France, the Marquis de Montcalm, was sent to Canada to organize campaigns and capture English forts. He found that the province was being ruined by a supreme rascal, the Intendant Bigot, a racketeer who could have given points to men of his breed in the present age. As intendant, Bigot controlled nearly every operation of colonial government and found a ready tool in the vain, incompetent governor, Vaudreuil. This man was Canadian-born and jealous of men from France, but Bigot was skillful in playing on his vanity and love of display. Vaudreuil knew what thievery was going on, but apparently connived at it and weakly submitted to Bigot's orders.

The official society of Quebec — Bigot and his gang as well as those who profited by their doings — lived extravagantly while the people suffered. These racketeers managed successfully to steal from the king, the colonial government and the people, to their own immense profit. The inhabitants, and the soldiers as well, were half-starved on small rations of bread and horse meat, while upper-class society of Quebec reveled in gambling and feasting.

No wonder that General Montcalm wrote despairingly to friends in France, "What a country, where knaves grow rich and honest men are ruined!"

Governor Vaudreuil resented the presence of this French general and insisted on his right as commander-in-chief of colonial forces to direct the militia and even countermand Montcalm's orders to his own troops. The general was thwarted in all his plans by the governor and was never able to organize unified campaigns.

Nevertheless, in 1758, General Montcalm defeated a large

army of English regulars and colonials at Ticonderoga. His own difficulties with mismanagement and interference by the governor were counterbalanced by the stupidities of the English General Abercrombie, one of the most inept generals ever sent to the American colonies.

On the whole, it was not going well for England in 1758 when William Pitt decided that Louisbourg must be captured to rob France of her seaport and open the way to Quebec. An invincible combination of army and navy was organized for the purpose. Ships were assembled at Halifax where the inhabitants watched with interest the training of soldiers and seamen for the great enterprise.

This siege was to be a different affair on both sides from that of 1745. Louisbourg was now protected by a French fleet, the fort was well garrisoned and commanded by a brave governor who was determined to hold it and save Quebec.

It was a formidable armada of British warships which faced the defenders of Louisbourg when the fog lifted on a June morning of 1758. They were opposed by the best that France could muster in soldiers and ships. In the long weeks of siege gallant and skillful fighting was done on both sides. Conspicuous among the leaders of British troops was a tall, youthful brigadier-general, James Wolfe, fighting his first campaign in America.

Slowly the defenses crumbled. When his ships had been burned or captured, his cannon put out of action and the outer defenses taken, the governor was forced to ask for terms, and complete surrender was demanded. Nevermore would the proud fortress protect Canada, nor would it serve the English. In order to prevent the French from re-taking it, the great bastions were razed in the following year. Nothing remains of Louisbourg today but a museum and grassy hummocks above a bleak shore.

Bonfires blazed and bells rang in Boston and London when the news of Louisbourg's fall was received. Military Halifax, crowded with triumphant army and navy men, went wild with joy. While the officers were entertained with balls and dinners, crowds celebrated in the streets and drank toasts all night in gallons of Jamaica rum.

General Montcalm in Quebec was dismayed by the fall of Louisbourg. He was well aware of the English plans against Quebec and exhausted his strength and patience in efforts to win co-operation from the governor for the organization of defense. His last orders from France had been to maintain a foothold in America at all costs and he had replied, "I shall do everything to maintain it, or die." With all his soldierly skill and deep loyalty to France, he worked to defend the last fortress.

Even when news came that the English fleet was in the river the general's plans were blocked by jealous interference. Montcalm sent a battalion to hold the heights of Levis across the river, but Vaudreuil ordered them to return to the city so that the important post was left open to the enemy.

The fleet was the largest ever yet sent to America, commanded by Admiral Saunders, with a large army under the command of the accomplished young officer James Wolfe who was now a general. One hundred and forty ships, carrying twelve thousand men, rounded the Île d'Orléans and appeared before Quebec in June 1759: transports and supply ships, great three-decker frigates with their cloud of sails — "a forest of great ships," Montcalm called them.

It was a fateful summer for the citadel on the heights where Montcalm, alert and watchful, tried to guess and forestall the moves of the enemy. It was fateful, too, for General Wolfe who, with his army and the aid of the fleet, must find a way to take this fortress which was protected by nature with bastions of sheer rock. General Wolfe was one of the most brilliant soldiers of England, but he was a frail and sickly man. Some of the time he lay ill with fever in his camp below Montmorency Falls, his mind tortured with the problem of how to get an army up those cliffs.

The French had well-fortified redoubts on the crest of the hills along the shore below Quebec and the approach to the rear by the St. Charles River was protected by fortifications. But General Wolfe was able to occupy the heights of Levis left unprotected by the stupidity of Governor Vaudreuil. Consequently the citadel was subjected to a constant and devastating bombardment. Houses and walls crumbled under the cannonading, but still the fortress held.

General Wolfe moved his troops from camp to camp behind the screen of ships, he laid waste villages along the shore and bombarded the town and fortifications from the fleet, but he failed in attempts to take the redoubts below Quebec. Constantly the ships moved up and down the river, while the general studied the ramparts of cliffs extending twenty miles or so above Quebec. Where could he find a vulnerable spot for the landing of troops?

Meanwhile, the summer passed and in the early September days both generals knew that success or failure was at hand. If Montcalm could hold out until the autumn storms began and ice was forming in the river, Quebec was safe. General Wolfe knew that he must take the citadel in September or retreat in humiliation, and the capture of that fortress was the crowning opportunity of his career.

In the beleaguered citadel the food problem was desperate. Quebec was cut off from the world by that forest of great ships in the river. Only from above, from Montreal and Trois Rivières, could food reach the city. At night provision barges glided silently down the dark river, hugging the north shore, to land in the cove called the Foulon two miles above Quebec. By a steep path up the cliffs supplies were transported to the citadel and the camp.

Montcalm realized the danger of that place where the cliffs could be scaled and had sent a battalion to guard the path, but once more the governor interfered. Declaring that the English could not fly up the cliffs, he ordered the soldiers back to the city. Only a small sentry post guarded the important spot.

General Wolfe's keen eyes had also seen the possibilities of that cove. On his reconnoitering trips up the river he observed washerwomen scrubbing clothes on the shore and saw that wash was spread to dry on bushes at the top of the cliffs. Therefore, there must be a path. A deserter from the French camp confirmed the existence of the path so the young General went ahead with a desperate plan, the last try to capture the citadel before the winter storms began.

On the night of September 12 a fleet of barges, filled with five thousand soldiers, moved silently along the north shore of the river in the darkness. A sentry challenged them and a voice replied in good French that they were provision barges from above. These were expected, so the sentry let them pass. Quietly the barges landed in the cove and General Wolfe with his officers led the regiments up the path to the heights. The sentinels were captured, and soon after dawn scarlet-coated British regulars and Scotch Highlanders in their kilts were forming in solid ranks on the Plains of Abraham.

The news that the British were on the heights came to General Montcalm while he was having an early morning cup of tea. Immediately there was bustle and confusion in the French camp. Montcalm hurried from place to place, marshalling his troops and sending them to the Plains.

Presently, in the bright sunshine, the opposing armies were drawn up in full view of each other on the open ground. Lines of British scarlet faced the white of French lines, the blue of the Canadian militia, and a wild array of bushrangers and Indians. Montcalm, on a black horse, rode along his lines, a gallant figure in full-dress uniform. He spoke to the men, encouraging them, then lifted his sword in the signal to attack.

The blue and white lines moved forward firing and moving on again, while through the smoke the British ranks could be seen standing stolid and silent until the French were close. Then devastating fire crackled from the scarlet lines, mowing down the French. They rallied and came on again, fighting gallantly, but the solid ranks, spitting fire and gleaming with bayonets, were too much for them. Their lines broke and the men started to retreat while Montcalm rode among them, trying to lead them back. He was badly wounded and was swept on in the tide of panic-stricken troops which streamed toward the city, pursued by shouting Britishers and Highlanders.

Montcalm would have fallen from his horse had not two soldiers held him up and led the horse through the Saint Louis gate. Women cried out in fear as the dying general passed, but he soothed them with quiet words and went on to the house of his surgeon to be tended.

In fifteen minutes the battle was over and Quebec was lost. Before dawn the man who had given his skill and devotion and broken his heart over a hopeless task was dead. On the battle-field there was sorrow, also, as victorious officers knelt beside young General Wolfe who died of wounds received in battle before he could be moved.

The ruined, starving city, filled with the wounded and dying, cut off from food and sunk in a mood of defeat, was surrounded by victorious troops. A few days after the battle the English

General Townshend marched his troops through the Saint Louis gate and lined them up before the Château to receive the keys of the city from the French commander. The fleur-de-lis was hauled down for the last time and the flag of Britain raised over Quebec.

General Montcalm was buried by torchlight in the Ursuline chapel, his body laid away in a great breach of the walls made by British cannon. Within a few days the English chaplain read funeral services for General Wolfe in the same chapel. Bigot the knave and Vaudreuil the fool, who had been instrumental in the ruin of their country, scurried away to Montreal.

The destiny of a continent was decided in that brief battle on September 13, 1759, although Montreal held out for another year. Then the last French post on the St. Lawrence surrendered to an English army and French empire in America came to an end. In the peace treaty of 1763 English merchants would have liked to have England receive from France the warm West Indies island of Guadeloupe, rather than what Voltaire called "a few acres of snow" in Canada. But William Pitt foresaw the value of Canada and the English colonials used their influence to obtain what they had always wanted, a British Canada.

The curtain was rung down on the tragic last act of a splendid drama. For over two hundred years men, and women, too, had played their parts on a vast wilderness stage. Explorers, traders, adventurers; nuns and spirited pioneer women; men of honor and courage imbued with a love for France, as well as fools and rascals who undermined the structure built by honest Frenchmen; one and all they did their bit in leaving the imprint of French character and civilization forever on North America.

France had not known how to foster and help the work of

her sons and daughters in the western continent.   Now, deserted by the mother country, the people rallied around their one secure bulwark—the Church.

In the country the sturdy habitants, rooted to their beloved *terre canadienne* remained a compact little world of tradition among sweeping changes.

II. The Kingdom of the Fur Traders

CHAPTER VI

The Adventurers of England and the Nor'Westers
[1670–1793]

LOCKED in ice except for a few months in the year, Hudson Bay long remained a region of mystery. The only visitors were a few navigators who steered their ships among the ice floes, searching for the Northwest Passage to lead them around the continent. It remained for two of those adventurous coureurs de bois of the seventeenth century to comprehend that the bay was the entrance to a valuable fur country and to lead English traders to its shores.

Medart Chouart and Pierre Esprit Radisson were natives of Trois Rivières on the St. Lawrence, a trading hamlet of sturdy frontiersmen. Pierre, when a boy, wandered too far into the forest one day and was captured by a band of Iroquois. The Indians thought him a likely lad and he was adopted by a family of their village. Living with his Indian family, hunting and going on war parties with the young braves, Pierre Radisson became half Indian himself. He understood and liked his savage friends and loved their wild, roaming life, but he was too thoroughly a Frenchman to remain with the Indians permanently. He took an opportunity to escape and returned to Trois Rivières to go hunting for furs with his brother-in-law, Medart Chouart.

They were a fascinating pair of adventurers, bold and imaginative, each abetting the other in ambitious schemes. Radisson's gay, boastful spirit and glib tongue made him the more colorful of the two, but in shrewdness and ability Medart Chouart was his superior.

Together they roamed afar among the Indians of the Great Lakes and among the Crees who inhabited the great northwest belt of woodland which was the source of much of the fur brought to Montreal. Woodlands of poplar, willows along the rivers, provided the industrious beavers with their favorite food. These animals, whose pelts were unusually fine because of the long cold winters of the region, built their dams along rivers which intersected the country.

Hunting and camping with the Crees the two adventurers collected a wealth of beaver pelts and persuaded distant Indians to bring their furs to Montreal. This enterprise brought them profits and praise from the Governor of Quebec. Medart Chouart was made captain of militia in Trois Rivières and bought himself a piece of land called *des groseilliers,* the gooseberry patch. He gave himself the title Sieur de Groseilliers and swaggered with all the airs of a seigneur. Radisson wrote, in the story of their adventures, "We weare Caesars with none to contradict us."

The Caesars already had an ambitious plan brewing in their minds. They wanted to explore the marvelous beaver country all the way to Hudson Bay and asked permission from the governor to make the expedition. When he made it a condition that half the profits should be his, the adventurers refused, and presently they slipped away quietly, without a license. For a long time they hunted and traveled with the Cree Indians and finally reached the bay. Looking out on its somber waters Radisson and his partner conceived the brilliant idea of reaching Hudson Bay by sea, to build a trading post and tap the fur wealth at its source.

With bales of furs worth thousands of dollars they turned up at Trois Rivières to be hailed as heroes by the townsfolk, but condemned as rascals by the governor. He got most of the profits from the furs by fining them great sums for going without permission. Medart Chouart was clapped into jail for deserting his post as captain.

Highly indignant over such reward for their labors, the two men, as soon as Medart Chouart was released, went to France to get backing from the king for their great idea. They knew that there were fortunes in furs in the Hudson Bay country, but they could not convince the king that their enterprise was worth while.

Next the schemers were seen in Boston and New York, trying to persuade ship captains to take them to the bay. In Boston they managed an interview with Sir George Carteret, privy councillor to King Charles II, who thought well enough of their plan to bring them to the attention of the King of England.

Into the London of 1666, devastated by the Great Plague, came the adventurers from Canada. King Charles was living at Oxford to escape the plague and there, at last, Radisson and Groseilliers, as Chouart was now known, were permitted to tell their story.

King Charles listened, then called his cousin, Prince Rupert, and some of his nobles to hear the tale. Before the lordly gentlemen, resplendent in great curled wigs and gorgeous silks, stood the bronzed and bearded forest wanderers clad in buckskin. They brought the fresh atmosphere of the wilderness into the royal audience chamber. Persuasive Radisson, the teller of tales, painted for the courtiers a great world of beaver and Indians, forests and waters. Groseilliers, the shrewd, probably pointed up the vivid story with quiet practical remarks. Prince Rupert listened with attention, for he was a far-sighted man who realized the possibilities of wealth in this venture.   King Charles depended on the counsel of their elder cousin, a grave, honorable soldier who had fought for Charles' father.

Prince Rupert was prepared to give the adventurers a chance, but the Plague, the Great Fire which followed it, as well as attacks by the Dutch, occupied the entire attention of the Court until 1668.   Then, under Prince Rupert's patronage, two little ships set sail for Hudson Bay, the *Eaglet* and the *Nonsuch,* with the hopeful Canadian adventurers on board.

It was Groseilliers, or Mr. Gooseberry, as the English called him, who carried through this first venture, for the *Eaglet* with Radisson aboard was damaged and forced to turn back.   Doubtless picturesque French curses filled the air when Radisson saw himself cheated of the adventure.

The *Nonsuch* made its way through Hudson Straits, sailed the full length of the bay and anchored for the winter.   The log hut in which Groseilliers and the English sailors spent the bitter months of cold was named Fort Charles, but later became Rupert House, a post where men have traded with the Indians for two and a half centuries.   Groseilliers' friends, the Indians, brought him quantities of furs and, when the *Nonsuch* returned to England the following summer, the adventurer was able to present the king with beaver pelts worth ninety thousand pounds.

That was proof enough to King Charles and Prince Rupert that the Canadians were right in their tales of wealth.   It was the fashion in the vigorous England of that day to form trading companies for commerce in foreign lands.   Such a company was formed by Prince Rupert, who was to be its governor, and a charter was granted by King Charles.   On May 2, 1670, The Governor and Company of Adventurers of England Trading into Hudson Bay received its charter.   The Adventurers were to be "true and absolute Lordes and Proprietors" of Hudson Bay and of all lands drained by waters flowing into the bay, with full rights to trade and govern in those territories. This was Rupert's Land.

On a modern map the Adventurers received the provinces of Quebec and Ontario north of the Laurentians, the whole of Manitoba and Saskatchewan, the southern half of Alberta and the southeast corner of the Northwest Territories. They did not then know that King Charles was handing to a company of traders more than a million square miles of territory.

Payment to the Crown as a symbol of obligation was to be "two Elks and two Black Beavers whensoever and as often as We, our Heires and Successors shall happen to enter into the said Countryes." This obligation was first paid two hundred and fifty years later when Edward, Prince of Wales, passed through Winnipeg on the way to his Alberta ranch, and again, in 1939, when King George VI and Queen Elizabeth toured Canada.

The company began its long career under the direction of able, energetic Prince Rupert and his associates. Trade was profitable for a few years in the posts built "at the bottom of the Bay" — Rupert House, Moose and Albany Factories — and at York Factory on the west shore.

Then the French moved to meet this challenge to their monopoly. The remaining years of the seventeenth century saw many clashes at the bay, as French expeditions came overland or by sea to oust the English. Ships of both factions were sunk off shore and forts were burned and rebuilt many times. At some periods the French had most of the forests, but the Adventurers always managed to maintain their continuous occupation of Rupert's Land by at least one post. Radisson and Groseilliers had their share in the fur trading they had initiated,

although they sometimes quarreled with the English and gave
their services to the French at the bay.

The Company of Adventurers were obligated by their charter
to explore Rupert's Land and to search from the bay for the
fabled Northwest Passage but nothing was done about it for
some time. Their traders at the forts were not adventurers
like the French and had no heart for venturing into the wilds.
When pressure on the company in England made it imperative
to attempt exploration Henry Kelsey, a young trader at one of
the forts, was chosen. He was a bold lad, keen, adventurous
and with a liking for Indians.

It was a pleasure for him to go off with the Crees, wintering
with them, making friends, and persuading tribes at a distance
to bring their furs to the forts. Henry Kelsey was the first white
man to see the musk ox and buffalo, the first English explorer
on the plains. He also traveled to the north in the Barren Lands
describing the country as being "all stones with a coat of moss
upon ym." First among Hudson Bay men, Kelsey learned to
understand and deal fairly with Indians, a practice followed by
the Great Company throughout its history.

Other men went out from the posts on exploring trips and
thereby the knowledge of the interior and of Indian life was
increased. The journals kept by these traders give interesting
first impressions of the western wilds of Canada and the Barren
Lands of the North.

Meanwhile, during the early part of the eighteenth century,
the English traders met keen competition from French adventurers who roamed the west, meeting the Indians in their own
territory. By setting up posts along the Indian trails and offering alluring trade goods they won the furs which the natives
would otherwise have carried to the posts on Hudson Bay.

Among these Frenchmen none were bolder or more determined than La Vérendrye and his sons of Trois Rivières. They were not only after furs but were inspired with the ambition of reaching the western mountains described by Cree Indians, beyond which lay the ocean according to the Indian tale.

Although La Vérendrye failed to get help from the governor for his explorations he and his sons pushed westward in 1731, going beyond Lake Superior to Rainy Lake and Lake of the Woods where they built posts. They did well with their trading and in successive years went on into the northwest, trading, and winning the furs the English hoped to get. Never did the dream of reaching the western mountains leave La Vérendrye's mind. Despite disasters and mounting debts he and his sons kept on with their explorations. On one journey they saw, far off, the crests of the Rockies, but the ambition of reaching them was never realized. Nevertheless La Vérendrye had blazed the trail to the Rockies for other men to follow, and his was the farthest west of any French exploration.

When Canada passed into the possession of England in 1763 French exploration came to an end, but during the next decade the English from Hudson Bay were enlarging the map of North America by expeditions to the north. Samuel Hearne was their most famous explorer. He was a young trader stationed at Fort Prince of Wales, a large stone fortress which had been built on a point beside the mouth of the Churchill River. Company officers were excited by pieces of copper which northern Indians brought to the forts and Samuel Hearne was ordered to explore to "Ye Norward" to see what he could find and to search for the Northwest Passage.

His first two attempts failed because his Indian guides deserted him after stealing his supplies. Nothing daunted, Hearne had the courage to leave Fort Prince of Wales in December of the next year, 1770, to face the rigors of the northern winter.

He and his Indian guide, Matonabbee, struggled across the desolate wastes of the Barren Lands, enduring blizzards and Arctic cold, following the Coppermine River. Summer brought heat and mosquitoes and the midnight sun which did not set. In July, 1771, Hearne reached the mouth of the Coppermine River flowing into the Arctic Ocean. He was the first white man to reach that sea overland.

His journal records much of interest about Indian life and Arctic travel. There was abundance of copper along the river, he reported, but it would be impossible to mine it. As for the Northwest Passage, his explorations convinced him that it did not exist.

Later, when he was governor of Fort Prince of Wales, Samuel Hearne suffered the humiliation of surrendering it to French ships. Long after Canada was lost to France the great French navigator, La Pérouse, sailed into Hudson Bay with three ships and prepared to attack Fort Prince of Wales. Hearne had only a small company of men, too few for defense. So the stone fort which was to have been the company's stronghold was surrendered without resistance. The French sailors did their best to pull down its thick walls before they sailed away. A log fort was later built at the mouth of the river and Fort Prince of Wales was never used again.

The Adventurers of England, after the conquest of Canada, were to meet new competition in the fur trade, this time from men of their own race. Adventurers from the old English colonies to the south hastened into the rich northern fur country and others came from England and Scotland, making their headquarters at Montreal. The English Frobisher brothers were among the men who made fur history in Montreal, but most of them were canny, energetic Scottish Highlanders, men such as William McGillivray, James McGill, Simon McTavish and Alexander Mackenzie. The town which had known the pioneer French fur merchants became the city of wealthy fur kings.

The color and adventurous daring of the old French trade was revived, for these men were individualists, matching their wits against their rivals. They were joined by sons of the French traders and coureurs de bois and by the canoemen who had paddled those traders over the waterways of the interior. French Canadian or half-breed, these men of the canoe became a unique type, the voyageurs of the new fur trade. The Montrealers followed the French routes to the west, took over abandoned French forts and adopted the customs and language of the former adventurers.

Competition was keen as these traders roamed the west with their stores of blankets, beads, paints, tobacco, knives, guns and brandy. Some of them were ruthless men who angered the Indians by bad treatment so that there were murders of traders who had abused them and great restlessness among the tribes.

In Montreal one group contended with another until they wisely joined forces about 1783 to form the North West Company. Leading spirits in the company were Simon McTavish and the Frobisher brothers. The Nor' Westers were men who knew the fur business at first hand, from their own trading and traveling among distant Indian tribes and through wintering in isolated wilderness posts. Every "wintering partner" had a share in the profits of the company. Such men, imaginative and daring, backed up their picturesque adventuring with hard-headed business sense, and they became invincible lords of the vast untouched northwestern wilds. The traders ranged the Great Lakes, followed the rivers south of them, scattered their forts over the prairies and the valleys of the Saskatchewan and Athabaska Rivers.

Fur kings in Montreal built themselves mansions and entertained lavishly. The lusty "wintering partners" found an outlet for their high spirits in the gargantuan banquets of the Beaver Club, an organization noted for its hospitality. Every visiting celebrity or traveler was entertained at the Beaver Club. No one could be a member who had not passed the test of a winter in the *pays d'en haut* as the far-off fur country was called. On the candle-lit mahogany banquet table pemmican brought from the Saskatchewan country was the *pièce de résistance,* but there were, besides, innumerable courses of rich food and countless bottles of wine were emptied. After hours of feasting the hilarious gentlemen, seizing swords, walking sticks or fire tongs to serve as paddles, sat themselves on the floor as though they were in a great canoe and swayed to the stroke of the paddles as they chanted voyageur songs.

The villages along the St. Lawrence between Quebec and Montreal were the homes of voyageurs who grew up to the trade of paddling canoes over wilderness waterways and passed on the work to their sons. Proud of their strength and skill, of their capacity for song and gay carousing, these swarthy men were a class apart in customs, superstitions and dress.

The voyageur wore moccasins and leggings of deerskin, a short shirt bound around the waist with yards of gaudy *ceinture fléchée,* a woven sash with arrowlike pattern in red, blue and yellow. Possibly these sashes were of Indian origin, but the women of the parish of Assomption became famous for the weaving of them. The *ceinture fléchée* was the pride of the voyageur and woodsman, and became a valued article, for the Indians could not resist them.

A deerskin pouch, embroidered with beads, hung from the voyageur's sash to hold his precious pipe and tobacco. Under the red knitted cap long black hair fell to his shoulders, framing his brown, alert face. For rainy weather he had a capote, a blanket cape with a hood.

During the winter the chief traders, called the bourgeois, came to the Laurentian villages to engage their crews for the great spring journey to the *pays d'en haut,* and in the spring the voyageurs began gathering at Montreal.

Brigades of canoes, sometimes thirty to a brigade, carried trade goods, food supplies and traders by the chain of waterways and portages to the distant northwest posts. The Montreal canoe, called the *canôt de maître,* was thirty to forty feet long, a shell of white birchbark which was strong enough to hold several thousand pounds of goods and a crew of fourteen men, yet was light enough to be carried on the heads of two or three men over portages. Canoes were decorated with insignia painted in bright colors on the prows.

When the great river was blue and shining in the sunlight of May and its shores were fresh with new green, the tip of Montreal Island above Lachine Rapids was alive with preparation for departure. Crowds of shouting voyageurs worked over piles of goods on the shore, while others reinforced the seams of the canoes with fresh spruce gum. There were cases of guns, kegs of powder and of rum and brandy, large sacks of goods weighing ninety pounds each, with two ears at the top by which they were lifted. The last act of the crews was to kneel in prayer in their own chapel of St. Anne. It was the last church or priest they would see for many a long month.

After an emotional hubbub of farewells to friends and families, the men settled themselves in their places, feathers in their red caps and at prow and stern of the cherished canoes. With a flash of scarlet paddles, dipping in unison, they were off, while from sturdy throats rolled the rhythmic chant of a voyageur song, perhaps *En roulant ma boule, roulant* or the lovely old French folk song *À la claire fontaine.*

Up the Ottawa went the brigades, through the Mattawa to the French River and on to Georgian Bay and Lake Huron, the ancient route to the west. There were many portages on that part of the route, to pass cascades or to go from one river to another. Quickly the goods were unloaded; each man took on his back two of the sacks, held by a strap which passed around his forehead. Sometimes the men vied with each other to see how great a burden they could carry. Other men took the canoes on their heads and all tramped over the rough forest path to the next waterway, where the canoes were expeditiously reloaded.

All day long the men paddled, without shifting position in their delicately balanced craft, or changed their labor to that of carrying heavy burdens over portages. At stated intervals in the hours of paddling rest times were measured by pipes. The headman gave the order, *"Allumez,"* and the paddlers leaned back against the thwarts, drew out their pipes and enjoyed the luxury of smoke and joking talk. Then the paddles dipped once more in time to the chant which woke the echoes in silent forests, resinous and fragrant.

At night the canoes were unloaded, drawn up on shore and turned upside down to make shelters for the men. Soon, over the blazing camp fire hung a huge kettle of boiling water in which dried peas bubbled and swelled, enriched with strips of salt pork or some kind of grease. From the fat in his kettle of food the voyageur got one of his names — *mangeur de lard* or pork eater. The men gathered around the kettle with their spoons, dipping in and eating ravenously. Relaxed around the glowing embers with their pipes, the lively fellows entertained themselves with boastful tales of prowess and arguments over the merits of their beloved canoes.

The canoe was as much a part of the voyageur as his skin. He loved its clean lines, its responsiveness to the turn of his paddle as he steered between boulders and through the swirling uproar of rapids. It was his home by day and his shelter at night. The men slept rolled in their blankets under the canoes while the boss of the outfit, clerk or trader, had a tent.

The stars were paling in the sky when the cry of the boss was heard: *"Lève, lève, nos gens!"* The men rolled out of their blankets to eat breakfast and pack the canoes in the sweet freshness of the wilderness dawn.

The brigades went on through Saint Mary's River and over the wearisome portage past the roaring rapids of the Sault Sainte Marie, into the vast and awesome Lake Superior. There the frail canoes must brave the open waters and treacherous winds of the lake. They hugged the shore as much as possible under the lee of great dark cliffs which stirred the men's superstitious imaginations. When gales blew, the crews had to make camp because the canoes would have been battered to pieces by the waves. The canoes carried sails and, when a light favorable breeze blew, which the men called *"la vieille"* or old woman, they were speeded on their way across the wide waters. The voyageurs propitiated the old woman by scattering a little tobacco on the water while they cried, *"Souffle, souffle, la vieille!"*

Grand Portage on the far shore of Lake Superior was first the meeting place of the brigades from Montreal and those from the interior. Then Fort William became the Nor' Westers great yearly rendezvous of traders, voyageurs and then rulers of the company from Montreal.

The brigades went ashore before approaching Fort William, so that the voyageurs might dress themselves for a grand entry in their gayest sashes, feathers in their caps and pennants floating from the canoes. Heralded by their chant, the men swept up to the frontier village of Fort William in magnificent style.

In June and July the traders and clerks of the North West Company, scattered over thousands of miles of wilderness, met with the aristocratic lords of the company from Montreal, for conferences on the business of the year to come and reports on the year past. The traders from the interior posts, with their canoes full of voyageurs and Indians, brought the winter's wealth of pelts to be checked and sent to Montreal. The brigades coming from headquarters at Montreal brought the trade goods and supplies for the next winter's work at the forts.

In the great wooden council hall and banqueting room of the company, hung with furs and Indian trophies, these "lords of the lakes and forests," as Washington Irving called them, held council and high revelry. The rulers from Montreal arrived with all the style of Highland chieftains in great canoes loaded with luxuries and immense quantities of wines and liquors. Magnificent banquets were held with all sorts of game, fish and venison and such wilderness delicacies as buffalo tongue and beaver tail. Hearty food was washed down with gallons of wine. Despite their feasting the wintering partners were able to confer with shrewd Scotch sense on the problems of the business.

While the lords reveled in their banqueting hall, the voyageurs from Montreal and from the interior spent days and nights of joyous carnival, singing and dancing with the dusky Indian and half-breed girls, squandering their wages in carousals.

Novices among the voyageurs took back to Montreal the great bales of valuable furs. Experienced men who had wintered in the country were called *hivernants,* and they went on with the clerks and traders to the distant posts with food supplies and trade goods. They traveled in smaller canoes called *canôts du nord*. Over the marvelous chain of waterways which threaded the northwest they went; by Rainy Lake and Lake of the Woods to Lake Winnipeg; there the brigades separated, some traveling by the Red and tributaries to the headwaters of the Mississippi, others following the Assiniboine and the Saskatchewan toward the Rockies.

Trading posts were built on lakes and rivers, near Indian encampments or convenient to their trails. Log houses, within a high strong stockade and great wooden gate, sheltered the trader, his clerks and voyageurs and the Indian wives that the men picked up for the season. Even the trader often had a "wife of the country" who expected to be left behind when her master returned to civilization.

The trader was ruler of a little kingdom of clerks, voyageurs and Indians during the long, lonely, bitter winter. In his log house the firelight from the hearth flickered over homemade benches and bunks, touching fur robes and snowshoes hanging on the wall. Early in the season the men caught fish which were frozen outdoors so that they lasted all winter. The posts in the buffalo country had pemmican made by the Indian women. Indians and voyageurs hunted what game they could find, and there was a store of dried peas or corn, but food supplies often were very low.

Christmas and New Year's were celebrated with gaiety. The men were given *regale* — a present of enough flour to make cakes and a pint of rum apiece. With Indian and half-breed women the men danced hilarious jigs to the squeaky tunes of a fiddle.

The voyageurs often had to make long journeys to other forts with their dog teams, braving icy winds and snowstorms. They took as much pride in their dogs as in the canoes, dressing the animals in gay beaded saddle blankets, with pompoms or bells on their heads. Little shoes of skin were made for the dogs' feet to protect them from being cut on rough ice or frozen snow. Riding and running, the men traversed the wintry wilderness; sitting on the sled to be dragged by the dogs until they were stiff with cold, then running beside them on snowshoes hour after hour. At night they scooped out a hollow in the snow to build their fire, and slept beside it with their dogs. The traders themselves became as tough and expert as their men in winter or summer travel in the wilds.

It mattered not at all to the bold Nor' Westers that their fur empire encroached on Rupert's Land, granted by royal charter to the Adventurers of England who had come to be known as the Hudson's Bay Company. The Nor' Westers were Canadians with their headquarters in the country, and they were versatile and full of initiative. The Hudson's Bay Company on the other hand had been in existence for a century — it was old, established, conservative. The committee of the Company in London made all the plans for the business and all orders for the men at the bay had to come by ship from London. The factors, as they called the traders, and their clerks were loyal servants of the Company who did their work efficiently, but they were as cautious as their masters. They stayed stolidly in their forts at the bay, using every means in their power to get the Indians to come to them. They had established friendly relations with the Crees, Chipewyans and Eskimos from the north.

The men of the bay spoke scornfully of the "Master Pedlars" of Montreal, but the time came when they had to meet that competition or go out of business. Samuel Hearne built the first Hudson's Bay fort in the interior in 1774 — called Cumberland House, near the Saskatchewan River. After that, the English of the bay matched the Scotch-Canadians of Montreal in building forts through Rupert's Land and on the Athabaska River. Often the forts were close together at important places and sometimes the rivalry was friendly. As time went on, however, competition for furs became bitter and war raged between the two sets of traders in the fur country.

Great rivers of the interior were the routes of the fur empire for both companies. The Churchill, Nelson and Hayes Rivers, flowing to Hudson Bay, were used by the English of the bay to reach the interior. Both companies had their forts on the Red and Assiniboine and on branches of the Saskatchewan, which was a great highway of Rupert's Land. The Nor' Westers also established posts on the Athabaska River.

The map was unrolling, fur traders were marking the courses of great rivers, opening the vast interior of Canada westward toward the Rockies and northward toward the Arctic.

Men with an itch for exploration found an outlet for their energies with the traders of Montreal. One of the most famous of them was Alexander Mackenzie, a young Scot, who came to Canada at the age of sixteen to be employed by a group of traders opposed to imperious Simon McTavish. By the time the companies had united in the North West Company Alexander Mackenzie was an important man. He became a wintering partner and was assigned to the Athabaska district.

The life of a fur trader did not satisfy this energetic, ambitious young man. He wanted to explore, and turned his attention to the Arctic which Samuel Hearne had reached by the Coppermine River. Mackenzie determined to find a way to the Arctic from Lake Athabaska. Perhaps, when he reached the frozen sea, he could find out something about that passage around the continent which still preoccupied men of adventurous spirit.

So he set out in the summer of 1789 from Fort Chipewyan

on Lake Athabaska. He had with him Indians and clerks in two canoes and was guided by an Indian called the English Chief because he favored white men.

Mackenzie was the first to follow the chain of lakes and rivers which led to the Arctic; from Lake Athabaska to Great Slave Lake, and thence into the Great River of the North which was to bear his name. Like all the exploring fur traders he kept a meticulous journal of his travels, recording weather and geographical conditions, observing the natives and their customs.

As they proceeded down the broad lonely river, Mackenzie's men, particularly the Indians, became uneasy and wanted to turn back. It took all the leader's persuasion, and he had a way with men, to get them to go on. Indians of the country warned Mackenzie that it would take him several winters to reach the sea, and that "old age would overtake them before the period of their return."

Indian warnings did not bother Mackenzie and the company went on. On July 11 the explorer sat up all night to observe the midnight sun, calling his men to see the wonder. He comments on the country: "The adjacent land is high and covered with short grass and flowers though the earth was not thawed above four inches from the surface, beneath which was a solid body of ice. This beautiful appearance, however, was strongly contrasted with the ice and snow in the valleys."

They came to a high place where they could see the river winding among islands to the sea, solid ice extending along the shores. They had reached the Arctic, and Mackenzie had explored the vast river which was to become a route for exploration and trade in the future. On the way back he observed banks of loose red shale, containing what he called "petrolio." This observant traveler was the first to see the petroleum shale of the Mackenzie region, so valuable in Canada's future.

Alexander Mackenzie had satisfied his explorer's instinct by following a great river to the Arctic. He was proud of the journey, but to his disappointment the North West Company was too busy in other directions to be much impressed by a route to the Arctic.

Next the explorer turned his attention to the towering ramparts of the Rockies which barred the way to the western ocean. There was a great deal of speculation at that time about the unexplored regions west of the Rockies. The voyage of Captain Cook to the northwest Pacific had fired the curiosity of Englishmen about a coast where natives had sea-otter furs to trade. Mackenzie knew that other English ships had sailed around Cape Horn to investigate the coast. There were rumors, probably started by Indians and passed from man to man, about a Great River of the West flowing into the Pacific.

Mackenzie's mind became obsessed with the idea that by venturing into the forbidding western mountains he might find the headwaters of that river and follow it to the sea.

CHAPTER VII

The Pacific Northwest
[1793-1815]

A SMALL log fort on the Peace River was the farthest outpost of the west in the spring of 1793. Alexander Mackenzie had built it and wintered there, in preparation for his journey over the mountains. Now, in May, he was setting forth to reach the Pacific by following the Peace River toward its source, hoping thereby to come upon the headwaters of the Great River of the West.

His voyageurs had built a huge canoe, large enough to carry provisions, arms, trade goods, and a crew of voyageurs and Indians, as well as Mackenzie himself and his young clerk, Alexander Mackay. The party paddled off in high spirits, following the Peace River through an upland country of trees and open glades where quantities of elk and buffalo grazed.

Wilder and wilder grew the river as they neared the mountains. Between precipitous banks the water tumbled in continuous cascades and rapids. In one canyon, where the current boiled over rocks hemmed in by steep cliffs, it seemed impossible to proceed. Mackenzie, with a long tow rope fastened to the canoe, cut a way up to the top of the cliffs, pulled his men up after him, and by degrees they towed the canoe through the raging waters. Beyond, to the horror of the men, they saw miles of rapids. Mackenzie let them rest while, with an ax, he began to clear a way through the forest. His determination roused his crew to shoulder the packs and the canoe, and to hack out a trail past the rapids to navigable water.

When the river forked, Mackenzie chose the southern branch.

On they went, struggling against the mad current in narrow canyons as they mounted higher and higher among rugged mountains. From distant icy peaks came the thunder of avalanches and they could see the snowy spume of their fall. At last they reached a tiny mountain lake, the source of the river they had followed, later called the Parsnip. They met an Indian who consented to guide them over the height of land to rivers flowing west. Exhausted as they were, the men, loaded with burdens, followed their indomitable leader across the Great Divide.

To their intense satisfaction they soon found a river flowing in the right direction and joyfully launched the canoe to travel with the current instead of combating it. Their relief was short, for the canoe was caught in a furious current which swept them spinning into wild whirlpools. The canoe was hurled against a tree, breaking the stern. The men jumped out and clung to it, as the water swept it across the river to crunch the prow against a boulder. At last they were whisked into a quiet eddy where they could drag the canoe ashore. Panic-stricken, numb and aching from the icy water, the men declared they would go no farther. Even the courage of the voyageurs was exhausted. Mackenzie wisely said nothing, but gave them a *regale* of rum to raise their spirits.

The men had the greatest respect for a leader who shouldered the worst of the labor himself and whose dauntless spirit did not quail before the most terrifying country. When the rum had warmed them, Mackenzie exhorted his men as stout northerners to conquer the difficulties and accomplish their purpose. The soaked goods were spread on the rocks to dry while the canoe was patched up with materials from their packs.

It took all Mackenzie's powers of leadership to keep the exhausted men going on the appalling river. Some of the time they risked their lives in furious rapids but, for the most part, it was necessary to cut a path through forests and carry goods and canoe around canyons choked with fallen trees and roaring with cataracts.   Hostile Indians threw rocks at them from the cliffs or shot arrows from the shelter of trees.

Mackenzie determined to make friends with these wild people who had never before seen white men.   He laid down his arms and walked toward them with upraised hands, in sign of peace, and gradually a few Indians ventured near.   Mackenzie managed by gesticulations and Indian sign language to make them understand that the white men were seeking the way to the sea.

He learned from them that the river they were following became impassable, but that the Indians had a trail between the mountains by which they reached the place where they traded with Indians who lived in houses.   These people obtained iron and copper from seacoast dwellers who were acquainted with white men and with their boats as big as islands.   One of the natives traced in the sand of the river bank the Indian route to the sea.

Deeply disappointed that there was no word of a great river flowing west to the ocean, Mackenzie decided to follow the Indian route.   He was then on the Fraser River and the spot where he left it, present-day Alexandria, is marked by a memorial.

The battered canoe was hidden and most of their supplies buried, to be retrieved on the return trip.   With heavy packs on their backs, the explorers set out, guided by the Indian who had traced the route, to go overland to the sea.   Soon the guide slipped away, but Mackenzie urged his men on, following a dim Indian trail through dense, luxuriant forests dripping with moisture.

Barefooted, ragged and exhausted they came, after some weeks of journeying, to Indian villages of wooden houses on a river. These people had white men's goods, but they were fearful and suspicious. Salmon, on which they lived, were caught in weirs set in the river. They abhorred meat, and the sight of a piece of venison among the white men's goods nearly caused a riot. The strangers were not permitted to bring meat into the village for fear the salmon would smell it and desert the river. Nor were they allowed to approach the river lest the salmon scent something strange and be frightened.

By diplomacy and persuasion the party of explorers made their way from village to village. Mackenzie knew how to deal with Indians, so that the explorers were kindly treated and fed on stews of salmon and berries cooked by means of hot stones in large wooden containers.

They were on the Bella Coola River now and, far in the distance, Mackenzie saw the shining line of the ocean. He managed to borrow a dugout canoe to continue the journey to the sea.

Salt air was good in their nostrils as the excited explorers paddled down the inlets, the goal accomplished after all their sufferings. To Mackenzie there must have been exhilaration in the sight of the breakers rolling in on the desolate, boulder-strewn coast. Fog and rain obscured their view, and Mackenzie refused to return until he could take astronomical observations and find out where he was. The men stretched themselves to sleep on the huge boulders. Next day the explorer made his reckoning. With a mixture of grease and vermilion he traced on one of the large rocks the brief, proud statement: "Alexander Mackenzie, from Canada, by land, the twenty-second of July, one thousand seven hundred and ninety-three. Lat 52° 20' 48" N."

The stubborn Scot had stretched the trail of the fur traders from Montreal over the vast plains and mountains, across the continent to the Pacific Ocean. He was the first white man to make the journey to the Pacific coast overland north of Mexico.

Two months before his arrival the ships of Captain Vancouver, exploring and charting for England, had visited the same stretch of the coast. So we are brought to the story of the explorers who reached the Pacific northwest by sea.

All over the known world, in the eighteenth century, ambitious men were thrusting out expeditions to find new territory, new commerce and riches. Spain had kept explorers from investigating the west coast of the American continent, although English ships, late in the century, sailed around the Horn to make the voyage to China. England had a vague claim to the northwest coast by the voyage of Sir Francis Drake in the reign of Queen Elizabeth.

White men were a rare sight to Indians of the coast north of California until the Russians reached Alaska.

Peter the Great of Russia was the first to send explorers into the seas between Asia and unknown northwestern North America. Vitus Bering, the Dane, was engaged to make voyages for Russia. With map makers and scientists in his company, the Dane traveled by boat and camel caravan, from Russia on the Baltic across Siberia to Kamchatka. There a ship was built and the explorers set out to sail blindly through the storms and fogs of terrible northern waters.

Map makers at that time believed there was a continent called Gamaland lying between Asia and the unexplored northwestern edge of the American continent. Vitus Bering, at the cost of his life, disproved that theory, for he found the strait which separated the two continents by a narrow waterway. His ship was driven ashore on the Aleutian Islands. Death came to most of the company, stranded among the rocks of those gloomy islands, and Bering himself died of scurvy. The few survivors who managed to return to Kamchatka on a homemade raft were noticed because they were clothed in sea-otter skins.

Russian fur traders, who had a lucrative commerce with the Chinese, realized the value of these soft, thick pelts. Soon ships of ruthless hunters haunted the wild Aleutians. Traders, who employed criminals and exiles of Siberia, enslaved and abused the Aleutian natives in their avaricious pursuit of furs for the Chinese trade. After Alaska had been explored the distant Czar organized the fur trade and the little Russian settlement of Sitka became the headquarters of the traders.

Geographers and navigators learned of the Russian discoveries and of their trade in sea-otter skins. The ambition of English traders was aroused, while the discovery of Bering Strait led geographers to think that it might lead to the long-sought passage around the continent.

To the ancient dream of the Northwest Passage was added a new belief in mythical straits on the Pacific coast, which would provide a way through the continent to the Atlantic. The charts of an old Spanish explorer, Juan de Fuca, had indicated such straits.

So it was that the restless seeking of geographers and explorers and the ambition of traders sent ships into Spain's private ocean. Their captains were to finish drawing the outline of North America, save for the Arctic northlands, by exploring the mysterious northwest coast.

The British Government sent out an expedition to search for the straits which, it was hoped, would connect the new fur realm of the Pacific with the traders on Hudson Bay. An experienced voyager, Captain James Cook of the Royal Navy, was chosen to command the expedition. English ships were then trading with China and harboring for water and provisions at the Sandwich Islands. There Captain Cook and his two ships made landfall in the spring of 1778 and soon set sail for the northwest coast.

Skirting the shores the sailors saw noble headlands descending in sheer cliffs to lines of foaming breakers. Above the headlands dim white shapes of lofty peaks hung mistily in the sky. Storms drove the ships off shore and Captain Cook missed the strait which would have led him into Puget Sound. He approached Vancouver Island and entered the harbor of Nootka on the outer side of the island.

On the shore, against a background of huge spruce and cedar trees, stood the large plank houses of an important Indian village, with housefronts painted in bold mythological designs. Long dugout canoes filled with women and warriors sped out from shore to investigate the strange visitor. The chief, draped in a robe of sea-otter fur, with a conical woven hat on his head, welcomed the white chief to the village. This was the first meeting of Englishmen with the proud natives of the seacoast.

The English sailors had a pleasant sojourn among the Indians. They were invited to a feast in the house of the chief, and entered through the yawning mouth of an enormous carved monster which formed the doorway. They marveled at the number of families crowded into the dim cavernous interior of the house, and at their painted chests, carved horn spoons and robes of soft fur. The simple Indians, not yet used to white men, gave up fifteen hundred beaver and sea-otter pelts for a handful of old nails.

From Nootka Sound the English ships went on past the long rugged island, its mountainous interior clothed in forests of immense trees; on through shining waters between islands and the deeply indented coast, majestic in its mountain-framed bays.

Captain Cook investigated Bering Strait, crossed to the coast of Asia and was seen by the Russians at Kamchatka. He called at the Sandwich Islands for food and water before returning to England. There, in a foolish quarrel with the natives, the captain of many voyages was killed. His journal returned with the ships to England. Captain Cook had concluded that neither the Strait of Juan de Fuca nor the Northwest Passage existed, but the story of the voyage and the sight of rich furs caused much excitement.

It was an age of trading voyages for the English, with whom seafaring New Englanders were in keen competition. Swift sturdy windjammers of the English and the Yankees sailed the seven seas. Adventurous captains were stirred by reports of northwest Pacific shores inhabited by natives with a wealth of furs.

English trading ships led the way around Cape Horn to call at Nootka Sound for rich sea-otter pelts which they carried to the port of Canton in China to exchange for tea and silks for England. Americans joined the race to get furs for the China trade. In Boston shipyards two ships were built for the Pacific — the *Lady Washington* and the *Columbia*. Commanded by Captain John Kendrick and Captain Robert Gray they sailed from Boston in 1787.

When they reached Nootka Sound the Americans found two English traders, Meares and Douglas, comfortably settled in a small fort, celebrating the launching of a small schooner they had built. Courtesies were exchanged between the English and American captains, but John Meares was careful not to give his American rivals any information about the fur trade.

Captains Gray and Kendrick discovered furs for themselves, as they sailed on up the coast, calling at Indian villages to fill the ships with fine sea-otter pelts for the run to China. When the

Columbia, first of the two to reach the home port, arrived in Boston in 1790, there was great rejoicing. She was the first American ship to round the Horn and make the voyage to China. Henceforth the fleet American trading vessels competed with the English in the Pacific.

Spanish governors in sleepy California ports awoke to the fact that the coast they considered Spanish territory was being invaded. At intervals navigators had been sent to explore the shores north of California before 1779. Bruno de Heceta had seen evidences of a great river entering the sea but could not find it. The Spanish did not have the resources or energy to make good their claim by establishing posts to the northward.

Now, however, the governors moved to make clear to the English that they were intruding on Spanish territory.

As Captain Gray sailed out of Nootka Sound on his first visit he met a Spanish ship under full sail. The American was allowed to pass, but the Spanish captain, Don Joseph Martinez, ousted the English from Nootka, pulled down their fort and captured one of their ships. A Spanish fort was built in its place and Spain announced her intention of holding the coast. Other English ships coming from China for furs were later captured.

The Spanish took pains to explore the eastern coast of Vancouver Island and formally lay claim to it. The pilot Narvaez sailed through the Strait of Juan de Fuca, explored Puget Sound and was the first to see the delta of the Fraser River and the landlocked harbor where a great city was to arise in the future.

England could not brook any interference with her shipping, even though the vessels were only unimportant traders. There were sharp controversies between the English and Spanish Governments, Spain claiming the coast by prior explorations, England by the fact of a post at Nootka. The countries were close to war but Spain, too weak to contend with England, withdrew her claim to the coast.

In 1792 Captain George Vancouver of the Royal Navy, who had been with Captain Cook on his Pacific voyage, reached the northwest coast with two ships, the *Discovery* and the *Chatham*. He was instructed to explore and chart the coast for England and to receive from the Spanish commander the post on Nootka Sound.

Captain Gray in the *Columbia* followed close on the Englishman's heels. Vancouver, as he passed the tall headland, Cape Disappointment, had been beset by fogs so that he failed to see, hidden by the Cape, the mouth of the Great River which both English and American explorers were seeking. Two weeks later Captain Gray found the immensely wide mouth of the river and saw the breakers roaring over the treacherous bar which made it so difficult to enter.

The stout *Columbia* sailed over the bar and Captain Gray explored for twenty miles up the river. The American was the first to enter the Great River of the West.

Later on, the ships of the Englishman met Captain Gray's *Columbia* in the Strait of Juan de Fuca. Captain Gray declared that he had found the river mentioned by the Spaniard, Bruno de Heceta, and showed his log and soundings to prove it. Vancouver, however, refused to believe that he had actually entered the river.

The English captain went his way, meticulously exploring and charting the coast of the mainland, entering each bay to see if it might lead through the continent. The names of the coastal waters bear witness to his passage: Puget Sound, Burrard Inlet, Jervis Inlet, Prince William Sound and Cook's Inlet. After exploring far up the coast of the mainland, Vancouver sailed around the island which was to bear his name and entered Nootka Sound to meet the Spaniard, Don Quadra.

Did the methodical Englishman note only coast lines and soundings on that voyage? Surely he must have been impressed with the rare beauty of silvery waters and forest-clad islands veiled in blue mist, overlooked by the towering white peaks of the Cascades and Olympics, faint as a dream against the sky!

At Nootka there was elaborate exchange of diplomatic conversation between Don Quadra and Captain Vancouver, accompanied by wining and dining, in which the Indian chief, Maquinna, in his otter-skin robes, took part. Before Vancouver returned to England the Spaniards had given up their post and withdrawn their claim to the coast.

In the course of his explorations Vancouver sent out one of his boats with Lieutenant Broughton across the bar and up the river which Captain Gray had named for his ship, the Columbia. The English boat passed up the river far enough to see, and name, the white cone of Mount Hood, rising above the forests. Vancouver claimed the river for England, stating that "it does not appear that Captain Gray either saw or was ever within five leagues of the entrance."

By the time Alexander Mackenzie inscribed his arrival at the Pacific on a rock, in 1793, the coast had been charted and claimed for England, while both an American and an English captain claimed the discovery of the Great River of the West. Russia held Alaska to the north and Spain had California to the south. England, having announced her possession of the coast north of the Columbia, did nothing to establish her claim by bringing settlers to the primitive country.

English and American trading ships made the great circular

voyage from home ports to the Pacific coast for furs, to China to sell the furs for tea and silks, and home again. This sweeping trade brought a fascinating mingling of peoples and cultures. In Britain and New England the homes of merchants and sea captains were enriched with the porcelains, lacquers and silks of ancient China. On their voyages the ships called at islands in the Pacific for food and water — Juan Fernandez Island off Chile, the Sandwich Islands (now the Hawaiian group) and, later, at some Spanish South American ports. The Englishmen and Yankees became acquainted with the exotic port of Canton.

Sailors brought away souvenirs from China or handicrafts, carvings, bark cloth and other curious articles from the Sandwich Islands and the Indians of the Pacific coast. Natives of the islands were taken on board as sailors, so that the coast Indians became acquainted with these people as well as with "Bostons" and "King George Men" as they called the Yankees and British. They mingled also with Russians and Spaniards, learning new ways and ideas from all the white men, passing the articles they obtained from them up and down the coast by trade among themselves. Very soon the unique Indian life and culture were changed by these contacts, their art was stimulated and the dramatic cult of the totem poles reached its height after men from the outside world had come among them.

While the fur of the sea otter brought men by ship to the Pacific northwest, the fur of the beaver and other animals led traders westward across vast primitive country not yet defined as Canada and the United States. The Nor' Westers were quick to follow Alexander Mackenzie's lead into the Rockies and the country of peaks, rivers and plateaus between them and the Pacific.

The mouth of the Great River of the West had been found,

but there was now a race between Nor' Westers and Americans for possession of the river by exploration.

Simon Fraser, a partner in the North West Company, with the trader John Stuart, followed Mackenzie's route by the Peace and Parsnip Rivers into the heights of the mountains, from which they explored in all directions. They found a lofty country where exquisite lakes were set among forested mountains. Great white peaks loomed through clouds above them. It was a country abounding in game and fish, inhabited by mild-natured mountain Indians who were willing to trade. Posts were built on lonely lakes — Fort McLeod, Fort St. James, Fort Fraser. The exploring traders called the country New Caledonia and, with a ceremony of musket shots and flag raising, they claimed the new inland fur empire for England.

Meanwhile an expanding young republic to the south was reaching out into the west. The vaguely defined Louisiana of the French had passed to Spain and back again to the France of Napoleon, and he had sold a territory of unknown extent to the United States. What were the boundaries of Louisiana? Did it extend westward beyond the Missouri River?

Thomas Jefferson sent Meriwether Lewis and William Clark to blaze a trail overland from the Missouri to the Columbia and to strengthen the American claim to the Great River by exploration. In 1806 those two intrepid explorers had completed their amazing journey over unexplored territory and had survived the dangers of the voyage down the Columbia to winter at its mouth.

The Nor' Westers thought that, in the south fork of the Fraser River which Mackenzie had followed, they had the upper reaches of the Columbia. But the source of the river and its course through New Caledonia were unknown. The Montrealers knew of the exploit of Lewis and Clark. They hastened to send Simon Fraser to explore the river for the company, to establish claim to the country north of the river before the Americans made their way in.

With the trader Jules Quesnel and a crew of voyageurs in two canoes, Simon Fraser was on his way in 1808. After passing the spot where Mackenzie had left the river the bold party in their frail canoes were swept into terrific canyons never before seen by white men. The turbulent river forged its way between mountain walls, sometimes only forty yards wide. The voyageurs were obliged to cut steps in the cliffs with their knives, to drag the canoes and goods to the top.

They came at last to an appalling sight. The river plunged with deafening roar into a narrow passage between precipices. It was impossible to climb the cliffs in order to pass by land. Fraser and his stout voyageurs looked at one another and resolved to make a dash for it. He wrote later: "All hands without hesitation embarked on the awful tide. Once on the water the die was cast; and the difficulty consisted in keeping the canoes clear of the precipice on one side and clear of the gulfs formed by the waves on the other. Thus skimming along as fast as lightning, the crews, cool and determined, followed each other in awful silence; and when we arrived at the end, we stood gazing at each other in silent congratulation on our narrow escape from destruction."

After that terrifying experience Fraser soon realized that the Indians were right when they told him the river was impassable. Hiding the canoes and most of their supplies the burdened men followed the course of the river by land up and down mountainsides, over cliffs, until they came to Indian villages and navigable waters. They obtained dugout canoes to continue their journey to the sea, through mountainous canyons and boiling rapids almost as bad as those they had already survived. When they reached the lowlands a new danger faced them from hostile coast Indians who howled around the canoes, beating their war drums.

Simon Fraser thought he had accomplished the feat demanded by his company, but when he took his reckoning, he found, to his dismay, he was in latitude 49°. He knew the mouth of the Columbia was in latitude 46°20'. After all that danger and suffering he had not explored the Columbia! The name of the Fraser, one of the most turbulent rivers of North America, honors the incredible journey of the leader and his brave men.

After the journey of Lewis and Clark, plans were brewing in the United States for organized fur trading on the Pacific. The fur merchant, John Jacob Astor, of New York, with the approval of the government, evolved a scheme for an American fur empire. Astor was in the habit of supplementing the furs he obtained from American trappers by buying from the Nor' Westers in Montreal. If he had posts in the Pacific northwest he could reap the harvest of furs for himself.

He planned to build a post at the mouth of the Columbia from which other posts could be established, while ships from New York would supply the forts and carry on coastal trade with the Indians. He formed the Pacific Fur Company and poured into the ambitious enterprise his accumulated wealth.

The ship *Tonquin* was to sail from New York, carrying traders and supplies to the Columbia, while an overland expedition was to follow the trail of Lewis and Clark from the Missouri to join the others at the mouth of the Columbia.

Astor employed experienced young traders of the North West Company to help his Americans learn the ways of the fur trade. French Canadian voyageurs were engaged to be his canoemen. These picturesque fellows made a dashing entry into New York, having come all the way from Montreal by waterways and portages and down the Hudson. Their gaudy costumes, French chatter and songs provided a nine days' wonder for New Yorkers.

The *Tonquin* sailed from New York in 1810, with an ill-assorted company of French Canadians, Scots and Americans. From the beginning the enterprise was ill-fated, for there was no authoritative leader and the different groups quarreled constantly. When they reached the Columbia there were more controversies between the Scots and the Americans before the post of Astoria was finally erected and the flag of the United States raised above it.

The captain of the *Tonquin,* with one of the Scottish traders aboard, sailed off up the coast according to schedule to trade with the Indians, a voyage from which they never returned. While trading in a bay of Vancouver Island the martinet of a captain became incensed with the wily Indians and knocked one of their chiefs overboard. Next morning swarms of Indians came aboard, ostensibly to trade, and at a given signal they attacked the ship's company with the knives they had just received for their furs. All the ship's crew were killed, with the exception of four men who escaped in a small boat and the ship's clerk, Lewis, who was wounded and hid below decks.

When the Indians, on the following day, came aboard the apparently deserted ship, a terrific explosion tore the vessel apart and scattered the mangled bodies of Indians over the bay. Lewis had fired the powder magazine, dying himself while he revenged the massacre of his comrades. Such was the dark beginning of the American enterprise.

The Nor' Westers had displayed no open opposition to the Pacific Fur Company, but there were ways to interfere with its success. Very likely they encouraged their young traders to accept Astor's proffered jobs, knowing that the Scots would be more loyal to their old company than to their American employer. One method of circumventing the Americans was to raise the flag of England at the mouth of the Columbia before they arrived. For this the North West Company chose David Thompson, trader, astronomer, surveyor and map maker for the company.

David Thompson was a strong, grave man, his rugged face framed in long black hair cut in a straight bang. He was an inveterate explorer and expert surveyor of wilderness country. The Indians called him Koo-koo-sint, the man who looks at the stars, and they admired and respected him.

For several years before the Pacific Fur Company rose as a possible rival to the North West Company, Thompson had been exploring for the Nor' Westers in the Rockies and the country beyond them. He discovered passes over the Rockies by which the traders could enter New Caledonia without following the difficult route of Mackenzie. Greatest of his exploits was the exploration of Athabaska Pass in the dead of winter with a hardy group of voyageurs and their dog teams.

Among those tremendous mountains, hemmed in by glaciers and snow-covered peaks, the voyageurs were frightened, but Thompson was elated over the majestic heights he was exploring. The party and the dogs slid and scrambled down the western slopes of the Pass and spent the winter at a place on the Columbia called Boat Encampment by fur brigades which followed the route in later years. The experiences of Thompson and his few sturdy men among the peaks and mountain passes were as amazing as the journey of Simon Fraser on his wild river.

The first time that Thompson found a branch of the Columbia River he exclaimed, "May God in His mercy give me to see where its waters flow into the ocean and return in safety!"

That wish was granted when, after several years during which he chased the elusive river through the mountains and plateaus of New Caledonia, he was given the order to reach its mouth before the Americans.

He set out with a crew of picked voyageurs and traders to win the race. At the junction of the Spokane with the Columbia he left men to build a fort and hurried on. With the voyageurs in full song and the Union Jack fluttering at the prow, the canoe swept along into the lower reaches of the Columbia. There, on the shore, stood the rough log fort of the Astorians! The Americans had arrived first.

The Scots and voyageurs who tumbled from the fort to greet the wanderers were old comrades. David Thompson and his men were welcomed and fed. They were supplied with provisions for their return trip up the river.

Misfortune continued to follow the Astorians. The overland expedition, after suffering incredible hardships during many weary months, finally reached Astoria, exhausted and depleted in numbers. Then, in 1812, England and the United States were at war. A British warship started the voyage to the Pacific to capture Astoria.

The Nor' Westers, too, moved to make an end of the American venture. A brigade of canoes, bringing officers of the company, made the tremendous journey from Montreal to the Columbia with the intention of buying out the Astorians. They were welcomed by one of their former employees, MacDougall, who was in charge of the post. He was very willing to negotiate with them and by the time the British warship arrived the deal had been concluded. Astoria was in possession of the Nor' Westers.

At the close of the war Britain and the United States agreed to restore posts each had taken from the other. The United States insisted that Astoria came under this agreement. It was too late, however, for American traders to make any headway in the northwest country. Posts of the Nor' Westers occupied the best spots on the Columbia and inexperienced Americans could not compete with the skill of these traders already firmly rooted in the territory.

By a treaty, in 1818, the country west of the Rocky Mountains was left open to traders of both nations for a term of ten years. Americans still claimed the Columbia region by right of the explorations of Captain Gray and Lewis and Clark, and the vaguely defined territory south of the river was visited by rival hunters and trappers. But from the Columbia River to Russian Alaska British and Scottish traders were about to create a fur empire under the flag of England.

CHAPTER VIII

Fur Is King in the West

[1800–1828]

WHEN the nineteenth century opened, the vast western wilderness was the battle ground of rival fur traders; the English of the bay and the Scotch Canadians of Montreal.

The Nor' Westers were checked in their southward moves when England and the United States agreed upon a boundary line from the Great Lakes to the Rockies at the 49th parallel. West of the mountains the Oregon country, as the Americans called it, was still open to the enterprise of all traders.

David Thompson, the great surveyor, explored and mapped the territory covered by the Nor' Westers' activities. His huge map of northwestern North America hung in the company's council hall at Fort William so long as that remained the yearly rendezvous. It was so accurate that it became the basis for all future maps of western Canada.

A new element of friction was introduced into the fur country by Lord Selkirk, a shareholder of the Hudson's Bay Company itself. He was a nobleman of idealistic character and philanthropic spirit, who embarked on an ambitious colonizing scheme through concern over the plight of poor Scottish crofters. They were being evicted from their little farms because the Highland chieftains, their lords, wanted the land for sheep raising. Lord Selkirk's first colonists were sent to Cape Breton Island where they managed to keep a foothold despite many hardships.

Farmers could do well on the western prairies, Lord Selkirk believed, but of course the Hudson's Bay Company was most unwilling to have men of the plow and the hoe invade Rupert's Land. Only the fact that the wealthy nobleman had bought a controlling interest in the company made it possible for him to obtain from the directors a large grant of land along the Red and Assiniboine Rivers.

Lord Selkirk called his tract Assiniboia and he planned to send settlers to the junction of the two rivers, a region of fertile grassy prairies. One of his arguments did have weight with the company; that settlers raising crops would help in the problem of supplying the western forts with food.

He had chosen, however, the place most likely to rouse the antagonism of the fur traders, particularly the rival Nor' Westers. The forks of the Red and Assiniboine were a rendezvous for traders of both companies and right on the route of the Nor' Westers to the interior. Forts of both companies stood near each other on opposite banks of the Assiniboine.

In 1812 and 1813 two companies of Scottish families were gathered by Lord Selkirk's agents and sent off to make new homes for themselves in Assiniboia. It was fortunate that they were sturdy people of a cold northern land, for their introduction to the New World was enough to tax their hardihood and stubborn Scottish courage to the utmost.

The colonists voyaged across stormy northern seas in company ships, to arrive at York Factory on the bleak lonely shore of the bay. From there they were sent by canoe up the Nelson River and over the length of huge Lake Winnipeg to reach Fort Douglas on the Assiniboine.

The difficulties of the first two groups were as nothing to the trials of the third party, composed of men with their wives and children. They were weakened by typhoid fever on the voyage and were dumped unceremoniously, in the autumn, at the small post at the mouth of the Churchill River. It was too late in the season to make the trek overland to York Factory, so the men at the post reluctantly sheltered the forlorn group through the winter in log huts.

Early in the spring they set out on snowshoes to reach York Factory. The men went ahead, dragging sledges laden with their stores, to make a trail for women and children who followed, while a Highland piper played his bagpipes to keep up their spirits.

One young man and his wife had to drop behind and build a shelter in the snow while the girl's baby was born. She survived that terrible experience and, as soon as she could travel, they went on, the young mother carrying her baby in her arms. At York Factory there was another long wait until the rivers were free from ice, so that they could complete their journey by canoe.

After such vicissitudes the wide rolling prairies, radiant in summer beauty, must have looked like a land of promise, when the colonists reached their destination in June, 1814. Bravely the Scottish families began their new life, undaunted by the reluctance of the Hudson's Bay men to help them and the open antagonism of the Nor' Westers in nearby Fort Gibraltar. Log cabins were built on the river bank and ground broken for seeding, while women and children adapted themselves to the toughest kind of pioneer life.

These staunch Scottish wives were not the first white women to reach the prairie lands. Some years before the French Canadian hunter, Jean Baptiste Lagimonière, had brought his wife, Marie Anne Gaboury, to the west. Her first baby had been born in an Indian tepee, a girl who was to become the mother of Louis Riel, the rebel.

Perhaps Marie Anne Gaboury was there to help the Scottish women learn the ways of life in the wilderness. At any rate, they found kindly neighbors for a while in the dark wives of half-breed hunters who lived along the river.

These half-breeds, called Métis by the traders, went out every spring to hunt buffalo farther west. It was an exodus of whole families, for it was the women's job to dry the meat of the fresh-killed animals and pound it up with fat and berries to make the pemmican which was packed in hide bags for winter use.

Pemmican, supplied by the Métis hunters, was bought by all the traders for the western posts. It was also the mainstay of existence for the settlers during their first difficult years. Every winter they migrated to Pembina in the buffalo country to be on hand for the spring hunt and to lay in buffalo meat for the families.

Smoldering antagonisms burst into flame when, in a time of great hardship, the leader of the colonists tried to prevent the Métis from selling pemmican to the western traders. It was easy then for the Nor' Westers to rouse the half-breeds against the intruders into the fur country. Settlers' cabins were burned and their crops destroyed. In a fierce encounter at Seven Oaks between the Scottish farmers and their enemies, several settlers, including the new governor of the colony, were killed. Fort Douglas was captured by the Nor' Westers, and families who had taken refuge there fled to Norway House, a post of the company at the head of Lake Winnipeg.

In the sub-zero cold of midwinter Jean Baptiste Lagimonière made the journey of eighteen hundred miles to Montreal on snowshoes, to tell Lord Selkirk of the disasters.

It was a blow to the idealistic colonizer but he refused to give up. He was the owner of the territory Assiniboia, granted to him by the Hudson's Bay Company, but he had not visited it nor did he understand the conditions with which his brave Scot-

tish people had to contend. Now he made the journey to Red
River with a company of Swiss soldiers who took Fort Douglas
from the Nor' Westers. Amid great rejoicing the scattered settlers were reunited and were comforted by the presence of their
benefactor.

Assiniboia was properly organized and plots set aside on the
Red River for a church, a school and a gristmill. Lord Selkirk's thoughtfulness extended to the Indians whose lands were
invaded by white men. He called a council of the Crees and
Salteaux and made with them the first Indian treaty. They
agreed to give him a strip on both sides of the two rivers "as far
as a white horse can be seen on the plain on a clear day." That
meant two miles, so that the farm plots, all with frontage on the
rivers, extended back that far.

The "Red River settlers" were there to stay, but the enmity
of the Nor' Westers followed Lord Selkirk to Montreal. He
became involved in lawsuits with them over his territory and
the troubles so undermined his health that before long he died.
Assiniboia was then governed by the Hudson's Bay Company.

The conflicts in the Red River region added fuel to the flames
of war between the rival companies. Both were being ruined
by the fierce competition for furs. The former friendly relations between traders and Indian trappers were being undermined by ruthless men who demoralized the Indians with liquor
and treated them badly. Having lost respect for the superior
white man, the natives fought to chase him from their lands.

As the fur contest advanced to the foothills of the Rockies,
traders met the resistance of the fleet hunters on horseback of
the strong Blackfoot confederacy. One of these chiefs had told
a Hudson's Bay trader that his people were "lords of the plentiful plains" and they now met the invasion of their good hunting
grounds by going on the warpath.

Both companies realized that the only way to save the fur trade was to unite. The Nor' Westers, indeed, were on the verge of ruin. Leading officers met in London to negotiate for union, encouraged by the British Colonial Office. The ancient and honorable Hudson's Bay Company held its charter from royalty, and it took parliamentary sanction to weld the two companies into one powerful organization. In 1821 they were united under the name and charter of the older Hudson's Bay Company.

The new organization possessed the advantages of both the former ones. They had the two great routes to the fur country, Hudson Bay and the St. Lawrence, but the Hudson Bay route became the important one. The system of profit-sharing "wintering partners" of the North West Company was retained, thus giving the traders the added incentive which salaried Hudson's Bay employees had lacked. When the initiative and boldness of the Nor' Westers was combined with the stability and prestige of the Hudson's Bay Company, the resulting organization was unbeatable.

The "Lordes and Proprietors" of the united fur trade were rulers over nearly half a continent, for their license to trade and govern extended over Rupert's Land and westward to the Rockies. By right of occupation the Hudson's Bay Company was soon to become ruler of New Caledonia and the Oregon country as well.

London was the headquarters of the company, but a governor was appointed to direct the work of the whole fur realm in Canada. Into the capable hands of the young trader, George Simpson, came the organization of the kingdom of the fur lords. He was a little Napoleon of a man, sturdy, stocky and dominating, a leader of men through his driving will and engaging personality. He had made a name for himself by skill-ful management of the trade in the Athabaska country, during the contest with the Nor' Westers, and the directors picked him for the tremendous task of amalgamating the posts and men of both companies into one organization. As Sir George Simpson he became the Governor of the Hudson's Bay Company in Canada.

Under his shrewd, forceful direction, order came out of chaos, every activity of the fur business was firmly knit into a smoothly functioning whole. Thus organized, the powerful company ruled the west for nearly fifty years.

Unessential posts were eliminated and their staffs of voyageurs and hunters were given land for homes on the Assiniboine, where the town of St. Boniface, French Canadian from its origin, came into being.

Trade with the Indians was stabilized on the basis of kindness, understanding and fair dealing, so that the men of the Hudson's Bay Company became to the natives the great white fathers who could always be trusted. The pernicious liquor trade was cut down so that the Indians received only small rations of watered rum.

The universal unit of barter was the beaver skin; one Skin, or One Made Beaver. Counters valued at one fourth, one half, "made beaver." When the Indian's furs had been inspected and accepted by the trader he received counters to the value of what he had brought, in the unit of beaver. With these in his hand he looked over the stores of the trading post, choosing goods; a long curved knife, useful for many purposes, a brass kettle, a gaudy woolen sash, a gun or a warm blanket, forerunner of the famous Hudson's Bay Point blankets of today. The trader took from the Indian's hand enough counters to pay for the goods he had chosen.   In some of the company's northern posts at the present time the Indians still do their trading with counters.

Beads in clear, cheerful colors — red, blue, yellow and white — were very popular with the Indian women.   They had become expert in adorning moose or deerskin shirts, moccasins and pouches with brilliant beadwork embroidery.   Indians and half-breeds preened themselves in these handsome costumes, adding a finishing touch of gaiety with a red woolen sash wound around the waist.

York Factory on Hudson Bay was the great depot for furs and trade goods.   It was a large establishment, with a warehouse for furs, quarters for clerks and traders, Bachelors Hall for the officers, kitchens and smithy.   The whitewashed log buildings were surrounded by a tall stockade and the Union Jack with the letters H.B.C. in the corner, floated from the flag staff.

Off shore, in the summer, were anchored the ships from England which had brought trade goods and supplies for all the posts, and would take back to London the winter's harvest of furs.   There came the brigades of canoes and York boats with their crews and the traders from the interior.   Voyageurs broke the silence of that lonely land with their songs and quarrels as they camped on the shore, trying to protect themselves by smoke smudges from the ferocious mosquitoes which then, as now, make life miserable in the northlands in the summer.

The company imported stolid, prudent young Scots from the Orkney Isles to be clerks and boatmen.   Their muscular strength was needed to handle the large, clumsy York boats, designed to carry quantities of freight.   The oarsmen had to rise from their seats with every pull on the long heavy oars.   In rough water the boats were often tracked by the men from shore, with ropes over their shoulders. By means of oarsmen and a square sail the York boats made good time on the lakes and rivers of the west. For the yearly journeys through the Rockies, and the Pacific northwest, the brigades traveled by canoe and pack horse.

Across the mountains the king of the fur country was Dr. John McLoughlin, chief factor of Fort Vancouver on the Columbia. This post was the headquarters of the Hudson's Bay Company in the Pacific northwest and John McLoughlin one of the greatest of the fur traders. He was a man of dominating character but deep humanity, who ruled his wilderness world like an autocratic father. The Indians called him Whiteheaded Eagle because of his mane of white hair, sharp beak of a nose and piercing eyes.

Fort Vancouver stood on the north bank of the Columbia near the Willamette River. It was an imposing establishment to the wild inhabitants of the region as well as to visiting dignitaries of the Company who came overland or by boat. The buildings were enclosed within a palisade twenty feet high, with a great gate secured by brass padlocks. In the Big House, McLoughlin and his wife lived in rather barbaric splendor, ruling their world of clerks, trappers and hunters. When the chief factor had distinguished guests they were entertained at dinner by Highland pipers.

More than a trading post was Fort Vancouver, for McLoughlin imported seeds and cattle and had some of his population engaged in raising wheat and meat to supply their fort as well as others in the region. With its fields and pastures, its log houses and Indian camps, Fort Vancouver was a startling sight to come upon in the solitudes of the Columbia.

In the early autumn John McLoughlin sent his brigades of hunters southward into California, Idaho, Nevada and Montana. French Canadian hunters and Indian trappers with their squaws assembled by the hundreds. They set off in a long train, mounted on gaudily decorated Indian ponies, to be lost in the forests and deserts for a year or more. Northward into New Caledonia, the brigades set out by canoe in summer with all the dash and bravado loved by their voyageur crews. Part of their journey through the mountains was made with pack horses.

When the Whiteheaded Eagle took to the trails with his lady to visit the forts under his direction, their horses were decked out in bright trappings. The chief was magnificent in high beaver hat, silk-lined cape and knee breeches. They were accompanied by a train of retainers on horseback. All this show was chiefly to impress the Indians of their domain. To them the tall beaver hat was the symbol of the white chief's prestige.

When the cavalcade was seen approaching a fort, the guns boomed and bagpipes wailed their thin wild music in welcome. The trader and his clerks came out to greet the chief factor with the greatest formality. All chief factors surrounded themselves with ceremony, knowing that it enhanced their prestige with the Indian tribes and almost equally wild half-breeds and French Canadians.

Their inspiration for show came from the chief of them all, doughty Governor Simpson himself, who enjoyed display and elegant social affairs. When he set out to visit the fur kingdom he fancied himself as the center of an impressive spectacle. He loved to sweep up to the posts in a dramatic fanfare of color and music, in his express canoe paddled by the most skillful voyageurs and Indians. His yearly visits to important posts brought vivid sociability into the monotony of the traders' lives.

The first of the governor's round-trip visits to all the posts from York Factory to Fort Vancouver, took place in the seventh year of his rule, in 1828. The fur kingdom had never seen the like of it.

A brigade of great canoes, containing chief factors, traders, clerks, and voyageur crews, left York Factory amid a din of cheers and gun shots which rolled over the empty, silent country. Their first stop was Norway House at the head of Lake Winnipeg, a post which became the headquarters of the new fur realm in place of Fort William.

Throngs of Indians, with their wives and children, had gathered there to see the Great White Chief whose godlike power awed them. Before their wondering eyes the governor's brigade sped toward the landing, brave with floating pennants, the gleam of scarlet paddles, the shrilling of bagpipes and the rollicking chant of the voyageurs. The head boatsman carolled the verses of *"À la claire fontaine,"* and the crews roared the chorus:

> *"Il y a longtemps que je t'aime*
> *Jamais je ne t'oublierai."*

In a huge canoe with the insignia of the Hudson's Bay Company painted on its prow, sat the lordly governor, elegant in broadcloth, ruffles and high beaver hat, among his wild, gaudily dressed crew.

There were *regales* and feasting for the crews and the Indians while the governor with his officers enjoyed a ceremonious banquet. Several days were spent in intensive work as Sir George Simpson spurred his officers, by his own driving spirit and capacity for work, to give the best that was in them.

Then the brigade went on, over the lakes and rivers and the weary portages, into the mountains where arrivals at the forts were staged on horseback, on to Fort Vancouver on the Columbia and Fort Langley at the mouth of the Fraser. The men at every post responded to the power and persuasion of the governor. By his skillful diplomacy he soon won the allegiance of traders, independent and hardened by years in the wilderness. The half-savage subjects of the fur kingdom adored the dramatic pomp of his appearances, while his autocratic rule, tempered by kindness, won their respect.

When the sociable governor paid visits to Lower Fort Garry on the Red River, there were celebrations at that center of society and business for the Red River settlements. Retired officers of the company added to the population in the villages which were strung along the river banks. The people were cut off from the world save for the yearly brigades of York boats bringing supplies from Hudson Bay, but they had an industrious, neighborly life among themselves.

New Year's Day and St. Andrew's Day were celebrated with balls at Lower Fort Garry, in the comfortable house of the chief factor. Often the governor was a guest of honor, to share in the dancing and drinking of toasts. The ladies' silken gowns, when they had them, came from London by way of Hudson Bay, and when they lacked slippers they danced the Red River jig just as merrily in moccasins.

For many years, while the west was the domain of the fur traders, the Red River settlements were an island of civilization in the vast sea of the plains.

The rule of the fur lords was an epic, a vivid period in Canada's story. The great company, after the union of the rivals, held its power through the character of the men who served it; from the chief factors to the clerks and voyageurs it was welded together by an esprit de corps, a staunch loyalty. The Hudson's Bay Company posts and the men who governed them were important in the building of Canada.

Men of the fur trade opened the west for those who would till the land and tame the wilderness. Adventurers and explorers blazed the trails, while the men who managed the posts of the united company with such integrity kept order in a vast wild land and eventually helped the incoming settlers.

While the fur empire was being built up in the west, the British provinces of Canada far away in the east, almost in another world, were advancing in social and political life. When their people turned westward, after the middle of the nineteenth century, the rule of the fur lords would be challenged by men in search of land and homes.

III. The Growth of English Canada

CHAPTER IX

The Beginnings of English Canada

[1763-1800]

ALONG the St. Lawrence, after Canada had been ceded to England in the Peace Treaty of 1763, the Canadian people waited in fear and uncertainty to learn their fate. They were abandoned to conquering England. French officials, troops and some seigneurs had left them to return to France. Between the people and their new rulers were the barriers of race, language and religion. Would they be torn from their beloved lands and cherished possessions like the Acadians?

When English troops under General James Murray took over Quebec the inhabitants were heartened to find the conquering soldiers helpful instead of harsh. Food was distributed to sick and hungry families and soldiers joined with townsfolk to re-build houses ruined by the bombardment. The nuns of the Hôtel Dieu and Hôpitale Générale, who faithfully nursed wounded English soldiers, were protected by General Murray, and their institutions, as well as that of the Ursulines, were given financial aid.

French officers, in the terms of capitulation, had asked and obtained for the people the right to practice their religion and to retain their goods and houses. It was also agreed that French Canadians were not to be deported. Great was the relief throughout the country when it was found that General Murray, who became military governor, intended to live up to these terms.

The French Canadians were fortunate in having the honorable, tactful gentleman, James Murray, for their first English governor. He sympathized with the plight of the conquered people and, being an ardent French scholar, appreciated their ancestral culture. His use of their language in official communications soothed the misery of being ruled by aliens, and there was no interference with their cherished religion.

The first plan of the British government for Canada was to wean the people from their French way of life by a liberal rule which would prove to them that they were better off as subjects of England than they had been under the rule of France. Thus it was hoped that Canada would become a loyal and useful Fourteenth Colony, added to the Thirteen Colonies farther south, to Nova Scotia and to Newfoundland.

Perhaps if Governor Murray had been able to carry out his tactful methods without interference this might have been accomplished. He understood that French Canadians were a people in their own right. In letters he called them "the best and bravest race on earth," for whom he had respect and affection. If sympathetically handled and assured of their rights, he was convinced that they would become loyal subjects of England.

During the years that he governed at Quebec, until 1766, Governor Murray had little trouble with the French Canadians themselves. Respect and liking were mutual between him and the upper-class townsfolk, the seigneurs and clergy. English soldiers, both in Quebec and Montreal, were soon on the most friendly terms with the inhabitants.

There was trouble a-plenty, however, with the colonial traders who flocked in from the older English colonies, avaricious for profits and control of the new territory opened up to English enterprise. They were greedy and ignorant, looking down on French Canadians as Papists and foreigners.

Constantly Governor Murray was in conflict with these traders, who raised an outcry when he appointed French Canadians to minor posts and protected their rights in the courts. English magistrates made common cause with the traders in trying to control the colony and reduce the Canadians to a people with no rights at all. English-speaking people of a better class, who moved in, and decent merchants from England disliked the loud-mouthed mischief-makers as much as did Governor Murray himself.

One of the objects of the colonial traders was to get their hands on the fur trade, and in this they were blocked for some time. The Indians made a concerted effort to drive the white men from their hunting grounds. Indians of tribes who had been friendly for many years with the French hated the English. Others, who lived in the Ohio Valley, were antagonistic toward colonial frontiersmen who invaded their lands.

Pontiac, a shrewd chief of the Ottawas, gathered the tribes into a conspiracy to attack the English forts and raid the villages. The war did not touch the Laurentian country but it blocked all contact with the western Indians. The warriors did not understand systematized warfare, with long sieges, so the effort of the native people to save their lands was a failure. The British government made ordinances to protect the Indians from ruthless traders and Governor Murray refused to give the greedy men in Montreal and Quebec licenses for trade in the west.

Eventually the organized opposition of these men to Governor Murray's management and the influence of their friends in London caused the governor to be called home to give an account of his rule. James Murray never returned to the Canada where he had hoped to make his home.

One good thing, however, had come from the colonies. Two Philadelphia printers had introduced the first printing press ever seen in French Canada and were printing on it the first newspaper the people had known, *The Quebec Gazette*. It contained news in the summer while, in the frozen winter, articles were printed "to please the Fancy and instruct the Judgement." The publication has continued to the present day under the name of *The Quebec Chronicle*.

Englishmen learned to endure the cold, snow and uncomfortable living of Quebec and some officers came to like the country. A few Scottish officers took up seigneuries along the river, married French Canadian girls and became lords of the manor in a new land. Their descendants are French-speaking families with Scottish names.

To officials in England, however, Canada was only acres of snow as described by Voltaire. William Pitt, who had wanted the new colony, was no longer in office and the succeeding ministry had little enthusiasm for the new acquisition in North America.

It was leaders of the American colonists who had urged the acquisition of Canada instead of a fertile West Indies island. The colonials had lived through years of violent forest warfare, they wanted the fur trade, and they considered Canada their conquest. They, too, wanted Canada to become a Fourteenth Colony, but one cut to their pattern, ready to join in their controversies with England.

Independent people of the Thirteen Colonies were increasingly rebellious against taxes and impositions laid upon them by an autocratic government. Some men were anxious to set Canadians against England and they came over the border, "preaching politicks" and putting disturbing ideas of liberty into the heads of the habitants.

When the upright, strong-minded soldier, Sir Guy Carleton, was sent to govern Canada in place of James Murray, he found trouble on every hand. In Canada there was dissatisfaction and, across the border, colonies on the verge of rebellion were a threat to Canadian peace. Sir Guy Carleton had been quarter-master general with Wolfe's army at the siege of Quebec. He had lived in the city long enough to know the people and, as he was not unwelcome to them, friendly relations were soon established. Upper-class French Canadians were pleased with his wife, a highborn English lady who had been brought up at the court of Versailles. She preserved in social functions the French formality so dear to Quebec aristocrats.

Governor Carleton studied the problems of the colony with a fair mind. The people had refused to become Anglicized and their discontent made them susceptible to propaganda from rebellious New Englanders. Some new plan must be adopted, one which would secure their loyalty by allowing them to remain French. Governor Carleton gave his support to the decision to make Canada distinctly a French Canadian province with the rights of the English-speaking minority protected.

In the Quebec Act of 1774 the people were assured of their Roman Catholic Church. The seigneurial system of land tenure was confirmed, much of the French code of civil law was retained, with the addition of the more humane English criminal code. There was to be a council to assist the governor and, when the time was propitious, a representative assembly would be granted.

The Quebec Act, called the Magna Charta of the French Canadian people, was accepted gladly by the clergy and seigneurs who saw their positions assured by it. These classes became staunch supporters of English order and authority. The habitants, who had been shaken by changing conditions from their old obedience, were not so pleased to have the seigneurs' rights retained. Nevertheless they accepted governmental changes calmly so long as they might continue to cultivate their lands and follow their traditional customs.

It was in the Thirteen Colonies that the Quebec Act roused intense resentment. The British government had greatly enlarged the territory of French Canada, including in it the western lands between the Ohio and the Great Lakes to the Mississippi. This was for the purpose of bringing that Indian territory under the government of Quebec so the activities of traders could be controlled and the land kept as a reserve for the tribes. People of the Thirteen Colonies were infuriated. Already, after Pontiac's war, frontiersmen had begun to travel westward from the Alleghenies and they believed those lands were their rightful field for expansion. It seemed to the colonies gross injustice to have them added to Quebec, a colony of which the people were both French and Papist. This act of the British government was one of the chief grievances accumulating against the mother country.

The Quebec Act did not go into effect at once, for in 1775 Governor Carleton's attention was concentrated on preparing Canada for invasion. The "shot heard round the world" fired at Concord on April 19 had great repercussions in Canada. Many English-speaking people who had come from the colonies were in sympathy with the rebels and the habitants were inclined to be very friendly to them.

A dynamic idea, born of eighteenth-century thought and nourished in the free air of the New World, had been tossed into the British realm of authoritarian rule by men of English blood; men who had conquered the wilderness and built their farms and towns by their own initiative and hardihood. They were dazzled by the vision of liberty and the doctrine of the rights of the common man. The conservative leaders tried in vain to control the flame of revolutionary feeling.

The Continental Congress feared that Canada would be used as a base for British operations against the rebellious colonies. They were also convinced that they had only to offer liberty to Canadians, oppressed as they thought under tyrannical British rule, to have them spring to join the rebellion.

Then a frontier Yankee individualist embarked on his own little war without orders, apparently opening the way to Canada. Ethan Allen and his Green Mountain Boys made their famous capture of ill-defended Crown Point and Ticonderoga. Inspired by this easy conquest, they went on to free Montreal from "British tyranny." They expected to be received with open arms, knowing that the town was full of sympathizers. When the Yankee crusaders reached Long Point, outside the city, they were disillusioned. They were easily defeated by British soldiers who marched out to defend Montreal.

The Continental Congress then planned an invasion of Canada to protect the rebellious colonies by taking it from England. It was hoped that friends within would make the invasion easy. New Yorkers, and men of Connecticut and New Hampshire, were to move from Lake Champlain to capture forts on the Richelieu River and proceed to Montreal. When the campaign was eventually organized it was under the command of Richard Montgomery, an English officer who had joined the revolutionists. Meanwhile, Benedict Arnold started a march from the Kennebec to the St. Lawrence with companies of Virginia riflemen and New Englanders, to capture Quebec. These moves were made in the year 1775.

Governor Carleton gathered all the forces he could muster for the defense of Montreal. He tried to call out the old Canadian militia of the seigneurs and their habitants. Although the seigneurs responded, the countrymen resisted all attempts of their officers and clergy to call them to arms. They had no mind to fight in this war on either side and only a few companies were assembled.

Despite the difficulties of welding untrained militia and frontiersmen into an army Richard Montgomery succeeded in his campaign against Montreal. Governor Carleton was obliged to evacuate the city and, although most of his soldiers were captured by the revolutionists on the river, the governor made a daring escape in a small boat, reaching Quebec in time to take charge of its defenses.

Benedict Arnold had companies of the sturdiest colonials and was an extremely skillful officer, but their march through the wilderness of Maine to the St. Lawrence country was a terrible ordeal. The men were ragged, sick and starving when they arrived in the first Canadian villages, where the habitants fed them, and supplied provisions for their further march. At the river they managed to collect enough boats to cross to the Quebec side, then after scrambling up the cliffs by Wolfe's famous route they marched across the Plains of Abraham with hopeful cheers.

Quebec was prepared for them, with sufficient reinforcements to hold the citadel itself. Benedict Arnold's summons to surrender was met by the stony refusal of Governor Carleton, every inch the British soldier, to deal with an officer whom he styled a rebel against his king. The invaders withdrew up the river to meet Montgomery, with whom they boldly planned the capture of Quebec. Such a citadel could not be attacked directly by the forces they had, but the officers planned to take the Lower Town with its stores and shipping. Then, they argued, the governor would be forced to surrender.

The Lower Town was protected by two barricades, one directly below Cape Diamond, called the Près-de-Ville, the other below the cliff, named Sault au Matelot.

It was during the first hours of the New Year of 1776, in a howling storm of wind and snow, that the daring attack took place. Unfortunately the garrison saw their signals so that the element of surprise was lost. Bells rang and drums beat to call the citizens to arms. In the bitter cold, in darkness and the confusion of the storm, fierce fighting took place around both barricades. Montgomery and some of his officers were killed at the Près-de-Ville while, in the wild street fighting around the Sault au Matelot, the defenders of Quebec were finally victorious.

For weary months the invaders continued their unsuccessful siege until, in May, British ships arrived. Reinforced by marines from the fleet Governor Carleton marched his troops out against the enemy camp and the colonials fled in haste, upriver to Montreal.

The occupation of Montreal was not a happy time for the Montrealers or their would-be deliverers. Many people had been in sympathy with the rebellion but close contact with the rough soldiers, who were fanatical in preaching their brand of liberty, soon caused friction. The unreadiness of the Montrealers to become rebels and their reluctance to accept the invaders' paper money, incensed the Americans. The phrase "not worth a ragged continental" had force in Montreal as well as in the rebellious colonies.

The Continental Congress made one more effort to win the Canadians by sending a distinguished delegation of commissioners to Montreal: Benjamin Franklin, Samuel Chase of Maryland who was a moderate, and the Carroll brothers of Carrollton. The Carrolls were Roman Catholics, one of them a great landowner, the other a priest, so it was hoped that they would have influence with the upper class and clergy. The Canadian aristocrats and churchmen, however, were firm in their refusal to take up arms against England.

The defeat at Quebec and the failure of the commission soon led the revolutionists to evacuate Montreal and return home. Despite the sympathy of some English-speaking Canadians and many habitants Canada had made up its mind. The French Canadians had decided that English rule would give them the best chance to keep their rights and their way of life. During the war there were no further invasions of Canada although the country was a base for British troops.

Canada remained a British colony while the rebellious Thirteen declared their complete independence of England. Henceforth two North American peoples were to go their separate ways. Thomas Jefferson set forth in immortal words the cause for which the Americans were fighting and the principles on which the newborn nation was to be founded.

England had lost the Thirteen Colonies but a British Canada was secured to her by the outcome of the American Revolution. The decision to fight and the desire for independence had been far from unanimous in the colonies. Hundreds of colonials — wealthy landowners, merchants, men who held important positions — were by nature Tories. They stood to lose everything under the leveling influence of democracy. Other honorable, intelligent people were intensely loyal to the king. They believed that the injustices under which the colonies suffered could be eliminated by discussion and compromise. Perhaps if King George III and his ministers had not been so stupidly lacking in comprehension of the colonials and their desires, these people might have been right. As it was, they were supporters of a lost cause.

Loyalist regiments were formed, which fought with the British armies. Bitter enmity existed between Loyalists and Patriots. To the Tories the war was no more than the revolt of a disloyal, ignorant rabble, while to the fighting Patriots those who defended England were people who betrayed their own countrymen to support the forces of oppression.

In the heat and anger of such a struggle tolerance was impossible. Revolution always brings to the top the disinherited, men who have never had a chance at a decent life. There were plenty of them in the colonies, to whom liberty meant opportunity for themselves and revenge on the people of wealth and position. Loyalist families were persecuted by mobs and driven from their homes to take refuge in towns held by the British.

After the war was over there was no place in the country for those who had openly supported the king and fought with the British armies. Their property was confiscated and they were forced to find new homes somewhere in British territory. Others who were unwilling to accept the Republic left of their own will.

Many of the wealthiest families who had friends in England escaped to the mother country during the war and others followed after peace was signed. Then hundreds of disinherited refugees crowded into New York to take ship for Nova Scotia or Canada. Sir Guy Carleton was sent to New York to undertake the task of evacuating the British troops and the refugees.

During 1783 a stream of ships left New York, crowded to capacity with people of all classes; aristocrats with their Negro slaves and whatever they had been able to salvage of their silver, clothes and furniture; merchants, farmers, artisans with their

families and bundles of possessions; officers and soldiers of disbanded Loyalist regiments.

Halifax was utterly swamped by the multitude of homeless
people, all begging Governor Parr for shelter, for food to keep
them alive, for land to settle on.   Nova Scotia, at that time, included all of the present Maritimes and it was a very sparsely
inhabited land.   There were villages of fishermen, small towns
like Annapolis Royal, and settlements of farmers in the most
fertile sections.   Many of them were New Englanders who had
migrated to adjacent and similar Nova Scotia long before the
Revolution, some to take over the farms of the Acadians, others
to settle on the banks of the Saint John River.   Halifax, the only
important town, was the English naval base, a garrison town
filled with snobbish British officers and aristocrats.   There was
also an influential group of merchants and shipowners who
profited from the West Indies trade — shipping lumber and fish,
and bringing back West Indies molasses to be converted into
rum in Nova Scotia.   They were like their counterparts in New
England ports, but they lived in a Halifax which was English
to its core.   Haligonians lived apart from the rest of Nova Scotia, looking down on the ordinary country people.

The Loyalists who poured into Nova Scotia had lost everything because of their loyalty to the king and for that reason
clung intensely to their allegiance.   Once more under the British flag they expected to be welcomed and provided for.   Some
among them alienated the natives by their airs of superiority
and their complaints of hardship in the land of their exile.
They felt that their sacrifices were not appreciated by a government which was more harassed by the problem of settling
thousands of refugees somewhere than grateful for their loyalty.

A large proportion of the newcomers in Nova Scotia, however, were fine people — men of intellect and education, as well

as families of humble social standing.   They adapted themselves with fortitude to the hardship of starting life all over again.

There was suffering for all while Governor Parr struggled with the complicated business of allotting land to the various groups.   Lumber and brick for building houses were inadequately supplied, government food rations were scanty.   New Englanders called the province Nova Scarcity in those years.

Groups of settlers were sent to Cape Breton and to Prince Edward Island.   Digby, Shelburne and other towns were founded by Loyalists.   Several companies came to Annapolis Royal, overwhelming that small town until their lands had been allotted and they had built their log cabins, gristmills and churches along the Basin.

The Reverend Jacob Bailey, himself a refugee from Maine, was the pastor of Annapolis Royal.   In later years he described in letters to a friend the bewailings of his Loyalist parishioners. To be sure, he said, things had not turned out as they had hoped, but they had the satisfaction of having followed their consciences.   He comforted himself with reflections on the fate of the revolutionists who had driven them from their homes. "The rebels, although they have succeeded in distressing us and humbling the British Empire, are much in the situation of the infernal spirits who, after they had seduced our first parents, instead of becoming more happy, plunged themselves without recovery into everlasting perdition."

Among the exiled people who entered Nova Scotia none were more successful in their pioneering than those who founded the town of Saint John and the Loyalist province of New Brunswick. During 1783 they came by the shipload to the north shore of the Bay of Fundy.   Many were officers and men of disbanded regiments with their families.

The first fleet sailed into Saint John harbor to deposit the forlorn people on an almost uninhabited shore, for only a few fishermen lived in the region. It was necessary to clear away brushwood and trees before the men could set up tents to shelter their families. Women watched with sinking hearts the disappearing sails of the ships, leaving them stranded in this unsettled wilderness. They shed a few tears before turning staunchly to the task of helping their men create new homes. Other ships brought additional settlers to the Bay of Fundy during that year.

Many families received grants of land along the beautiful Saint John River, in a peaceful country where shore meadows were nourished by spring floods. They prospered, and before many years had passed they were living comfortably among their fields, with good houses and plenty of servants.

The town, which had been christened Parrtown by the governor himself, soon had its name changed to Saint John by inhabitants who did not feel kindly toward him. They blamed him for their trials while waiting for allotments of land and building materials. Before long the humpy hills around the harbor were sprinkled with houses, and energetic people were developing their community life.

It was not long before social distinctions were once more in force among people who had shared adversity in common. Saint John was divided into Upper Cove, inhabited by the aristocrats, and Lower Cove, home of humbler folk. Negro slaves who had come with their families were settled in a district of their own where their descendants live to this day.

The Saint John settlers were pleased with their location. They had an excellent harbor, good fisheries and unlimited supplies of lumber in the forests which covered the land. Fishing and lumbering led to the days of Saint John's importance.

The settlers on the Bay of Fundy were dissatisfied with their dependence on Halifax, far away and difficult to reach. They asked for a government of their own and, in 1785, the petition was granted. The province of New Brunswick was established with its governor, legislative council and assembly. Fredericton on the Saint John River was founded to be the capital.

Prince Edward Island also had its provincial government. Save for Cape Breton Island which for a time was a separate province, the sprawling English colony of Nova Scotia was shaping into the political divisions which constitute the Maritimes today.

Isolated from Canada on the St. Lawrence the Maritimes began their separate existence. The governor of each province was appointed by the British Colonial Office and the same was true of Quebec. British North America was a group of provinces each ruled directly by England. The colony of Newfoundland, far away from other British possessions, had no contact with them except through fisheries.

It is estimated that as many as 28,000 exiles from the Republic settled in the Maritimes. These people and the English of Halifax were bound to the mother country by affection and strong allegiance. The New Englanders who had come before them added a leaven of Americanism to Nova Scotia and maintained the link of friendliness with people of the New England coast.

While fleets of ships brought a new population to Nova Scotia and New Brunswick, hundreds more of the refugees crossed the border into Quebec or trekked on foot with their children and a few possessions through the forest trails of upper New York to cross the Niagara River; all of them longing to find help and happiness under the British flag. Those who came up the Richelieu River settled in towns along the St. Lawrence; others went to the Niagara frontier and the north shore of Lake Ontario. The various groups founded a new province.

Among the settlers were many officers and men of New York regiments which had been organized by Sir John Johnson. He was the son of Sir William Johnson who had been baron of a wilderness estate and leader of the Six Nations of the Iroquois. The Glengarry Highlanders from New York with additions from the old country settled a whole county in the new land. There were New York farmers of Dutch extraction, Hanoverian German soldiers, Mohawk Indians who had fought for England under their great chief Joseph Brant. The civilian people were mostly artisans and farmers with their families.

The country was unbroken forested land when it was laid out in townships and plots for farms. Companies of settlers were brought up the St. Lawrence and over the lake in bateaux. After each head of a family had drawn the number of his allotment of land from the surveyor's hat, he set off with wife and children to start his new home in the "bush." Trees must be felled to make a clearing for his log cabin, stumps must be burned or rooted out so that with spade and hoe the land might be prepared for planting.

Gradually groups of log cabins connected by woodland trails brought human activities into the solitudes of the bush. The ring of axes, shouts of men and laughter of children were cheering sounds to lonely settlers. Smoke rose from chimneys of clay and sticks, indicating homes where women stooped over the glowing logs to cook food for their families.

These people began their new life in the forest with little beyond their courage and their willing hands. They had no money, no household goods, very little clothing. The government issued to the families tools such as axes, spades and hoes, saws to be used by several men in common, seed wheat, cows and materials for clothing.

The people learned to make trousers and petticoats of deerskin, coats from Indian blankets, boots from hide. Having no money they depended on barter and, in times of necessity, often exchanged a plot of land for a few pounds of flour, a cow for eight bushels of wheat, or a horse for some elemental food supply.

The first few years were a time of back-breaking labor and extreme hardship: 1788 was known as the "hungry year" when the crops failed. It was a slow business to get supplies to the settlements. Everything had to be transported in heavy flat-bottomed bateaux up the St. Lawrence and over Lake Ontario. The western settlements were cut off from Canada by wilderness and the long water journey.

Undaunted by loneliness and poverty the courageous people forged ahead in their task of home building. Little villages grew out of the bush. In the clearings wheat, flax and potatoes flourished among the stumps, and cows and horses were added to the homesteads. Presently there were a few gristmills to grind the wheat and a few sawmills to produce lumber for building.

In the log cabins, furnished with rough homemade furniture, there was a cheerful, homelike life. Scottish, English and German, the settlers were neighborly folk. Bees were organized by the women to spin and weave flax or make quilts. There were logging and house-raising bees when men assembled to help a new settler start his home. The bees gave the people an opportunity for hearty fun accompanied by heavy eating and drinking.

Some few pioneers traveled as far as the old French settlement around the fort on the Detroit River. The fort was in United States territory after the Revolution, so that some French Canadians crossed the river to be joined by new settlers.

The British government allotted to the loyal Mohawk Indians

lands along the Grand River flowing into Lake Erie. There the Mohawk villages were ruled by Joseph Brant, the intelligent chieftain who became almost more English than Indian. He paid visits to England and had his portrait painted by Romney. The little church he built for his Christianized people was the first Protestant place of worship in the new settlements. During his last years Joseph Brant lived in dignity in a large house on his own estate, attended by Negro servants.

It cost the British government great sums to provide tools, food, and materials for thousands of Loyalists both in Nova Scotia and Canada. Thus the people were recompensed, as far as might be, for the losses suffered by remaining loyal to England. Sir Guy Carleton proposed further a sort of badge of honor. He made an ordinance that all those who had supported England before 1783 might place after their names the letters U.E. signifying their adherence to the principle, unity of empire. Local boards were instructed to register all such persons to differentiate them from other settlers. In Canada, today, people who are descended from United Empire Loyalists have much the same pride of ancestry as New Englanders whose ancestors were pilgrims on the *Mayflower*. Indeed, the United Empire Loyalists are regarded almost with veneration.

The new English-speaking population changed the racial balance of Canada, for the French were no longer the majority. Government under the Quebec Act did not satisfy people of English or Scottish stock. Much as they hated republicanism they had been accustomed to democratic assemblies in their old homes. By 1791 the new settlements were sufficiently organized to demand English law and representative government.

It was the difficult task of Guy Carleton, now Lord Dorchester, to reconcile the French and English elements when he returned as governor-general of Canada. The French Canadians were much disturbed by the influx of Scottish and English settlers and were further upset by the French Revolution.

Fiery Citizen Genêt, representative of the French Republic in the United States, was determined to rouse the French Canadians against England and to unite them with revolutionary France. Naturally the reaction of the clergy and aristocrats to the Revolution was one of shock and abhorrence. They wanted no dealings with Frenchmen who discarded their religion for the Goddess of Reason and who not only revolted against their divinely appointed king but executed the royal family and nobility. The habitants, simple and ignorant people, did not understand political ideas but were upset by French agitators and their extravagant promises.

Republican France was more alien to French Canada than Protestant England with its parliamentary government. The upper ranks of the people cast in their lot with England but they clung to the Quebec Act as the guaranty of their racial and religious rights. Since it was evident that the English-speaking Canadians would not be satisfied with this, the British government evolved the Constitutional Act, separating Canada proper into two provinces.

Lower Canada was Quebec province where French Canadians were an overwhelming majority. Westward from the Ottawa River the new settlements became Upper Canada, the nucleus of present-day Ontario. Each province was to have its governor and its legislature consisting of a legislative council appointed by the governor and an elected assembly which had limited power.

French Canadians had never known representative government and they entered into the new system in a doubtful frame of mind. The people of Upper Canada, of course, were glad to live under a parliamentary system something like that of England.

On December 17, 1792, the first legislative assembly of Quebec met in the old Bishop's Palace with all the pomp and ceremony of British government.   The band, the speech from the throne, scarlet-coated officers and uniformed guard, ladies in gay frocks in the gallery, made it a vivid scene.   Half of the Upper House and two-thirds of the Lower House were French Canadians. For the first time men of the French race sat with their English fellow subjects in a parliamentary assembly.

Colonel John Graves Simcoe was appointed lieutenant-governor of Upper Canada.   He was an energetic gentleman, a staunch Empire man to whom everything about the British form of government was exactly right.   He hoped to make his province of Loyalist people into a little replica of British parliamentary rule, with upper-class gentlemen firmly in control. Republicanism was anathema to Governor Simcoe and he intended to prevent the people from developing any democratic ideas they might have brought with them from their old homes.

The small town of Niagara was chosen for the capital of Upper Canada.   There Governor Simcoe and his wife came, in the summer of 1792, to take up their residence in the small plain building known as Navy Hall.   The first legislature of Upper Canada assembled at Niagara in September of that year.   There were nine members in the legislative council and sixteen in the assembly.   They journeyed with their wives by boat or over woodland trails to present themselves, in the best attire they could muster, for their first session.   Many had taken the time from the harvesting which needed their attention.   Nearby settlers and Mohawk Indians crowded into small Niagara for the occasion.

Primitive surroundings did not prevent the truly British governor from opening his little parliamentary assembly with ceremony. Accompanied by a military guard he appeared on horseback, dressed in scarlet full-dress uniform with a cocked hat on his head. His lady wore brocaded white satin.

Governor Simcoe and his wife became popular with the people, for they took a great interest in the advancement of the province. Over rough trails and in uncomfortable bateaux they traveled assiduously, visiting the settlements. The governor directed the building of roads through the bush to make communication easier. It was he who founded the town of York on the site of the old Indian trading place, Toronto. York was to be the capital of the province, but in Governor Simcoe's time it was little more than a military garrison with a few blocks of houses near the water front. The streets were rough trails deep in mud and obstructed by tree stumps. The town found a way to make its topers useful by ordering each drunkard to remove a stump. From the town to Lake Simcoe a trail was ambitiously sketched out, and named Yonge Street.

The governor believed that many Americans were dissatisfied with the Republic and only needed an invitation to put themselves once more under the sheltering wing of King George III. In order to add to the population he offered free land to Americans who were still loyal to England. Many pioneer farmer families migrated to Upper Canada, willing enough to swear allegiance to King George for the sake of free land. They made good settlers, but their American character and point of view became a disturbing element later on to reactionary men in the Upper Canada government.

At the close of the eighteenth century, readjustments had been made between French and English Canadians and the provinces had weathered one contest with their aggressive neighbors to the south. Separated by wilderness and immense distances from the western realm of the fur traders, British Canada proceeded to develop its political and social life.

CHAPTER X

The Provinces Grow Up

BRITISH NORTH AMERICA, at the beginning of the nineteenth century, was a group of scattered provinces, each more closely linked to England in interest than to its neighboring province. People of various racial stocks were learning to live together in Upper and Lower Canada.

Montreal was, already, a bilingual city of two peoples. English merchants, and the Scottish and English fur lords of the North West Company, spoke French and lived in amity with their French neighbors. Three of them — McGill, McTavish and one of the Frobishers — married into French Canadian society. English John Molson, whose famous brewery was a thriving concern, endeared himself to the countryfolk by dressing like a habitant. James McGill was to give the wealth made in the fur trade to found the college which became McGill University. In both Quebec and Montreal, people of Protestant faith had raised their churches of a different ecclesiastical architecture beside the older Roman Catholic churches of the French.

Stately Quebec was the home of the governor-general whose presence created an official society composed of English officers and their wives and upper-class French Canadians. Balls were brilliant with the scarlet and gold of British uniforms and the fashionable elegance of ladies. The lovely wild countryside made a perfect setting for romantic excursions of gay young officers with their pretty companions.

Canadians were too much occupied with their own affairs to worry about the newborn nation which was expanding so lustily south of the border. British officials and army officers, however, watched anxiously the rising tide of resentment in the United States against the former mother country. Deep anti-British feeling was an aftermath of the War for Independence, and many Americans were not inclined to sympathize with England when she was engaged in a life and death struggle with Napoleon, the conqueror of Europe.

American ships were sailing to all the ports of the world, building up a sea-borne commerce which was seriously threatened by the war between France and England. When the warring countries instituted a blockade, each trying to prevent neutral ships from reaching the other's ports, the United States government insisted on the right of its merchant marine to trade with all countries. Both French and English naval vessels interfered with American commerce, seizing ships and goods destined for enemy ports, and protests from Washington brought no relief.

The real quarrel was with England, however, for commerce suffered more from English seizures, and there was also in American minds a grateful memory of help given by France in the Revolution. The greatest wrath was aroused by the right England claimed to stop American ships on the high seas to take off British-born seamen who had deserted to join American crews because of better conditions. It was not easy to verify the birth of sailors who were all English-speaking, and American as well as British seamen were seized.

Despite the indignation aroused among shippers, merchants and seamen over interference with American activities, the clamor for war did not come from the seaboard states. There the conservative men of property, members of the Federal party founded by Washington and Hamilton, were convinced that another war with England would be ruinous. It was the radical anti-British Democrats, party of the southern planters and western frontiersmen, who swept the country into war, having their own reasons for stirring up trouble with England.

Thomas Jefferson, the leader of the Democrats, was himself a man of peace. He was opposed to the building of a large navy because it would involve entanglements with European nations. The destiny of America, he believed, was that of an agricultural nation, expanding westward. Following this conviction he bought Louisiana from Napoleon and sent Lewis and Clark to the Pacific.

It was under Jefferson's successor, President James Madison, that the crisis came. The Congress which met in 1811 was dominated by a group of fiery young men called the War Hawks, led by John C. Calhoun of South Carolina and Henry Clay of Kentucky. Under the ostensible reason for war, to maintain American rights on the seas, ran another current; the conviction of aggressive, westward-forging men that it was the "manifest destiny" of Americans to control all of North America. In Congress Henry Clay cried: "I would not stop at Quebec or anywhere else, but I would take the whole continent." War with England would make it possible to march on Canada and eliminate British rule from North America, so thought the War Hawks.

The fur trade and the Indians were involved in the plans of the westerners. England had been slow in evacuating Detroit, Michilimackinac and other posts which were in American territory by the boundary fixed after the Revolution. Frontiersmen were convinced that the English used their position along the border to encourage the Indians in their raids on settlements. The natives were fighting desperately to keep the pioneers from their lands in the Ohio and Mississippi valleys. The frontiersmen also had their eyes on the northwest and its wealth of furs.

At this time the middle-western tribes had found a great leader in the Shawnee chieftain Tecumseh, the finest of the Indian chiefs who tried to save their people from extermination. His great dream was that of uniting all the tribes in a native empire powerful enough to keep white men from encroaching on western Indian lands. To this end he would make use of either the British or Americans to win concessions and good treaties for his people. But even Tecumseh could not keep the tribes from being lured into individual treaties with the United States government whose policy was to prevent the tribes from acting together.

American frontiersmen, unfortunately, never thought of Indians as people with rights to their ancestral lands and they advanced into the territory they wanted regardless of treaties. If the Indians resisted they must be exterminated or pushed on into less desirable country. Tecumseh came to realize this and decided that the best chance for his people lay with the British. He thought that war was coming so he marched his warriors across the border and offered their services to General Isaac Brock.

On a June night in 1812 American officers from Fort Niagara were dinner guests of the British officers in Fort George just across the river. A messenger brought a despatch to the British colonel. He read it, cleared his throat in embarrassment and announced: "Gentlemen, this is serious news. President Madison has declared war on Canada."

The startled officers of both countries pulled themselves together and the dinner was finished with elaborate courtesy. Then the officers shook hands and the Americans returned to Fort Niagara. Henceforth the men in the two forts facing each other across the narrow river must regard one another as enemies.

So the sprawling, chaotic war, which never should have taken place between Canadians and Americans, began along the lakes and around the forts on the banks of the Detroit and Niagara Rivers. Canada had nothing to do with the war between England and the United States on the high seas, where the small American navy acquitted itself very well. The United States might possibly have settled the question of rights for her merchant ships without going to war, however, and the invasion of Canada had little justification.

England was too engulfed in war to provide Canada with many troops. In the United States there was no unity, for the people at large were indifferent and New Englanders were so opposed that flags were put at half mast when war was declared. The regular troops and the raw militia failed to co-operate and there were few good commanding officers. Although these armies were larger than the forces Canada could muster, the British and Canadian soldiers made up for lack of numbers by their superior training and discipline.

American politicians and frontiersmen still believed that Canadians were so dissatisfied with British rule that they would offer little resistance to invasion and would see that it was to their advantage to join the Republic.

On the contrary, when General Hull marched his troops across the river from Detroit and issued a bombastic proclamation to the people, he met firm resistance. Very soon the general marched back to the American fort at Detroit.

For the people of the Canadian provinces, held together only by loyalty to the British Crown, the war brought the first glimmer of national feeling as they united to defend their own soil.

It was a fantastic war, fought in frontier territory on both sides of the lakes and rivers; a war of forts taken and re-taken, of tiny fleets of war vessels engaging in battles on the lakes. There

On the St. Lawrence

Notre Dame de Victoire, Montreal

Street Scene, Quebec

Sous le Cap Street, Quebec

Baude Street and City Hall, Quebec

Old Houses Below the Château Frontenac, Quebec

Porcupine Needlework

Old Silver

Quebec Arts and Crafts

Wood Carving   Habitant Bedspread and Wood Carving

Place D'Armes, Montreal

Château de Ramezay, Montreal

Old Mill, Île aux Coudres

An Outdoor Oven, Charlevoix County

Champlain Market, Quebec

Habitant

Old Houses, Île D'Orleans

Government House, Halifax, N. S.

Ox Cart on Road, Digby,

Hackett's Cove, Nova Scotia

Maude Lake in Schreiber District

School Car, Ontario

Cobalt, Ontario

Farmer in a Wheat Field
Alberta

Reaping on the Prairies

Threshing on the Prairies

Hutterite Children, Manitoba

ainians' Greek Orthodox Church, Gonor

Manitoba Farmer

Harvesting Beets, Manitoba

Lac les Arcs and Mount Lougheed, Exshaw, Alberta

ndian Mother and Child   Indian Tepees near Banff

Pulp Mill on British Columbia Coast   Totem Pole at Alert Bay, Vancouver Island

Prince Rupert, British Columbia

Arrival of First Train at Vancouver

View of Vancouver Harbor

Farming near Regina, Saskatchewan

Elk Falls, Vancouver

Lumber Camp, Carrot River

Big Timber, British Columbia

Indians on Vancouver Island

Inner Harbor, Victoria, B. C.

Loading a Komatik at Moose Factory

Trading Furs

Leaving Fort Norman

Springtime View of Yellowknife

The Season's Last Trip Out from Yellowknife

were blunders on both sides and victories for each, but the Canadians, defending their land, fought with more conviction than their opponents.

General Hull at Detroit, alarmed by the war whoops of Tecumseh's Indians in the woods and the sight of marching British regulars, surrendered the strong fort to General Brock without attempting to defend it. Commodore Perry soothed American pride when, with his six small ships, he won a naval victory on Lake Erie over a small British fleet. That made it possible to retrieve General Hull's blunder and re-take Detroit.

Canadians have their hero in General Isaac Brock. The blond, military Englishman was an inspiring leader who put heart into all the soldiers by his bold, confident spirit. His skill in strategy and quickness of decision brought victories to the Canadians until he was killed at the Battle of Queenston Heights.

Queenston was important, for it was the key to the Niagara peninsula. Attack was expected there or at Fort George where General Brock was when he received news that a large force of Americans had crossed the river at Queenston. Canadians, when they recall the battle, see the red-coated figure of their general galloping on his white horse to Queenston to take command. The Americans had captured the Heights and the British cannon. General Brock led his men straight up the slopes to take it back, his tall, bright-colored figure a fine target for American guns. When he fell, his men rushed on, captured the position and chased the enemy back across the river. That battle is a proud historical memory for Canadians.

Closely linked to the splendid figure of the British soldier is that of the lithe, bronzed Indian Tecumseh. General Brock appreciated his Indian ally, and Tecumseh, after meeting the general, said to his warriors, "This is a man."

The Indians were faithful, valuable allies, contributing their bravery and native craft to many battles. It was a sad day for the Indian race when their great chief was killed in battle. He was buried in the forest by his people.

The inhabitants of the countryside did their best to help the war, and Canadians cherish the somewhat legendary story of Laura Secord. The story goes that she learned of an American plan to surprise the British at Beaver Dam, after the battle of Queenston, and she set out to warn the British camp. Innocently driving her cow and swinging her milkpail, she got through the American sentries and walked all day through the forest by roundabout trails to reach the British camp. So they were warned and the American attack was a failure.

French Canadians proved their loyalty when nine hundred of them and two hundred Indians defeated an American force at Châteauguay. This victory and another at Crysler's Farm freed Montreal and Quebec from danger.

The capture of York by American troops was the cause of much bitterness on both sides. The defenses were poor and the troops too few to hold the town so the British officer in command decided to retreat to Kingston. The powder magazine was fired to prevent the stores from being used and it exploded just as the Americans were marching in, causing much loss of life. The soldiers believed that it had been timed purposely to cause the slaughter. Rage over this probably had something to do with the act of irresponsible men in burning the government buildings and barracks. Although the deed was disavowed by the American government Canadians were greatly angered. The burning of Niagara village added to the resentment. In retaliation British troops, when they occupied Washington, set fire to the White House and other government buildings.

At last the inglorious war came to an end, leaving bitterness, particularly on the Canadian side, which took long to heal. There was peace once more along the lengthy frontier, where boundaries were now more fully defined. Never again would the battered forts be rebuilt on either side for war between people of the same ancestral stock. Those which have been restored are now museum pieces. The Great Lakes were demilitarized, their waters free to both countries.

Americans learned at last that their neighbors did not wish to become part of the Republic, and the men of Manifest Destiny turned their attention to the vast west.

On the part of the United States the invasion of Canada was a deplorable blunder, but for Canadians there are proud memories of the success with which their ancestors defended their land.

Stirred to new patriotism and united by the struggle, the people of Upper and Lower Canada turned to the development of their country by improving communications.

Canals were necessary to facilitate transportation over the waterways which were the only feasible route between Upper and Lower Canada. It was a long wearisome journey in flat-bottomed bateaux from Montreal, past innumerable rapids in the St. Lawrence, to the lakes. Crews of rough French Canadian boatmen propelled the bateaux by oars, by poles in the rapids, and by the use of sails on the lakes when the wind was favorable. Larger Durham boats were introduced by Americans who had used them on the Mohawk River. They were clumsy vessels with square stern and rounded bow. Weighted with freight they made slow progress, by means of a large sail and by the labor of the boatmen, who tramped up and down the narrow gangway along the sides, sending the boat forward by the steady push of long poles.

Neither bateaux nor Durham boats had quarters for the unfortunate passengers who had to travel in them between Upper and Lower Canada.   They huddled among the barrels and bales of freight, exposed to all the vagaries of weather.   At night they camped on shore with the crew or sometimes found shelter in a primitive inn or farmhouse.

At frequent intervals progress was interrupted by rapids. The passengers walked over the portage trails or rode with the freight in wagons.   Sometimes the boats were tracked by the crew who, with ropes over their shoulders, dragged them through raging waters while they scrambled along rocky shores or waded waist-deep in icy water.   At the long portages farmers with teams of horses or oxen pulled the heavy Durham boats through the rapids.

It took courage to travel between Upper and Lower Canada before canals were built and steamboats introduced.   The hardy people took it in their stride, however, including the ladies in their bonnets and voluminous skirts.   They traveled despite all obstacles and cheerfully endured the slow, tiresome journeys.

Even before the War of 1812 travel between Quebec and Montreal was improved by the introduction of the new marvel of the steamboat.   In 1809, two years after Robert Fulton launched his *Clermont* on the Hudson, the *Accommodation,* built by the public-spirited brewer, John Molson, made her maiden voyage from Montreal to Quebec.   Citizens crowded the wharf to see her depart, regarding the strange vessel with awe and admiring the bravery of the ten intrepid souls who took passage on her.

Off she went, with a tremendous churning of paddles, while billowing clouds of black smoke rolled from her tall thin funnel and the Union Jack streamed proudly from a masthead.

The *Accommodation* left Montreal on a Wednesday afternoon and reached Quebec on Saturday morning, but thirty out of the sixty-six hours of the trip were spent at anchor during the nights. The vessel had no lights, nor were there lighthouses or other navigation signals to guide her through the channels in the darkness. On the return trip the boat's six-horse-power engine was not strong enough to propel her through Saint Mary's Current below Montreal, so that the captain of the new-fangled steamboat had to suffer the humiliation of having his vessel towed by ox-teams from shore.

Two years later a larger steamer, the *Swiftsure,* was launched and did service for the government during the war. By 1818 Molson's St. Lawrence Steamboat Company had six additional steamboats plying between Montreal and Quebec.

Meanwhile the first steamer on the Great Lakes, the *Frontenac,* was built on the Bay of Quinté and launched in 1816. She was a schooner-rigged vessel with paddle wheels and one funnel. People who traveled on her between York and Kingston thought her a floating palace, with accommodations as elegant as those of a hotel. The *Frontenac* was eclipsed later on by the *Canada,* the largest and fastest lake steamer of her time.

Steamboat transportation had come to Lake Ontario, and between Quebec and Montreal, while trade and travel between Upper and Lower Canada were still hindered by many rapids in the St. Lawrence. There was a great improvement when the long, tumultuous Lachine Rapids above Montreal were circumvented by the Lachine Canal which was finished in 1821. With processions of boats and schooners passing through the canal, up from Quebec and down from the lakes, Montreal expanded as the junction between east and west. Laden with barrels of flour, peas, pork, salt and rum, the boats made the journey up to lake ports, to return with the grain and potash of Upper Canada settlements. Later on other canals were built to pass rapids in the St. Lawrence, making a long chain of efficient waterways. On the lakes primitive bateaux were replaced by trim two- and three-masted schooners, trading back and forth between Canadian and American ports with grain and lumber.

At the place where the gathered waters of the inland seas tumble from Lake Erie over the steep escarpment of Niagara, travel from Lake Ontario to the upper country had always been interrupted. For generations voyageurs and traders had left the Niagara River below the thundering cataracts to carry goods and canoes over the portage trail. In the days of bateau transportation, goods were loaded on ox-carts at Queenston to be drawn across the peninsula to towns above the falls. Passengers made the crossing on foot, on horseback, or in jolting stage-wagons, and wheels and hoofs widened the old trail into a road of sorts.

It was a great day for trade on the lakes when the Welland Canal was built to carry boats past Niagara Falls, and was opened in 1829. It was possible then to travel by water, with few interruptions, all the way from the upper lakes to Montreal and Quebec. Farmers, who were beginning to cultivate the fertile Niagara peninsula, rejoiced at the sight of boats being towed along the canal past their fields and orchards.

Steamer travel in the large vessels had become very comfortable, although small boats plying between local ports were primitive and crowded with immigrant families going to the settlements. Even they, however, were preferable to travel on land in Upper Canada before the middle of the nineteenth century. Journals of the period describe the woes of those who traveled by wagon or stage over the abominable roads.

The main routes between towns and settlements had grown from pioneer trails but had not improved in the process. They were a terror to travelers who were transported over them in crude stagecoaches. For some time the coaches had no doors because of the necessity of fording flooded streams in the spring.

Passengers scrambled in and out through the windows. In spring the roads were well-nigh impassable with hub-deep mud, cavernous holes full of water, or stretches of corduroy road where logs had been laid over the bottomless mud. The only rest for battered travelers was to be found in primitive taverns which were dirty, crowded with hard-drinking men and ill-supplied with food.

Even more painful were the journeys of farmers and villagers in their springless carts, over the forest roads between villages. They were hardly more than trails between solemn aisles of virgin forest trees — maples, oaks, pines and beeches. Struggling horses dragged the carts over tree trunks, around stumps, in and out of muddy abysses, while the miserable occupants were thrown back and forth until every bone ached, and were nearly devoured by ferocious mosquitoes.

Families who had cleared a place for their farms in the forest, or whose parents had done the pioneering so they now lived in comfortable villages, hated the dense encroaching forest. To them the magnificent trees were enemies to be destroyed.

A vivid description of life in the bush was written by a cultivated English lady, Anna Jameson, who was living in York in 1837. She was a writer with a lively curiosity about this new land, who dared to set off all by herself to study the country and people. Anna Jameson traveled by small steamers on the lakes, which stopped frequently at landings to take on wood for the engines. She journeyed in the rough stage-wagons and was battered black and blue in farmers' carts.

Like every distinguished visitor to Upper Canada she wanted to meet the famous but irascible Colonel Talbot who lived like a lonely old eagle in his log manor house above Lake Erie. No one ever knew how the haughty gentleman would receive him, but Anna Jameson must have been very charming, for he entertained her courteously. She described the large log hall of his manor, hung with bearskins, his fields and cattle, and the people who lived in the villages and on the farms of the Talbot Estates.

Irish Colonel Talbot had received grants of thousands of acres in the bush during the early years of the nineteenth century, and had become a colonizer on a large scale. English, Scottish and Irish families seeking opportunity in a new land as well as American pioneers were settled by the colonel on his acres. He was an iron autocrat to his people and became a fierce, reactionary old gentleman, but his enterprises peopled a large territory in Upper Canada.

Anna Jameson sympathized with the lonely, hardworking life of families in the sparsely settled country. It was a saying of pioneer times that "he who has been once to church and twice to mill is a traveler." Various seasons of the year, however, brought the people together for work and fun.

Settlers of the most prosperous districts celebrated the harvest by assembling their produce for exhibition and sale in the fall. These small fairs were forerunners of the agricultural fairs which became so important an element of Ontario country life later on. Most farmers had their "sugar bush" of maple trees, for the pioneers had learned from the Indians to make sugar from the sap of the sugar maples. In a primitive country, where cane sugar was almost unknown, maple sugar was an important market product. While the snow was still on the ground the trees were tapped and the work of boiling down the sap began. Probably the young people helped with the work but, aside from labor, "sugar-eating bees" in the groves were spring festivals for romantic youths and girls. Children, too, came with spoons and ladles to get their share of new sugar.

Winter was the most sociable season, for then the mud holes and corduroy were buried deep in snow and it was easy to travel in box sleighs over the frozen surface. Wrapped up in bear-skins, families thought nothing of driving fifty miles or so for surprise parties or short visits with friends.

Entertainments among the country folk had the rough hearti-ness of pioneer communities but in the garrison towns on Lake Ontario — Kingston, Niagara, York — life was patterned after that of English towns and social distinctions were sharply drawn. The presence of government officials and English of-ficers gave a formal tone to social affairs. These provincial aristocrats amused themselves with evenings of whist, dinner parties or balls. When, for New Year's Day, St. Andrew's Day or the King's Birthday, official balls were given in the govern-ment house at York, the élite of the whole neighborhood came from far and near to be present. Ladies in silks and velvets danced the night through with elegant gentlemen and officers in the candle-lit ballroom.

"Muddy York," the capital, was redeeming its reputation by building board sidewalks in the town, and it had become a pros-perous community of brick houses. Well-to-do gentlemen had their country estates along the rough length of Yonge Street. In the eighteen-thirties York became a city and its British name was changed to the original Indian name, Toronto. A group of reactionary, ambitious men controlled the wealth and power of the province, causing political dissensions which were soon to reach the stage of rebellion.

A new channel for transportation between Upper Canada and Montreal was opened by a third canal. It linked the Ot-tawa River with Lake Ontario by way of the Rideau River and Lakes. It was undertaken by the British government in 1826 to provide an alternate route between Montreal and Lake Ontario in case another war with the United States made the St. Law-rence route impracticable. Fortunately the Rideau Canal was never needed for military purposes, but it brought about the founding of the future capital of Canada.

Near the place where the Rideau and Gatineau Rivers join the Ottawa the northern terminus of the canal was placed. That junction of three rivers had a history as old as that of the Indian tribes who once were lords of the beautiful forested wilderness. There the tribes came to trade and to throw offerings of tobacco to the Manitou of the foaming Chaudière rapids and cascades. By a trail in the woods they carried their canoes past the white waters to continue up the Ottawa. Later the fur traders followed the portage trail. It became a wagon road for the young settlement, and now stately Wellington Street of the capital follows the course of the ancient trail along the bluffs.

When Colonel By of the Royal Engineers arrived with his army of sappers, laborers and engineers, the site of the future capital was a cedar swamp and the wooded bluffs above the river had their primeval beauty. Settlers had trekked through the wilderness to build the village of Richmond near by, and across the river was the lumbering village of Philemon Wright, the ambitious Yankee from Massachusetts.

From his camp, built on the bluff, Colonel By directed the labors of the canal builders. Bytown became a rough settlement of log houses inhabited by Irish laborers, a few tradesmen and lumberjacks who spent their summers carousing and fighting after their long winters in the woods.

When the canal was opened in 1832 steamer transportation brought respectable, ambitious citizens to organize community life. They did their best to make Bytown more than a lawless settlement of floating population.

Down the great river in the spring came the huge timber rafts from the lumber camps of the forests. Philemon Wright inaugurated the lumber industry of the Ottawa Valley at the opening of the nineteenth century.

After exploring the country he brought a group of settlers, traveling over the snow in sledges drawn by horses and oxen, to the site of his village. Within a few years there were a grist-mill, sawmill and tannery at Wright's Mills, which soon had its name changed to Hull. The first raft of squared timber from Wright's lumber camps floated down the rivers to Quebec in 1807.

The powerful Ottawa, river of the northern woodlands, stained brown with minerals and forest humus, first knew the canoes of Indians and traders, then the rafts of the lumbermen. They were a breed of Canadians as colorful as the earlier coureurs de bois and voyageurs. Scotch, French Canadian, Indian and half-breed were the lumberjacks and raftsmen of the Ottawa Valley.

In the solitude of winter woodlands the men felled the forest giants, cut them into lengths of squared timber and dragged them with ox-teams through a track in the forest to the river banks. When the ice went out in the spring, thousands of squared timbers were steered by the lumbermen from the rapid stream into quiet waters where they could be assembled in cribs. The cribs were built into huge rafts on which the men lived, cooking over a fire built on a bed of sand, sleeping in bark shelters or little huts. Sails were raised to speed them on their way as they went down the rivers. Later on, about 1835, timber chutes were built beside dangerous cascades over which the rafts, men and all, slid down as though on toboggans to smooth waters below.

From Lake Allumette on the Ottawa to Wolfe's Cove at Quebec, a distance of nearly eight hundred miles, the rafts jour-

neyed in about six weeks. It must have been a rare spectacle
to see those enormous flotillas of timber, with their occupants,
carried along with the current down the superb rivers.

At Bytown, their first stop, and at Quebec, their destination,
the men in their blanket coats, red sashes, caps and huge boots,
enlivened the streets. They made for the taverns, wild for drink
and sport after their months of solitude. Their wages were
spent in mighty carousals and brawls.

In the basin before Quebec lay the great lumber ships waiting
for the masts and the loads of oak and pine timbers for the
staunch hulls of ships. When England was cut off from Baltic
timber during the Napoleonic wars she turned to the wealth
of the Canadian forests, and from that time to the decline of
wooden ships the lumber trade flourished. Sawmills of the
country also produced quantities of sawn lumber for building
purposes.

Canada had built ships since the time when La Salle built
and launched his tiny *Griffin* on Lake Erie in the seventeenth
century. Water transportation led to the growth of shipyards
at lake ports for the construction of schooners and steamers. At
Quebec sailing vessels were launched from yards where the
French had built the small ships of an earlier age.

Lumber for the Quebec industry came from the forests of
the province as well as the Ottawa Valley. French Canadians
had their winter camps in the woodlands and their log drives
on wild rivers. The lumberjacks and raftsmen were provincial types as characteristic of the country as the habitant farmers.
Out of their winter barracks in the woods and their rafting on
the rivers grew a new crop of folk songs to be joined with the
old chansons of France and of the voyageurs.

From the shipyards of Quebec in 1831 was launched the
steamer which was the first to cross the Atlantic entirely under

steam. That claim was made for the American ship *Savannah,* but her engines were helped out by sails during the voyage.

The *Royal William,* launched at Quebec, was built to win the subsidy offered by the government of Lower Canada for a steamer which would ply between Quebec and Halifax. Great crowds cheered her departure on her first voyage, and she made three trips successfully. The owners lost money on the venture, however, and decided to send her to England to be sold. The *Royal William* made her famous voyage, was sold to Portugal, then to Spain and ended her career as the *Isabella Segunda.*

Shipbuilding developed naturally in the seafaring province of Nova Scotia. Among the new population of Loyalists were many energetic men from American coast towns who had the sea and the love of ships in their blood. As sailors or owners or workers in the shipyards they helped to build up the marine industry which brought prosperity and fame to Nova Scotia and Saint John, New Brunswick.

Shipowners profited during the War of 1812 by trade with New England, despite war, and by active privateering. With the return of peace the gaunt skeletons of ships in the making were seen in many a Nova Scotian cove, and the racket of hammers and saws was a good sound, signifying prosperity. Barks and brigs and graceful clippers under clouds of sail left the harbors for the ports of the world. Grand Banks schooners of Lunenburg made that town of German population famous among codfishers.

Nova Scotia knew its greatest prosperity and importance in the age of the sailing ship. The Bluenose sailors and captains, their sturdy fishing schooners and fine fleet windjammers, were known and respected on every sea. Nova Scotians were labeled Bluenoses in the early days because in the harsh sea winds their noses were always pinched and blue with cold. These seamen were of the same character and lived on the same sort of coast as the Yankee skippers and sailors with whom they competed.

In Halifax English and Loyalist aristocrats maintained their rather snobbish social life. There were villas in the fashionable town of Windsor, and horse racing and hunting, sleighing parties and balls occupied this exclusive society. King's College was founded at Windsor by intellectual Loyalists solely for the education of gentlemen's sons who were members of the Church of England. Other denominations started their little colleges and Dalhousie University was founded by men who believed that higher education should be open to all students, regardless of religious creed.

The beautiful Georgian building, Government House, in Halifax, was the residence of the lieutenant-governor and the scene of the most official social affairs. In equally beautiful Province House the legislature functioned, and in the assembly representatives of the people contended with the autocratic Tories who controlled the government. Liberal Nova Scotians were faced with a reactionary group as unyielding as the clique which ruled Upper Canada. In all the provinces, during the eighteen-thirties, a conflict was going on between men who demanded some right to manage their own affairs, and their governors, who ruled with the aid of powerful Tory factions.

CHAPTER XI

Rebellions in 1837

AT THE TIME the Canadian people were seeking some control of their government the democratic idea was challenging the rule of aristocracies in Europe as well as America. There were revolts on the continent and in England liberals were bringing about reforms in the parliamentary system. In the United States the democracy of the frontier found its leader in rough, but honest and powerful, Andrew Jackson of Tennessee.

In Canada the colonial system of government no longer satisfied a vigorous people. When Upper and Lower Canada were organized under the Constitutional Act, after the American Revolution, the British ministry decided that the American colonies had been lost because they had been allowed too much political liberty. British statesmen did not intend to permit tendencies toward democracy to make headway in the remaining provinces of British North America and their governments were organized with this in view.

The governors and executive councils of the provinces were appointed by the British Colonial Office and were responsible only to the Crown through the colonial secretary. The legislative councils were chosen from the privileged classes. The elected assemblies, representing the people, had no control over the governing officials and their policies. From the point of view of England and the governors it was the job of the assemblies to attend to local matters such as roads, waterways, trade between provinces, and to vote supplies for these works, leaving government to the chosen few.

Except in Lower Canada the people were largely of Scottish and English stock, not content to live under such autocratic rule. In Upper Canada American settlers added to the reform element, while the Ulster Irish generally supported the reactionaries. Aside from the particular grievances of each province the fundamental demand of all reform groups was that the governor, the executive and legislative councils, be responsible to the people in their governing. This was to be accomplished, the reformers hoped, by making the legislative councils elective instead of appointive, by having members of the executive branch of government sit in the assemblies, and by giving these elected bodies complete control of the purse strings of the provinces.

To the British ministry and the local Tories such a scheme of government for colonials was unthinkable. If the colonies had equality in self-government with the mother country it would give them the status of an independent nation, and what, then, became of British rule?

In the early stages of the controversy there was no thought of disloyalty to England; rather, the quarrel was with the haughty local oligarchies who managed to perpetuate power and privilege within their own groups. In the eighteen-thirties the struggle of years was reaching a crisis.

Nova Scotians found their leader in "plain Joe Howe" of Halifax. He had grown up in close companionship with his father, a Puritan Loyalist from Massachusetts, who had the position of King's Printer in Halifax. Young Joseph was nourished on the Bible and Shakespeare and learned the printing business in his father's shop. It was natural for him to find in journalism the outlet for his liberal ideals and his passionate love for the people and landscape of his province.

The big, hearty, jovial young man traveled on foot and on horseback from one end to the other of the province, rejoicing in its farms and orchards, its rocky, spruce-trimmed coast.   He was at home in fishermen's cottages, in farmhouses and among the townsfolk, and he taught the scattered people of the country-side to love their land and take pride in being Nova Scotians.

Joseph Howe's paper, *The Nova Scotian,* became the mouth-piece of the Liberal party in their controversies with the Tories who ruled the province.   Howe's witty and eloquent writings drew to him the men of ability and intelligence who worked with him to win responsible government.   The executive and legislative council met behind closed doors to conduct the gov-ernment without consulting the assembly.   The council was composed of bankers, judges, aristocrats and the Bishop of the Church of England.   The power of this church, whose mem-bers were the upper-class minority, was a sore point in Nova Scotia, for the large bodies of Presbyterians, Baptists and Metho-dists had no equality with the established church.   Howe added to his unpopularity with the people of privilege by championing the cause of religious equality.

No one among the leaders of the Canadian people in their fight for responsible government expressed more eloquently than Joseph Howe the principles for which they were opposing the British government and their local oligarchies.   When he was elected to the assembly, in 1836, by the Liberal party, he declared these principles in forceful words.

"In England," he said, "one vote of the people's representatives throws out a ministry and a new one comes in which is com-pelled to shape its policies by the views and wishes of the major-ity; here we may record five hundred votes against our ministry and yet they sit unmoved, reproducing themselves from among their own friends and connections, and from a narrow party in the country who, though opposed to the people, have a monopoly of influence and patronage.   In England the people can breathe

the air of life into their government whenever they please; in this country the government is like an ancient Egyptian mummy wrapped up in narrow and antique prejudices — dead and inanimate but yet likely to last forever. We are desirous of a change, not such as shall divide us from our brethren across the water, but which will ensure to us what they enjoy. All we want is what exists at home — a system of responsibility to the people extending through all the departments supported at the public expense."

The Liberals and their fearless leader carried on their battle with the Tories at home and in England slowly, by constitutional methods, while in Upper and Lower Canada the struggle for reform reached the stage of open revolt. Nova Scotia profited, however, from the work of the extremists who forced the mother country to deal with the problem of reform in colonial government.

In Lower Canada the efforts of the assembly to win control over the executive council were greatly complicated by racial antagonism. The relations between French and English had grown worse since the days of Sir Guy Carleton. The people had been restless and dissatisfied under governors who vacillated between repression and conciliation. Bad feeling was caused by the tendency of English Canadians in the ruling clique to look down on the French as inferiors. Sensitive French nationalism was always on the defensive, fearful of losing its rights. French Canadians had been stirred to anger by a proposal of British statesmen to unite Upper and Lower Canada in one province, thus submerging the French in the mass of English-speaking people. Their vigorous opposition had put an end to the plan of union for the time being.

As elsewhere, the assembly in Quebec was demanding control of the officials by control of the purse strings, and the majority of the members were French Canadians. The ruling group, called the Château Clique, or the Bureaucrats, were English-speaking men of wealth. There were, however, some English leaders working with the French for reform. The questions of taxation and funds for public works became a struggle between an English minority engaged in commerce and the French majority which controlled the assembly.

Louis Papineau, the speaker of the assembly, was the leader of the radical Patriotes. The handsome French Canadian was a man of fiery eloquence and violent feeling. He seems to have been carried by his own emotion and oratory beyond constructive thinking, but he inspired ardent young men with the dream of a free French Canadian nation. Moderate Liberals were antagonized by Papineau's violence, and government resistance to reform grew with his attacks.

In this tense situation the Patriotes began to think in terms of rebellion, harking back to the early days of the American Revolution. Phrases in their resolutions were reminiscent of the Declaration of Independence and they formed societies called *Fils de la Liberté,* like the American Sons of Liberty. In the village of St. Charles a liberty cap was raised on a pole at a meeting and enthusiasts swore to defend the cause of their country.

When matters reached this stage the Catholic Church threw its influence against the Patriotes, for the clergy thought they were better off under England than under radical French Canadians. Priests warned their people of the sin of rebellion, so that most of the villages around Quebec remained quiet when open revolt occurred in 1837. Most of the disturbances took place in the vicinity of Montreal and in villages on the Richelieu River.

English Canadians countered the *Fils de la Liberté* by forming constitutional societies to uphold British institutions. Young men of both parties were arming and drilling in preparation for trouble. It was a tragic situation when fellow citizens of two racial stocks came to open conflict. In Montreal, English Canadians of the Doric Club clashed with the *Fils de la Liberté* in furious street fighting. Windows in homes of prominent English Canadians were smashed by Patriote fighters, and young men of the Doric Club wrecked the office of the Patriote newspaper.

Government troops moved into Montreal, roads were barricaded, and there was a hunt for leaders of the Patriotes. Most of them escaped to join their countrymen in the villages. Volunteers were raised in the city to join with the troops in battles which took place in various villages.

Louis Papineau had raised a whirlwind by his revolutionary oratory but, when simple French Canadian countryfolk were being killed in battles, the leader was not with them. Papineau wanted separation from England and a republican government, but he could not bring himself to accept the armed rebellion he had instigated by his leadership. Whether by advice of his associates or his own desire he escaped over the border into the United States.

Some French Canadians were stirred by a few hotheaded leaders to vain hopes of becoming a little independent nation. They won nothing by the revolt but suffering and disillusionment, but the controversies in the assembly helped to awaken England to the necessity of change in colonial government.

The quarrels in Upper Canada had also reached the stage of revolt and there was some communication between Louis Papineau and William Lyon Mackenzie, the radical leader of the people in that province.

The situation in Upper Canada was different from that in the

French province, or that in Nova Scotia with its close bond with England. Upper Canada was a pioneer province and its people of farm, village and town had the democratic instincts and desires of pioneer communities. Families whose Loyalist forebears had fled from republicanism about fifty years earlier found that some measure of self-government was necessary to their happiness.

Their hope for civic advancement and prosperity lay with their representatives in the assembly. The provincial government functioning at Toronto was, however, in the hands of a particularly reactionary group called the Family Compact, not because the families were related, but because they managed to perpetuate among their own snobbish group their power over the life of the province.

Anna Jameson, who wrote so observantly of her travels in Upper Canada, described the situation in Toronto. Perhaps her comments give a fair picture of the social clique which composed the Family Compact. In 1837, the year of crisis, she wrote: "Toronto is like a fourth or fifth rate provincial city with the pretensions of a capital city. We have here a petty colonial oligarchy, a self-constituted aristocracy based upon nothing real nor even upon anything imaginary; and we have all the mutual jealousy and fear and petty gossip, and mutual meddling and mean rivalship which are common to a small society of which the members are well known to each other. It is curious how quickly a new fashion or folly is imported from the old country, and with what difficulty and delay a new idea finds its way into the heads of the people or a new book into their hands."

Added to the control over politics, money and social welfare, which roused the opposition of the liberals, was the power of the Family Compact to control church resources, through the position of the Church of England.

When the provincial government was organized one seventh of the public lands was set aside as clergy reserves, to support a Protestant clergy. As the members of the governing clique had from the beginning belonged to the Church of England that body had become the powerful religious body of Upper Canada. Yet this was the church of the aristocratic minority. Methodism was exceedingly popular with the people and the Presbyterian Church of Scotland as well. Both these denominations had a great following but they could not share in the resources of the clergy reserves, nor were they allowed equal status with the Church of England. Archdeacon Strachan, head of this church in Upper Canada, was a member of the executive council in the government and a Tory of Tories. He used his political power to favor his church, so that the struggle for responsible government was complicated by the campaign to secure religious equality.

There were fine men of progressive ideas among the Liberals of Upper Canada; men such as Marshall Spring Bidwell, Robert Baldwin and John Rolph, who were the equal in professional position and more than the equal in brains of the Tories. They would have been glad to have accomplished their aim by constitutional methods, but the Family Compact, and the governors who listened to them, would not move an inch from their entrenched position. The repressive measures went so far as the arrest and persecution of a leading liberal.

As milder methods failed, the man who was a born agitator, never so happy as when he was fighting opposition, became the leader of people determined to win their rights. William Lyon Mackenzie was a peppery, excitable Scot, a small man with a big leonine head and burning blue eyes. He gave up his business of chemist and bookseller to publish a newspaper, *The Colonial Advocate,* in which he carried on propaganda for his radical views and attacked men who were his political enemies with bitter personal abuse. He and his paper were hated in government circles. Once when he was out of town some hotheaded young men of the ruling families broke into his office, destroyed the printing press and scattered the type in the bay. This outrage brought sympathy to Mackenzie and the people began to see in him their champion.

When he was elected to the assembly Mackenzie carried on in the House, as well as in his newspaper, fierce attacks against his opponents and the abuses in the government. The fiery little Scot, shaking with excitement as he launched his furious attacks on privilege, aroused so much resentment among Tories in the parliament that they had him expelled. When a new election was held the people voted him in again, but he was not permitted to take his seat. Persecution and his fearless fight for reform made Mackenzie a hero to the people, who showed their appreciation by electing him Mayor of Toronto, when that city was incorporated.

The battle between Reformers and Tories came to a crisis in 1837, under the arrogant governor, Sir Francis Bond Head. He listened to the councils of the ruling clique and misjudged the dangerous situation.

The democratic farmers and townsfolk in the sparsely settled countryside responded readily to plans of the liberal leaders for organization to gain their rights. Mackenzie traveled about, holding meetings and organizing groups. Men were inspired by his words to begin secretly drilling with old muskets and forging pikes in the blacksmith shops.

He and a few of the more radical spirits went beyond the wishes of the moderate reformers in their declaration for separation from England as the only solution for the province, and in their plans for armed revolt.

The governor invited trouble by removing troops from Toronto so the rebels would be tempted into action. They did as he had hoped. The radicals, led by Mackenzie, planned a march on Toronto, to seize the arms in the barracks, capture the governor and set up a provisional government. The march was intended to coincide with a rising of the Patriotes in Lower Canada. Defeat came to the Patriotes, however, while Mackenzie's plan was under way. In both provinces the revolt of inexperienced, badly led people was doomed to failure.

Everything went wrong with the march on Toronto. It was planned that bands of armed countrymen were to meet at Montgomery's Tavern some miles out of the city on Yonge Street. Mackenzie was in the country, starting the companies on their march when John Rolph, working in the city, changed the date to an earlier day because the governor had got wind of their plans.

Companies of farmers and townsfolk were marching through mud and rain to the rendezvous at Montgomery's Tavern. It was too late to notify them of the change of date, and only a few bands had arrived on December 3. They were so footsore, hungry and exhausted that they refused to march on to the city at Mackenzie's urging. That delay meant defeat, for the governor had time to assemble militia and prepare defenses.

The first brush between militia and rebels on Yonge Street would have been comic had it not been so disastrous to the rebel cause. Each party fired a volley, each thought that its own company was being mowed down, and they ran from each other at top speed. The only experienced soldier among the rebel leaders was Colonel Anthony Egmond, a veteran of the Napoleonic wars. When more companies arrived he and Mackenzie tried to organize the men in a patch of woods to meet the attack of new militia regiments coming out from town.

The sight of the regiments marching over a hill and the first crash of cannon balls in the woods shattered the resistance of the bewildered, disheartened countrymen. They ran for their lives through the woods and by muddy back roads to reach their homes. Many prisoners were taken but Mackenzie escaped to make his way across country to the American border with a price on his head. Many times he narrowly escaped capture, but he was sheltered by friendly farmers who passed him on from one refuge to another.

In Buffalo the rebel leader found sympathy and was able to collect money and men to set up a provisional government on Navy Island in Canadian waters just above Niagara Falls. Most of his men were reckless, irresponsible Americans, always ready to join a fight.

Mackenzie brought about strained relations between England and the United States by obtaining American help for his rebellion. Canadian volunteers made the situation worse when they crossed the river to an American harbor to seize the small American steamer *Caroline* which Mackenzie used for a supply boat. They captured the crew, set the vessel afire and turned her adrift to rush over Niagara Falls in a blazing spectacle.

For three weeks the leader of a lost cause held out on Navy Island. When he retreated once more to the American shore he was arrested and kept in jail for a while for violating the neutrality laws of the United States.

At that time the upper New England states and New York, along the border, were frontier territory, where many people were so enthusiastic over their new democracy and so anti-British that their sympathies led them to aid the Canadians in throwing off "British tyranny."

Canadian refugees were sheltered by countryfolk, and the secret societies called Hunters' Lodges joined with exiled Ca-

nadian leaders in the attempt to keep the rebellion alive.   The
Hunters' Lodges were organized and carried on by honest agitators as well as irresponsible troublemakers.

There were battles along the border during 1838, particularly
in Lower Canada.   They resulted only in burned houses and
barns and the imprisonment of miserable people who thought
that they were fighting for liberty.   Then began the migration
of unhappy French Canadians to New England factory towns.

It was some time before the danger of war between England
and the United States, caused by many violent incidents, was
averted by the will of both governments to keep the peace.

William Lyon Mackenzie lived in the United States for some
years.   When he was pardoned and returned to Canada in the
eighteen-forties he sat once more in the assembly, a disillusioned man.   Close contact with a rude, unruly democracy had
dampened his ardor.   The grandson of the visionary who tried
to bring freedom to the people became a powerful political
leader.   Prime Minister William Lyon Mackenzie King guided
Canada through some crucial years of the twentieth century.

The revolts in Upper and Lower Canada were the work of
sincere fiery agitators who led discontented people into suffering
and defeat.   They did their work, however, together with the
more moderate agitation of constitutional reformers.   England
was startled into the realization that there must be changes in
colonial government if Canada was to remain British North
America.   Through blood and suffering and civil conflict the
provinces had made one step forward toward self-government.

CHAPTER XII

The Provinces Become a Dominion

CANADA was set on the road to nationhood by the keen political understanding of Lord Durham, a nobleman with a radical mind and real devotion to the good of the Empire and of Canada. He was sent out as high commissioner in 1838 to bring the chaotic provinces to order and to study and report on the troubles of Canada.

Rebellion had failed, leaving misery and confusion in its wake. Lord Durham banished those ringleaders who were in Canada while Mackenzie and Papineau were forbidden to return to the country. In honor of the coronation of young Queen Victoria he declared a general amnesty for all but a few of those who had taken part in revolt, believing that they were discontented people who had been led astray by agitators. Some of the most active rebels had been executed, to the great grief of the people.

During his five months in Canada the high commissioner conferred with all the warring factions while an able corps of assistants gathered further information for him. The report which he presented to the House of Commons analysed with insight the troubles afflicting Canada and proposed remedies. The *Report on the State of British North America* was a statesmanlike document which is considered by historians to have laid the foundations for the united Dominion of Canada.

Lord Durham recommended the union of Upper and Lower Canada in one provincial government under a governor-general, as a solution for their difficulties. Thus, he believed, the French Canadians would be gradually merged in the English-speaking population and could not remain a distinct French unit in a

British land. He proposed that this be brought about by the consent of the political parties in both provinces. That was a difficult thing to accomplish in the state of animosity which existed. It took all the skill of brilliant, tactful Lord Sydenham, who succeeded Lord Durham as high commissioner, to win the consent of English and French leaders to union. The French party yielded for the sole reason that they realized it was their only chance for any self-government as a province of the Empire.

The British Parliament accepted the Report and the Act of Union was passed. It remained for Lord Sydenham to put into practice the principles of government proposed by Lord Durham. Canadians were to have parliamentary rule with control of domestic policies, and governors were instructed to work in harmony with the wishes of the legislature when it did not interfere with the interests of the Empire. The British government had not yet fully accepted the principle of responsible government.

In the Maritimes, which had not suffered the disasters of rebellion, the reform party managed to bring about satisfactory changes during some years of excited controversy. There were greater difficulties in Upper and Lower Canada.

Each province was to have an equal number of representatives in the union parliament. The country was divided into self-governing municipalities so that Canadians were able to advance rapidly in the management of their local affairs.

Kingston was chosen for the capital of the united Canadas and there, in 1841, the first parliament thrashed out their problems under the masterful direction of Lord Sydenham. It was his will and not that of the Canadians which prevailed. Under the succeeding governor-general, Sir Charles Bagot, a Canadian administration was formed which represented the interests of the two peoples. It was headed by two moderate reformers, Robert Baldwin of English blood and Louis Hippolyte La Fontaine of French blood. The Canadas were now known as Canada East and Canada West.

Through some years of storm and stress Canadians learned the processes of popular government under governors who sometimes aided and sometimes hindered, according to their character and convictions. The knotty problem of how the governor-general was to be responsible to the Crown and at the same time responsible to the people of Canada caused many conflicts. In parliamentary sessions Canadian politicians were as turbulent, as factious and as selfish in their views as the men who battled in the Congress of the United States. Riotous elections were as common in Canada as across the border. In both countries independent North Americans, in a republic and as provinces of an empire, struggled through trial and error toward their differing ideas of democracy.

The year 1849 was a time of crisis for Canada. Montreal, which had become the capital, had been booming a few years before from the trade between the upper and lower country. Merchants and the provincial government had gone deeply in debt for ambitious enterprises of canal building, dredging of river channels and building of docks. Fleets of barges brought the wheat of the lake country to be converted into flour in Montreal's mills.

Canadian commerce prospered because of preferential tariff arrangements with England. Then the mother country adopted free trade, which brought prosperity to the English but ruin to Canadian merchants. At the same time Americans, who had seized on the possibilities of the newfangled railways, constructed lines from the Atlantic coast to meet the lake traffic. Canadian products went by rail to New York and Philadelphia while Montreal's once busy waterways were left empty and desolate. During the business depression came thousands of starving Irish immigrants fleeing from famine at home. They arrived dying of ship's fever and involved the whole city in suffering and disease.

British statesmen, at this time, decided to accept the desire of Canadians that their government be responsible to them through their elected representatives, rather than to the British government through the governor. The colonial office informed Lord Elgin, the governor-general, that the wishes of the assemblies should no longer be resisted. He was a believer in Lord Durham's theories for Canada, but he saw that the two races must share in government. In 1848 Lord Elgin called upon the French and English leaders of the majority party to form an administration.

This caused great agitation among the Tories, who were further annoyed because Louis Papineau, who had been pardoned, once more sat in the assembly and stirred up French discontent with his old fervor. Bitter feeling increased over the Rebellion Losses bill.

For years claims had been presented to the government by people whose property had been destroyed during the upheavals of the rebellion. Some of the petitioners had been at least sympathizers with the rebels and most of those who had suffered losses were French Canadians. So, in this time of gloom and depression, the smoldering hatreds of the rebellion period were revived.

When it seemed likely that the obnoxious bill would pass there were stormy meetings and feeling was especially bitter in Montreal. From bankrupt merchants and mobs in the street there rose a clamor against compensating rebels when the government was in financial straits and the people in need. Nevertheless the bill passed and Lord Elgin signed it because he believed it his duty to abide by the will of the majority.

Immediately fury broke out in Montreal. From a monster mass meeting a mob of rioters streamed to the parliament buildings, smashed the furniture and set the buildings afire. While the flames leaped against the night sky and precious records were destroyed the mob cheered the spectacle.

Every time Lord Elgin appeared in the streets his carriage was surrounded by jeering crowds, throwing stones and rotten eggs. When he came from a government meeting at the Château de Ramezay his carriage was followed to his country home by crowds on foot, on horseback and in cabs. Never did a governor of Canada suffer such abuse, and all because he had stood by the principles of responsible government for which some of the people had fought! For several days Montreal was in the hands of rioting mobs. The fury of ignorant men had been roused by the agitation of the privileged class, so that the Tories, opposed to reform, were pretty well discredited. Order was soon restored but, because of those riots, Montreal lost the chance to become the national capital of Canada.

New troubles followed on the heels of the riots. Canadian merchants, despairing of their future and feeling that England cared nothing for their welfare, looked across the border at the big, thriving democracy. They were dazzled by the rapid advancement of the Americans and thought that their salvation lay in joining themselves to that successful country. Times were topsy-turvy indeed in the unhappy Canada of 1849, for this time it was the merchants and upper class, chiefly of Montreal, who signed an Annexation Manifesto. The Tories of 1837 demanded separation from England while English-speaking reformers and some French Canadian leaders of 1837 were the loyalists of 1849.

All the agitations of that troublous time died down and were soon forgotten as prosperity returned. Business picked up and immigration increased. Old navigation laws which had prevented Canada from trading with foreign nations were repealed and Montreal became once more, and in a larger way, a busy port. A forest of masts rose beyond the docks as in 1850 nearly a hundred foreign vessels came to the port.

Lord Elgin was rewarded for patient, diplomatic effort when he obtained the signing of the Reciprocity Treaty with the United States in 1854. Natural products were to be admitted free of duty in both countries, and American fishermen were to have the privilege they had long desired of fishing within the territorial waters of the Maritime provinces. Nova Scotia was not pleased with this agreement, but as trade brought prosperity to the province it was accepted. Another provision was the right of Americans to use the water system of the St. Lawrence and canals, while Canadians were given similar rights in Lake Michigan. So began the mutual use of the magnificent system of waterways which lies between the two countries.

Canada had never known such prosperity as that which followed the Reciprocity Treaty. At last trade could flow freely in its natural channels, north and south. For the first time there was a real and friendly link, through trade, between the lusty Republic and its northern neighbor.

Canadians followed Americans into the excitements and speculative schemes of the railway age. Travel in Canada was still, in the eighteen-forties, a combination of steamboat on the waterways and stagecoach on the terrible roads. Lake and river had always been for Canadians the natural route for travel, and the provinces had been too much involved in political dissensions to get down to the important business of improving roads. Stagecoach travel produced a camaraderie of the road as battered passengers recounted their adventures around log fires in country inns. The cities — Toronto, Kingston, Montreal, Quebec — had their stagecoach inns, forerunners of travelers' hotels in the railroad age.

The people of the Canadas were turning their eyes westward, but the west, to them, extended as far as Lake Huron. The fertile, beautiful lands along Lakes Ontario and Erie were yielding produce to the farmers and northward to Lake Huron colonizing companies were turning the wilderness into farms and towns. The prosperity of this western country must be aided by railroads.

Few people gave any thought to the enormous region of plains and mountains extending to the Pacific, the realm of the fur traders. That country was known only to a few travelers besides the men connected with the fur trade, who were secretive about the fertility of the plains.

As they emerged from political troubles into a time of economic advancement it was necessary for the provinces to be joined by effective travel routes that they might co-operate. It was difficult enough to transport people and goods between Canada East and Canada West, but the only connection with the distant Maritimes was by a slow sea voyage. It was easier for people in any of the provinces to cross the border into the United States than to go back and forth between the provinces.

Politicians and business men of the Canadas went to work on ambitious railway schemes. Short lines were built, the majority of them in Canada West. It was planned to make connection with an American line to Portland, Maine, to provide an outlet for Canadian products to the sea.

In the Maritimes political leaders gave their attention to plans for an intercolonial railway. They wanted to link Halifax with Saint John on the Bay of Fundy and continue to Portland for the increase of commerce between the Maritimes and New England. It was their hope, also, to overcome their geographical isolation from Canada by a railroad from Halifax to Quebec.

Joseph Howe, the Nova Scotian, gave himself to the promotion of the Intercolonial Railway. Meeting with other Maritime leaders, routes were worked out to satisfy both Nova Scotia and New Brunswick. Joseph Howe went to London to win backing from the government for the scheme. He returned triumphant with the promise of a large loan to guarantee the funds the provinces could raise.

Long before his contemporaries Joseph Howe envisioned railroads pushing on across plains and mountains to create a British North American nation extending to the Pacific. In a speech to the people, after his return from England, he cried exultantly: "I venture to predict that in five years we shall make the journey hence to Quebec and Montreal and home through Portland and Saint John by rail; and I believe that many in this room will live to hear the whistle of the steam engine in the passes of the Rockies and to make the journey from Halifax to the Pacific in five or six days."

It was to be more than five years before Joseph Howe could travel to Quebec by train and he would not live to see the fulfillment of the rest of his prophecy. Disappointment came to him when, in the following year, the British Colonial Office withdrew its promise of support. Bit by bit the Maritime provinces built sections of their railroads until, in 1860, Halifax had connection with the Bay of Fundy and Gulf of St. Lawrence while New Brunswick had a line from Saint John to the Gulf. The Intercolonial Railway did not achieve its connection with Canada until after Confederation.

Politicians of the Canadian parliament went ahead with a scheme to amalgamate their railroads and connect them with

Portland in the Grand Trunk Railway. England had been in a fever of railroad building in the eighteen-forties and English promoters and contractors had a large share in the company which eventually carried through the Canadian project. In 1860 the Grand Trunk Railway was completed from Lake Huron to the Atlantic. The Victoria Bridge, a magnificent structure for its time, was built to carry the railroad across the river at Montreal and on to the United States.

Small wonder that Montrealers celebrated with the gaiety and love of spectacle characteristic of them when the Prince of Wales came to open the Victoria Bridge in 1860. Through flag- and flower-decked streets the son of beloved Queen Victoria passed between cheering crowds. People crowded the river bank to see the arrival of the royal party and to watch the prince lay the last stone of their wonderful bridge.

The ceremonial ball given in honor of Prince Edward was held in a huge pavilion decorated in Victorian style with bowers and grottoes, while fountains spouted claret and champagne. Lovely ladies of Montreal society sailed through the dances in their most fashionable spreading crinolines, escorted by courtly gentlemen in frock coats and high stocks.

Canadians enjoyed the thrill of their first railway journeys as much as Americans had done somewhat earlier. To be sure they were jounced unmercifully over the rough tracks, they were exposed to wind and sparks from the engine, and were nearly asphyxiated by the smoke of wood-burning locomotives. But this was progress, Canadians were catching up with their big neighbor in modern transportation. Now the people of Canada and their produce could travel from Montreal downstream to Quebec, west to the cities of Canada West, or over the river and on to New England and even to Chicago, on branches of the Grand Trunk Railway.

With prosperity, civic life and education were advanced in Canada West. Public education was helped by having the revenue from the disputed clergy reserves applied to that cause. Several small colleges were already in existence. Queen's College in Kingston was founded by learned Scotsmen, and honored with a royal charter from Queen Victoria. Most colleges had come into being to provide higher education for students belonging to one or another religious denomination. It was something new, therefore, when Robert Baldwin, the reformer, proposed a state university which should be non-denominational and open to all ambitious students. Bishop Strachan protested against such a godless institution but, due to the efforts of Robert Baldwin, the University of Toronto was started on its splendid career despite the bishop.

Social life in the towns of the pioneer province was simple, but reaching toward culture. People enjoyed evenings of lectures, oratorical readings and music, or the receptions of the Scottish, English and Irish societies.

In the French Canadian province education was in the hands of the religious orders and the country people were illiterate. Young men of upper-class families received their professional training in the Collège de Montréal or the ancient Seminary of Quebec and Laval University. Girls continued to grow up under the care of the Ursulines and other teaching orders of nuns.

In Montreal people of wealth and sophistication, both French and English, created a social life lavish in its festivities. It was, however, in old Quebec that art and culture flourished.

The lumber industry and shipbuilding kept the working population busy, and the directors of those industries, as well as old seigneurial families, had money to enjoy the good things of life. Among these they counted music and drama. People of talent, both French and English, found appreciation in Quebec and audiences were never lacking for concerts or performances of Shakespeare.

It was in Quebec that Cornelius Krieghoff, a painter of Dutch extraction, found inspiration for his work and sale for his pictures. He was a member of the convivial bohemian set of artistic people who gave color to the life of the town and countryside by their merrymakings.

Winter night carnivals, down the river at Montmorency Falls, were the favorite amusement of the bohemians and society folk. Over the frozen river came the brightly painted carrioles, horses trotting to the music of sleigh bells, while under the buffalo robes laughing girls snuggled close to their escorts. No one minded if a carriole upset occasionally, toppling a young lady in billowing crinolines upside down in a snowdrift. Sometimes Lord Elgin and his lady were present, in their fine sleigh, with outriders, and red pompoms nodding on the horses' heads.

The spray of the cascades, tumbling over the cliffs, was frozen into an icy cone called the Sugar Loaf from its shape. The boldest of the merrymakers climbed the cone by steps cut in the ice, to shoot down the glittering slope at terrific speed on toboggans. There were supper parties in ice grottoes carved out by a clever restaurateur in the back of the Sugar Loaf. Many revelers went on over the snowy roads to one country inn after another, spending the nights in song and wine drinking.

Cornelius Krieghoff joined the winter night revelers, sketching in the midst of the hilarities, and found other subjects for paintings in the villages, where he made friends with the habitants. He, who was one of the earliest of Canadian painters, recorded for posterity the festivities of old Quebec and the charm of the Laurentian countryside and its people.

In the mid-nineteenth century French Canadian country life was at its best. Political troubles had passed away. At peace on their farms the habitant families followed the traditional ritual of plowing, planting and harvesting. They had their winter night *veillées* for song and the telling of legends; their Sunday mornings at Mass with the time of visiting and exchange of neighborhood news which followed. In the big cosy kitchens of the farmhouses women worked at their looms and spinning wheels, producing not only homespun cloth but the rugs and coverlets of a charming folk art. Wood carvers of great talent, in village shops, carved pulpits and saints for parish churches.

The long narrow ribbons of farms became ever narrower as the farmers divided their land among their sons, until there was not enough land to go around. Younger sons took to the lumber camps or migrated to New England, following the lure of town life as described by relatives who had gone there. Away from their beloved river, the farmers pushed farther and farther into the virgin woodlands of the north, hewing out new farms. A sympathetic Frenchman, Louis Hémon, who lived among the people, at a later time described that life in the charming little masterpiece, *Maria Chapdelaine*.

Aside from the traditional life on the St. Lawrence the Canadas were moving toward great change. There was a growing interest among thinking men in the idea of the federation of the provinces. It was not a new idea, for statesmen, Sir Guy Carleton and Lord Durham among them, had raised the question at various times. Geographical obstacles had made it seem impossible to bring under one central government groups of people who were separated by vast distances. Now, however, the railroads were bringing the provinces closer together. If Canadians were to become more than mere colonials, if they were to advance in prosperity, they must unite. Political differences between Conservatives and Liberals, between French and English, were making government in the united Canadas unsatisfactory, so that politicians of these provinces took the initiative in plans for federal union.

The interest in union grew in the early sixties, as Canadians were once more threatened by danger from across the border. Again they were involved in a crisis of affairs in the Republic. The struggle between the principles of federal union and states' rights, between free and slave-holding states, led to the Civil War or the War Between the States. The sympathies of most Canadians were with the North. Runaway slaves, passed along by the underground railway, crossed into Canada at villages on Lakes Erie and Ontario, to be welcomed with sympathy and started on a new life as free men.

England, however, favored the South and because of her activities the tension became so great between the United States and England that it seemed as though there might be another war. If that happened Canadians foresaw that an army released from civil war would turn against Canada. In order to be freed from fear of their aggressive neighbor the Canadian provinces must band together and become a nation.

The call of the west was heard as well. Statesmen realized that there was a huge rich territory in the hands of the Hudson's Bay Company which might well be taken over by advancing American pioneers unless Canada became strong enough to claim it for British North America.

Confederation of the provinces was brought about by a small group of able men who were so deeply convinced of its importance they put aside party differences to accomplish it. Totally opposed in character and political ideas were the two men who were most instrumental in winning English-speaking Canadians to the idea of federation. George Brown, the Liberal, editor of the Toronto *Globe,* and John A. Macdonald, a lawyer of Kingston and a Conservative, had been opponents throughout their political careers. By the time they had become leaders of their respective parties they were not even on speaking terms. For the sake of Canada's destiny they put aside their personal animosities and worked together faithfully to bring about the union of the provinces. Both were men of Scottish birth, with a strong feeling for the Empire. They believed it essential for Canada to preserve her connection with England.

George Brown was very popular with the democratic people of Upper Canada. He was a man of vigorous, expansive ideas who looked westward from his provinces. Canada's western boundary should be the Pacific Ocean, he declared. Through his speeches and his forthright articles in the *Globe* he had great influence.

John A. Macdonald was as subtle and wily as George Brown was direct. He had made a success of law and politics by native ability, without the aid of money or family, and he was a master hand at politics. His diplomacy, and cleverness in handling men, made it possible for him to smooth out differences in the momentous conferences over confederation.

Associated with these two men was the French Canadian, George Étienne Cartier. He had been a follower of Papineau but had changed his views and become the leader of the Conservative party in his province. French Canadians had not enjoyed union with Upper Canada and the proposal for a larger union met intense opposition from the radical party. Cartier's achievement in winning consent for confederation was a triumph.

It was difficult to persuade the Maritimes, so isolated from the rest of Canada. They could be protected by England's sea power, so did not share the fear of the other provinces in regard to the United States.   They were considering the union of their three provinces — Nova Scotia, New Brunswick and Prince Edward Island — under one government.   Their delegates met at Charlottetown, Prince Edward Island, in 1864, to discuss the plan.   To this conference came the Canadian leaders — Brown, Macdonald and others — to present their scheme for union of all the provinces under a national government.   Their plan provided for local legislatures in each province, with representatives in the national parliament.   That appealed to the independent Maritime men who hesitated over union of their three provinces because it would involve giving up their individual legislatures.   They agreed to meet with the Canadian delegates at Quebec to discuss plans for confederation.

When decisions so important for the future of Nova Scotia were being made Joseph Howe was not present.   He was no longer in politics, for the Conservative party, led by Dr. Charles Tupper, was in power.   Howe had refused the invitation to attend the Charlottetown meeting because he was too busy with his work as commissioner of fisheries.

The man who had been the first to put into eloquent words the idea of a British North American nation, extending from sea to sea, was not ready to help in the founding of that nation when the opportunity came.   Joseph Howe's great-hearted enthusiasm had been dampened by many disappointments and he had turned from large visions to a local patriotism.   It was difficult, too, for a man of his egotism, accustomed to power and the applause of the people, to surrender leadership in provincial affairs to Dr. Charles Tupper.   He gave only a lukewarm interest to the proposal for confederation, believing it best for Nova Scotia to unite only with her sister provinces.   So it was Dr. Tupper and not Joseph Howe who attended the Quebec conference.

In that ancient city the delegates met in October, 1864, to plan a new nation. The Fathers of Confederation spent fourteen days of intensive work, meeting in secret conferences to the annoyance of Canadian and English journalists, and created the basic plan for confederation. It was then ready to be presented to the provincial parliaments and to the British government.

Their aim was to keep Canada united to England through a governor-general appointed by the Crown, and at the same time to provide self-government for the young nation through a national parliament. The individualistic provinces were to be assured of management of their local affairs through provincial parliaments headed by lieutenant-governors. The Fathers of Confederation planned Canadian governmental institutions on the model of the Mother of Parliaments in the old country.

In Nova Scotia the people's opposition grew and they protested against the plan in angry mass meetings. They were suspicious of Canadian politicians and feared that their interests would be swamped in a national parliament. Joseph Howe threw in his lot with the people and led the campaign against confederation with vigorous pungent speeches. Dr. Tupper won the day, however, in the Nova Scotia legislature, and New Brunswick followed suit. Prince Edward Island did not join the other provinces until a later time.

The British North American Act, which is Canada's constitution, was passed by the British Parliament and became law in 1867. Canada celebrates her birthday in the same week of July as the United States, for the Dominion of Canada came into being by royal proclamation on July 1, 1867.

Nova Scotia tried to withdraw and there was talk of annexation to the United States. Joseph Howe realized that this would happen if Nova Scotia did not remain in the Dominion, so changed his attitude. Dr. Tupper and John A. Macdonald persuaded him that he would be protecting the interests of his beloved province if he agreed to confederation and accepted a post in the national government.   To the people it seemed that their champion had betrayed them and old friends in Halifax crossed the street to avoid speaking to him.   It was a hard thing for the warmhearted man who cared so much for the friendship of the people.   They understood, later on, that he had acted for their interest and Joseph Howe regained his place in the affections of Nova Scotians.

In the buildings of Victorian Gothic architecture, set high on the bluffs above the Ottawa, the first parliament of a new nation held its sessions.   The once lawless settlement of Bytown had become Ottawa, a prosperous little town.   Its citizens were immensely proud because, in 1857, Queen Victoria had chosen it to be the capital of the united Canadas.

Overshadowing the frontier town, the Parliament Buildings spoke of the deep allegiance of Canadians to the mother country and its institutions.   Below the bluffs the great river sweeping by sang of the "true North, strong and free," of a people who were setting out to fulfill their national destiny.

The coalition of Conservatives and Liberals did not last long. George Brown withdrew in 1865 and his colleague in confederation, as Sir John A. Macdonald, became prime minister. For many years this masterly statesman was to lead the new nation.

The Dominion of Canada began its existence with four provinces — Quebec and Ontario (which had been Canada East and Canada West), Nova Scotia and New Brunswick.   To extend that Dominion from sea to sea was the compelling urge of the national leaders.

Separated from the provinces by wilderness and the Great Lakes, the Red River settlements were growing on the verge of the prairies. But a Canadian, in order to reach those towns, must travel into the United States by train and return by steamboat on the Red River. Beyond lay the vast and fertile prairie lands, the domain of the Hudson's Bay Company. It was time that fur traders should relinquish their hold on such wonderful lands to men who would farm and build towns. Far away on the Pacific coast the Crown colony of British Columbia and Vancouver Island carried on a life of its own, entirely separated from Canada in the east. Already Americans had gained a large slice of the Pacific northwest through the Oregon boundary controversy.

The winning of these enormous territories of plain and mountain, with their potential riches, stirred Canadians to a new era of adventurous expansion. Westward the vigorous young men turned their eyes and westward streamed the pioneers to win for British North America a dominion extending from ocean to ocean.

IV. The West Is Won

CHAPTER XIII

The Prairies Are Tamed

UNDER the huge dome of the prairie sky little villages and farms edged the two streams of the Red River district in the eighteen-forties. Between the trading post of Fort Garry and the Stone Fort or Lower Fort Garry on the Red River lived descendants of Lord Selkirk's Scottish settlers and retired men of the Hudson's Bay Company with their families. Across the river from Fort Garry, French Canadians and the half-breed Métis had their village center in St. Boniface and their farms were scattered along the river banks. All the farmers wanted frontages on the rivers, the water highways, so that the farms stretched back from the banks in narrow ribbons like those along the St. Lawrence. Beyond were communal hayfields and pastures for horses and cattle.

After the union of the warring fur companies in 1821 the inhabitants, governed by the Hudson's Bay Company, had been able to develop their farming and their community life.

Once a year came the brigades of York boats from Hudson Bay, bringing supplies which came to the bay in ships from England for the forts and settlements. Everything the people wanted to make life more civilized came to them by that long sea and river voyage: furniture, pianos, silks and broadcloth for dress clothes, feminine fineries and even carriages for the prosperous families. Such things as plows, spades, hoes and nails were more precious than gold since they had to be imported from England.

Iron being so scarce, the early settlers invented the typical pioneer wagon of the Canadian plains made wholly of wood, the Red River cart. The parts were fastened together with wooden pegs, or thongs of rawhide, and the two great wheels were bound with rawhide in place of tires. For any journeys beyond the settlements people traveled in these carts drawn by oxen or horses, or rode on Indian ponies. They followed the practice of Indians and traders in traversing the frozen plains with dog teams in the howling winds and snows of severe winters.

It was a hard-working life, but one of neighborly sociability. The villages had their little churches and schools, their societies and entertainments. There were balls and festivities at the Stone Fort which was the social center of the settlements and the residence of the chief factor of the Hudson's Bay Company for the district. The Métis, too, had their hilarious gatherings when they danced the Red River jig and other pioneer dances to the squeaky music of fiddlers. The bells of their church at St. Boniface were dear to everyone of French Catholic faith and they were ministered to by a beloved bishop. The Gray Nuns cared for the health of the settlers and taught the children in their school.

Far to the west on the grassy plains the buffalo still roamed in great herds and were the mainstay of life for the Indian tribes. The hides and fur robes, the pemmican made from the meat of the buffalo were for many years essential to the Red River people, and the Métis continued their springtime migration westward for the buffalo hunt. In caravans of Red River carts the families set out, with the men riding alongside on Indian ponies. Song and shout and the continuous shrieking and groaning of ungreased wooden axles on the carts marked the progress of the procession.

While the provinces in the east were developing trade and transportation and working over their political problems the Red River people lived in a world of their own, separated by leagues of wilderness from the more advanced eastern communities. The villages of Assiniboia made a small nucleus of settlement on the illimitable plains.

In the northwest there were small settlements of Métis and a few pioneers near Fort Edmonton on the north branch of the Saskatchewan River. Over the vast territory, lifting gradually in rolling land toward the foothills of the Rockies, trading posts and missions marked the only incursion of the white men into Indian domains. Following the trails of the fur traders the missionaries came to teach and convert the Indians and to minister to the tiny clusters of settlement.

Father Lacombe, a splendid pioneer priest called the Black-robed Voyageur, was beloved among Métis and Indians. Methodist missionaries came, with a deep sense of their responsibility to bring civilization into the wilds. Their wives and children accompanied them to the great lonely land, helping to make the small mission settlements near trading posts into havens for the Indians, where they would find help in hunger or sickness and kindness from people who took the trouble to learn their languages. Reverend James Evans did an invaluable service for the whole northwest when he worked out a syllabic alphabet for the Cree language, a sort of shorthand by which Indian syllables could be transcribed. He made a primitive press, type and ink, so that he might print Bible passages in this script for the Indians to read. Although the alphabet was made for the Crees it could be adapted to other Indian languages and was later applied also to the Eskimo tongue. Church of England missionaries also came into the northwest, working among the Crees, training some of their converts to minister to their own people. They had a strong mission at the old trading post of The Pas.

The missionaries traveled great distances by canoe, dog team and Indian pony in their work among the Indians. They understood the native people and their real friendliness exerted a great influence in keeping peace between Indians and whites later on. From the missionaries and from the men in the Hudson's Bay posts the Indians knew that they would meet kindness and straight dealing.

Rupert's Land, extending to the Rockies, and the north country so far as the fur traders had penetrated, was still the undisputed domain of the Hudson's Bay Company. They had a monopoly of the fur trade and ruled Assiniboia, the Red River district, with a firm hand. Change was coming from the south, however, and that change was to bring to an end the exclusive control of the fur lords.

In the eighteen-fifties the isolation of the Red River district began to be broken. American pioneers were settling the new state of Minnesota and the town of St. Paul was a growing center. The Red River towns were cut off from Canada in the east but there was nothing to prevent communications north and south. The great plains rolled on into Minnesota without a break and the Red River was an easy water route. Very soon the Red River people had a mail route, by pony and cart, to the nearest American settlement. When the railroad reached St. Paul it was easier for the Hudson's Bay Company to transport their furs to St. Paul and ship them east by rail than to continue the long sea route by way of Hudson Bay to England.

During the spring and summer, long trains of Red River carts loaded with furs creaked and crawled over the trail from Fort Garry to St. Paul. On the return trip they brought supplies for the settlements. Announced by the squeaking, groaning wheels and escorted by long-haired, swarthy Métis carters, these new fur brigades made a sensation in St. Paul. The shaggy ponies, fierce dogs, the men in French caps and vivid sashes, elk-skin trousers and moccasins, brought the atmosphere of the northern wilds to the more settled people of the American town.

During the eighteen-fifties some new inhabitants came to the Red River district and a village, later to become Winnipeg, began to grow around old Fort Garry. Two young men from Toronto brought a printing press and, in 1859, began the publication of western Canada's first newspaper, *The Nor' Wester.*

The Red River people, watching the progress of Americans in Minnesota, were becoming restive under the rigid rule of the Hudson's Bay Company and its monopoly of the fur trade. Any trapper who tried to ship his pelts across the border to make profit for himself met swift punishment if caught by agents of the company. The inhabitants also felt the need of better government to help them in the development of their resources.

Complaints of the company's methods were sent to London and, as its age-old charter was to expire in 1859, petitions were made to the British Parliament not to renew it. A parliamentary committee was appointed to investigate the affairs of the Hudson's Bay Company. The decision was made that the northwest should belong to Canada as soon as government was strong enough to take care of it.

For ten years more the Hudson's Bay Company continued its rule over Assiniboia, although with lessening control. During those years more people came into the district as communication with Minnesota was improved by a little steamboat which ran on the Red River between a point near the border and Fort Garry.

In the east the Canadian leaders who were working for confederation included the acquisition of the northwest in their schemes for the development of the country. Half a continent, they argued, was too large a reserve for the scattered agents of a trading company and a few thousand Indians.

The question was decided after confederation was accomplished and the new Dominion of Canada had acquired a national government. In 1869 the Hudson's Bay Company surrendered to the British government its two-hundred-year rule of Rupert's Land. Traders gave up to settlers, but the company made a good bargain. The British government bought Rupert's Land for $1,500,000 and, in addition, the company retained one twentieth of the fertile belt and five hundred acres around each post. Rupert's Land and the Northwest Territories were handed over to Canada and the new Dominion thus gained an area many times larger than its four provinces.

With their usual businesslike efficiency, the officers of the company adapted themselves to new conditions. The fur trade continued without the monopoly. The company boats and barges became freight and passenger carriers on the rivers. Traffic in the northwest increased when flat-bottomed sternwheel company steamers, after crossing Lake Winnipeg, were dragged through the rapids at the mouth of the Saskatchewan and proceeded up that river to Fort Edmonton. The supply depots at the fur trading posts became general stores, serving the new settlements as they grew. From this small beginning the Hudson's Bay Company has developed in modern times its wholesale business in the blankets, whiskey and tobacco for which it had long been famous, and its chain of splendid department store familiarly known as "The Bay" in the largest western cities. So the great company, which had explored and opened the west, has continued to be a power in Canada.

Meanwhile the first move of the Canadian government in

Assiniboia was so tactless, so lacking in consideration for the feelings of the old inhabitants, that it resulted in insurrection. The Métis had been the first settlers in the country. Even before the arrival of the Scottish colonists they had lived along the rivers. They had made up the majority of the population. Newcomers from the east were not popular and even the English and Scotch were inclined to think of Canada as alien.

Trouble began when, in 1869, the government surveyors arrived to divide the land into large square sections, and to lay out roads. Immediately the Métis were roused to alarm for their hereditary lands. The surveyors' lines cut right across their narrow river-front farms.

Excitable and credulous as they were, the Métis were easily led by such a dramatic personality as the French Canadian who took up their cause. Louis Riel's father had been a leader among the Métis and his grandfather was the coureur de bois, Jean Baptiste Lagimonière, who had helped Lord Selkirk in the early days of the settlement. Louis Riel was a vain, ambitious, violent man, not without experience and education, for he had lived at Montreal. He and his followers were French and Catholic and they expected the French of Quebec to aid them in gaining their rights.

The Hudson's Bay Company had relinquished its rule, so that there was no real authority in Assiniboia. It was easy for Louis Riel and his angry Métis followers to seize Fort Garry and set up a provisional government. The ambitious leader probably expected to establish a French state in the west. When a governor was sent to take over the new territory, Louis Riel's armed men met him at the American border and refused to let him enter. Men who opposed the new dictator were shut up in a dank jail of Fort Garry.

Matters were brought to a head by Riel's arbitrary act in

executing an Irish Orangeman, Thomas Scott, who had defied him. Immediately the racial and religious feeling, always smoldering, burst into flame. A French Catholic had murdered a Protestant Irishman and the fat was in the fire. There was wild excitement in the east between the Orangemen of Ontario and the French of Quebec.

Early in 1870 the Canadian government at Ottawa moved to end the disturbances by making of old Assiniboia a new province of the Dominion, and troops were sent to aid in the establishment of constitutional government. When this news reached Fort Garry Louis Riel's friends began to waver and he himself changed his attitude. He hauled down the flag of his provisional government and raised the Union Jack over Fort Garry. Then, before the troops and the new lieutenant-governor arrived, he escaped into the United States.

Despite this stormy beginning, the province of Manitoba was successfully organized. Its boundaries were laid out, its provincial government set up, and in 1870 Manitoba became the fifth province of the Dominion of Canada. Under the new government the Métis received grants of land in return for the surrender of their ancient claims.

Between Manitoba and British Columbia lay the vast empty Indian domains. The next problem for the Canadian government to settle was the Indian question. South of the border American pioneers had advanced across the west with ruthless disregard of Indian rights and had been insufficiently checked by the government. In Minnesota and Dakota the Sioux had been on the warpath, terrorizing settlers. The Canadian leaders took note of the bloody Indian wars in the American west and moved, with justice and decency, to prevent any such troubles in Canada.

A summons was sent to the chiefs of tribes inhabiting Manitoba. Their "Great Mother" Queen Victoria, ran the summons, bade them come together to discuss the treaties under which they would surrender a good part of their ancestral lands to the white man. It was not the first treaty for some of the tribes, for Lord Selkirk had bought from them the land along the Red and Assiniboine Rivers for an annual rental of one hundred pounds of tobacco.

In the summer of 1871 a thousand Indians, brave in their warpaint, feathers and beaded deerskins, gathered at Lower Fort Garry to meet the government men. They had come in force with all their families. It was only one of the many colorful gatherings which had taken place at the historic stone fort. Queen Victoria was represented by a commissioner and with him were the lieutenant-governor of Manitoba and several Hudson's Bay men, who were always trusted by the Indians for their fair dealing.

Such a powwow as this, lasting a week, was hugely enjoyed by the Indians. They feasted on the queen's food and spent many happy hours in oratorical harangues. Each band was asked to elect its delegate to sign the treaty, and after much chanting and speechmaking they were chosen. Around the conference tent, outside the gray stone walls of the fort, the proud Indian delegates squatted on bright-colored blankets — Red Eagle, Bird Forever, Flying Down Bird, Centre of Bird's Tail, Whip-poor-will and Yellow Quill.

The government men needed all their tact and diplomacy to persuade the chiefs that they could not keep the greater part of the new province, as they demanded. It was made clear to them that hundreds of new settlers would come in and that unless they accepted reserves of land and annuities now they would lose everything. The chiefs saw the point and yielded.

Every Indian family of five was to receive thirty-two acres of land. Each chief was to be paid twenty-five dollars a year. In addition, each man, woman and child was to receive an annuity of three dollars (later raised to five) as well as an immediate gift of three dollars. As the families settled on their allotted lands they were to be presented with implements and animals to start farming. The chiefs who signed the treaty were pleased with the gift of a uniform, a buggy, a flag and a silver medal.

The medals caused some trouble because the chiefs did not think them sufficiently imposing. Hurriedly, at Ottawa, large new medals were made, but they were electrotypes, silver-plated. Months later, when the third treaty was being made with Indians living near Lake Superior, a chief caused the white men to blush by proclaiming that he was ashamed to wear over his heart a medal bearing the image of his Great Mother made of such base metal. After that, treaty medals were made of solid silver.

As settlement advanced, other treaties were made with the tribes inhabiting the great plains and the Northwest Territories. The Indians never had cause to regret their trust in the word of the government and they themselves were true to their bargain. Every year, to this day, throughout the vast west and the northlands, "treaty money" is paid at posts of the Hudson's Bay Company or of the Royal Canadian Mounted Police. Indian agents and police officers have charge of paying to every man, woman and child the annual five dollars "for as long as the grass shall grow."

With the fertile, grassy prairies opened for settlement, pioneers came in from eastern Canada and the United States. Crowded into the jolting springless Red River carts under a canvas top, pioneer companies with their women and children journeyed over the trails to take up land and break the virgin earth of the prairie for wheat fields.

Among them came the first Europeans to find new homes in the Canadian west. In 1874 the first bands of Mennonites came from Russia to take up grants given them beyond the Red River settlements. They were Germans who had migrated to Russia to practice their religion of pacifism. Then, when the attempt was made to force them into the czar's army, they moved on again, across the ocean. Within two years there were six thousand of them farming happily on the open prairies, the first to prove that the treeless plains made good farm land. During the eighteen-seventies Icelandic fishermen also reached Manitoba and began their town of Gimli on the shores of Lake Winnipeg. So, early in its history, did Manitoba province become a haven for Europeans seeking opportunity and good land.

With settlers and adventurers pouring into the empty plains, inviting to lawlessness and trouble with the Indians, the Canadian government moved to bring law enforcement into the wild land. From the towns of Manitoba to the Rockies the new pioneer territory faced two thousand miles of the American border which must have some policing. Lawless American traders peddling whiskey to the Indians were a menace. So, in 1873, was created that famous force of riders, the Northwest Mounted Police, three hundred strong at its inception. They were stalwart men, perfect horsemen and sure shots, striking figures in their tight scarlet coats, pill-box caps worn jauntily, and blue trousers with a gold stripe.

Symbolism means a great deal to Indians. Just as the tall beaver hat of the chief factor had been made the insignia of the King George man in the early days, so these scarlet-coated riders represented to them the Great Mother Queen Victoria under whose government they lived.

From their lonely little forts scattered over the immense territory the Mounted Police rode out, two and two, to keep order in a lawless land.   Swift and relentless in their pursuit of evil-doers, they had behind them the power and prestige of the distant government and they ruled by their own force of personality, their honesty, justice and tact.   Law went with settlement in the Canadian west, and the country was spared many disturbances.   Canadians did not experience the lawlessness and Indian wars characteristic of the American west.

While the rolling plains were unfolding to hopeful advancing pioneers, young Manitoba was growing rapidly.   Steamers plied on the rivers and carried people and freight by Lake Winnipeg and the Saskatchewan to the other nucleus of settlement around Fort Edmonton.   James J. Hill, a Canadian who lived in St. Paul, put the steamer *Selkirk* on the Red River in 1872 to make regular trips between the towns of Moorehead and Winnipeg.

Talk of railroads was on every tongue in ambitious Manitoba. The government had promised British Columbia to build a railway across the plains to the coast.   When that was done Manitoba would be linked to east and west, and how she would grow! In the meantime the most feasible way to reach the province was still by train from Montreal to Chicago and St. Paul and then by steamboat on the Red River.

It was thus, in 1877, Lord Dufferin, the governor-general, came with his lady to visit the prairie province of the Dominion. A special event of that visit was of great importance to Manitobans. The Countess of Dufferin was to drive the first spike of the railroad the government was proposing to build from Manitoba to Pembina on the border, to meet an American line advancing to that point.

The Countess of Dufferin, an observant lady with a lively sense of humor, described amusingly in her journal their adventures in Manitoba.   The citizens of small Winnipeg laid themselves out to do honor to their distinguished guests. They were entertained with a formal ball at Government House. Lady Dufferin commented on the style of the dresses and dancing and reminded herself that, a few years before, the ladies would have danced the Red River jig in moccasins instead of being so correct and fashionable. The guests were invited to evenings of songs and recitations and to an outdoor exhibit of games. On this occasion a sudden thunderstorm drenched the ladies' gowns and feathers.

The countess was goodnaturedly amused over the torrential thunderstorms of the prairie summer and the deep, gluey mud in which their carriage was bogged down every time they drove outside the town on the rough roads. She had never imagined anything like the vast flat sea of prairie grass and flowers under a great arch of sky. The sense of space and freedom in this big land impressed her deeply.

Lord Dufferin and his wife endured the roughest journeys to visit the groups of people who wanted so much to see the representative of Queen Victoria. At an Indian reserve the braves, in their best Indian finery and cherished articles of white men's wear, danced and drummed and sang for them. The new Mennonite settlers far out on the prairie prepared a celebration for the governor-general. The people raised a welcoming arch hung with flowers at the entrance to their village, presented specimens of their wheat, flax and musk melons, while their leaders made speeches of thanks to the representatives of the Queen. Girls in their peasant costumes served Russian tea in glasses. The governor and his wife were astonished at the productive fields and good thatched houses, the result of a few short years of work.

Before the visit ended the countess drove the spike which initiated the building of the new railway. Next year, 1878, the first locomotive for that road came up the river on a flatboat, decked with flags and evergreens. Winnipeg greeted it with a joyous clamor of bells and whistles. That pioneer engine with its flaring smokestack now rests in the park before the Canadian Pacific station in Winnipeg, with its name, *Countess of Dufferin,* painted on its side. It is kept spruce and shining, a memento of the coming of the railroad to the prairies. The first train reached St. Boniface that same year and soon regular schedules were arranged by way of St. Paul to Toronto.

Wheat, the first shipment of the golden wealth of the prairies, was sent east in 1876. It was carried by steamboat and rail to Duluth, thence by the Great Lakes to Toronto.

As the government surveyors worked over routes across the plains for the transcontinental railroads each little town along the Red River dreamed of becoming a great city by having the line pass through it. Winnipeg won by building a bridge to St. Boniface to bring the trains of the line from Pembina across the river.

The pioneer people of the west eagerly awaited the sight of gangs of laborers laying the shining rails across the plains—the rails which would end their isolation, bring them population and provide a route for their wheat to the markets.

CHAPTER XIV

Gold and Lumber in British Columbia

LONG TRAINS of prairie schooners were winding over the western plains of the United States while the provinces of Canada were busy with political struggles. Some few pioneers had trickled over the mountains into Mexican California, but the famous gold nuggets which were to send the Forty-niners rushing to California had not yet been found in Sutter's mill-race.

The Oregon Trail turned northwestward to reach the Columbia River, growing wider and more deeply rutted each year from countless wheels and hoofs and feet of men. Missionaries had led the way to the Columbia to convert the Indians, and after them came the pioneers in great companies of white-topped wagons.

When they reached Fort Vancouver on the Columbia John McLoughlin, the Whiteheaded Eagle, was kind to the families who often arrived starving and exhausted. He supplied them with food and made no effort to prevent them from farming on the rich lands of beautiful Willamette Valley. As the farms and settlements grew, there were sometimes disturbances between the Indians and settlers. Then the Indians came to the Whiteheaded Eagle saying, "Shall we kill?" But, every time, McLoughlin protected the settlers.

American pioneers had found a new land of promise and nothing would keep them from it. The men of Manifest Destiny clamored for possession of the whole "Oregon country." American claims to the Columbia were based on the journey of Lewis and Clark and on Captain Gray's discovery of the river's

mouth.   Also, forts of Astor's Pacific Fur Company had been
built in the interior.   But northward from the Columbia River
New Caledonia was occupied by the trading forts of the Hudson's Bay Company and England claimed the coast by right of
Captain Vancouver's explorations.

These claims did not deter the frontiersmen from their ambition to have the country from the line of Mexican California to
54° 40', the boundary of the Russian colony in Alaska.   "Fifty-
four-forty or fight" made a fine campaign slogan for politicians,
and helped to elect President Polk.

The new president declared that he looked the British lion
in the eye, but, in the long negotiations between the British and
American governments, England won her claim to the 49th
parallel as the boundary from the Rocky Mountains to the sea,
deflected southward to include the whole of Vancouver Island.
The Oregon boundary question was settled in 1846.   It left the
Hudson's Bay Company posts on the Columbia in American
territory.

John McLoughlin knew that men would farm where there
were good lands and, since England had not sent settlers to the
Columbia, it was inevitable that American pioneers would occupy that fertile region and claim it for the Republic.   He and
Governor Simpson, of the Hudson's Bay Company, prepared for
the change they saw coming by sending chief factor James
Douglas to build Fort Victoria near the southern tip of Vancouver Island.   When the posts on the Columbia were given
up, Fort Victoria became the headquarters of the Hudson's Bay
Company in the northwest.

Log buildings within the high stockade housed the fur warehouse, the supply shops and the men.   Outside were the wheat
fields and cattle pastures of the company, the farms of a few settlers and Indian villages.   There the dark, powerful and strong-

minded James Douglas ruled the whole territory for the company. He and his gentle half-breed wife, daughter of a trader, had for companionship only a handful of settlers' families.

England sent a governor, Richard Blanshard, to rule this little group on Vancouver Island. In 1850 he brought British law to the northwest but his stay was short and unsuccessful. The Hudson's Bay Company, controlling trade and employing the inhabitants, was the real ruler. England then appointed James Douglas to be governor of the colony of Vancouver Island, while at the same time he ruled the fur posts for the company.

Ships from England came around the Horn to bring supplies to Fort Victoria for all the posts. The company's little paddle-wheel steamer *Beaver* was the first steam vessel in the northwest Pacific. She voyaged up and down the coast, sailing into rivers and inlets to carry supplies to the posts and collect the Indians' furs. Although the company did not encourage individual settlers it engaged in farming enterprises of its own. Wheat and cattle were raised on company lands. Gristmills and sawmills were run for the benefit of the posts and of settlers. When Indians brought "black stones" to one of the forts it was discovered that there were seams of coal at Nanaimo in the northern part of the island. The company then imported miners and went into the coal-mining business. Fort Victoria remained a sleepy little place and the fur country of the mainland seemed secure from invasion. The rule of the fur lords was about to end, nonetheless, in dramatic fashion.

Trading schooners often came up the coast from San Francisco which, in the eighteen-fifties, had changed from a small Spanish village to the feverish town of the gold miners. Sometimes bearded men in high boots came on the schooners to Fort Victoria. They bought pork and flour and pickaxes at the trading store of the fort, paid for with gold dust from their pouches.

Then they sailed on the *Fraser* across the waters to Fort Langley and disappeared up that turbulent stream. Some of the men came back to Fort Victoria with gold dust and a store of nuggets, but the traders paid little attention to it. Indians had always found small amounts of gold on the river bars and it had seemed unimportant.

Nevertheless rumors began to spread that there was rich gold on the Fraser River. Men who went back to San Francisco with full pouches added to the excitement. The prospectors of California turned with a rush to the new Eldorado.

In March, 1858, sailing ships disgorged a gold-hungry mob at Fort Victoria. They swamped the quiet village, besieged the company store for food and tools, crowded the company's steamers to cross to the Fraser. All that summer they came in ever-increasing streams. Fort Victoria became a city of tents, and the fever spread to the clerks of the post. They deserted to go prospecting, while trappers gave up hunting furs to search for gold. Crews deserted the ships as soon as they arrived even as other sailors had done earlier at San Francisco.

From Fort Langley the crazy horde tramped and scrambled upstream on foot or with pack horses, following narrow Indian trails along the shore and on the edge of cliffs. In canoes and dugouts and rafts they braved the boiling waters of the Fraser rapids. In the first six months of 1858 five hundred thousand dollars in gold was taken from the rich bars of the Fraser. Some men were getting as much as eight hundred dollars a day. This news brought more hundreds to the river. Prospectors lived through the snows of that winter in order to be first on the ground in the spring to follow the gold up the river, hunting for the mother lode which was the source of the gold in the gravel bars.

Yale and Hope were booming mining camps with their log

saloons, boarding houses and stores. Up the river beyond, the gravel bars swarmed with men, digging, washing and sluicing for gold.

Governor Douglas watched the rush with alarm and took quick action, remembering what had happened to Oregon. At Fort Victoria each prospector was required to buy a license at twenty shillings a month for mining privileges under the British Crown. This did not stop the men, who often evaded the payment by going overland from American territory, but the governor kept some check on the number going to the mining camps.

England also remembered Oregon. The British ministry moved to establish government in the mining country before it could be taken over by Yankees. Governor Douglas was asked to resign from the Hudson's Bay Company to become the governor of New Caledonia, to be renamed British Columbia, and of Vancouver Island. In November, 1858, at Fort Langley the new colony was proclaimed.

When British Columbia became a Crown colony, the rule of the fur lords in the northwest came to an end. The trade of the Hudson's Bay Company continued, but they no longer had the monopoly and civil government controlled the country. The day of the fur traders gave way to the day of the prospectors, and they opened the country for settlers.

Judge Matthew Begbie was sent from England to bring British law to the mining country. Holding court in the largest camps he became a terror to desperadoes, for his judgments were swift and stern. The lowliest Indian or Chinese, however, was as sure of justice as the richest miner, so that the "Old Man," as the miners called him, came to be deeply respected in the camps.

By the end of 1859 there were camps along the Fraser at Chilcotin, Soda Creek, Alexandria, Quesnel, far up the river.

As the prospectors moved on from lower bars Chinese came in, to wash over the claims left by careless white men. They soon found their place in the camps as cooks.

How the men got through to the upper Fraser is a mystery, for they were traversing some of the wildest, most precipitous country of the northwest. Panting steamers, with men crowding every inch of space, dragged crowded rafts up as far as Yale. From there the prospectors, mostly on foot and burdened with packs, scratched out trails along the cliffs, crossed from one precipice to another on swaying Indian bridges of poles, hacked their way through dense forests of giant hemlocks and Douglas firs. Over some of the way they could follow the fur traders' trails, going from fort to fort, but most of the trek was through virgin wilderness. Many men gave up and came out penniless, many were drowned in the rapids or died of fever or starvation. Other hundreds made money, spent it in extravagant celebrations, and went on to seek new fortune.

When the Fraser bars were all occupied and their riches exhausted, the imaginations of the adventurers were inflamed by the discovery of a new and much more wonderful gold country in the interior. Prospectors were then finding gold in gravel benches above the shores of inland lakes and in creek beds beyond Quesnel on the Fraser River. They were branching out into a beautiful high country of plateaus and pine forests eastward from the Fraser. The herds of caribou, hunted by the miners for food, gave the country its name, but they spelled it in their own fashion, Cariboo.

In the autumn of 1860 four men set out from Cariboo Lake in this interior country to explore an untouched wilderness of peaks, ravines and plateaus. They followed a likely looking creek and soon excitement mounted as each pan of gravel they washed yielded a larger store of big shining gold nuggets. Winter snows were beginning but the men dared not leave their claims. Two stayed to guard the discovery and build a log cabin, while the other two returned to Cariboo Lake for supplies. Try as they would to keep the secret, prospectors hanging around the store at the lake sensed that a new strike had been made and followed them to the creek. More came on their heels, claims were staked on the new treasure creek and men slept in holes in the ground to guard them.

In the spring the news of gold in the Cariboo leaked out to the world and a frantic rush began over mountain and canyon and up the rivers to the new territory. Every creek produced riches; from one, only four hundred feet long, fifty thousand dollars worth of gold was taken in six weeks, another yielded a hundred thousand dollars in a few weeks. At Williams Creek the miners found that gold-bearing gravel lay far down under a bed of blue clay. The first digging yielded a thousand dollars worth of gold, and from then on men dug and burrowed like moles in the creek bed and hillsides. In one year two and a half million dollars in gold was taken from Cariboo claims.

The wild days of the Forty-niners' rush to California were repeated in British Columbia. On came the adventurers from the United States and Europe and Canada in the east. Across the Isthmus of Panama, around the Horn, from San Francisco and Victoria, overland from Canada, on foot, by pack horse and raft, through the most primitive country they streamed to the Cariboo. Barkerville on Williams Creek became the central camp. It was crowded with miners, and prices of provisions and supplies were fantastic. Flour was three hundred dollars a barrel, boots fifty dollars a pair!

Far away in Canada a group of about seventy Canadians and Englishmen, who were poor but adventurous, determined to seek their fortunes in the Cariboo. They called themselves the

Overlanders. In 1862 they left St. Paul in Minnesota to reach Fort Garry by the first steamer to run on the Red River. At the Fort they outfitted the party with blankets and pemmican, with ponies and with oxen to drag the two-wheeled Red River carts.

From Fort Garry the Overlanders went forth in a long procession of ox-carts to follow the trail of the fur traders from fort to fort across the plains. Their way lay over the trackless prairies, beautiful in midsummer luxuriance of tall grass and multitudes of flowers.

At Fort Edmonton on the north branch of the Saskatchewan the wanderers were greeted with cheers and gunshots. Their supplies were replenished and they started for the mountains with a guide and extra pack horses. It was hard going now, as they struggled over rough country where the horses sank to their bellies in treacherous swamps, and they had to build rafts to ferry carts and animals across rivers.

At Jasper House, the last fur post before Yellowhead Pass in the Rockies, carts were abandoned and they set out with the oxen and pack horses to climb through the perilous pass, high among peaks and glaciers. Despite many misadventures the party came through and reached the headwaters of the Fraser River. Joyfully they followed the stream, for they knew it would lead them to the Cariboo. In a few days, however, the Fraser showed its true nature, for it plunged into canyons in swift rapids.

The adventurers were at a loss what to do. The season was getting late and they must push on, or be caught by the snows of winter. Finally one group decided to go overland in search of a white man's pack road described by the Indians. Others resolved to run the rapids of the Fraser to Fort George. They traded horses for Indian canoes and Indians helped them to construct huge rafts from trees which they felled. The rafts had railings to which the oxen and horses were tied, and cooking was done by building fires on large flat stones so they would not have to stop to camp.

With buoyant confidence these inexperienced men launched themselves in canoes and on rafts on the furious river which had nearly been the death of those hardened men of the wilderness, Alexander Mackenzie and Simon Fraser.

By a miracle the rafts survived the terrifying rapids, sometimes completely submerged, but bobbing up again through the surging waters. At the worst places some of the company packed the supplies over perilous Indian trails while the others guided the rafts through the rapids. The canoes were smashed and some of their occupants lost. At last the river widened and became quieter, and in the distance the exhausted wanderers saw the little log buildings of Fort George. The men in the fort were amazed beyond words at the apparition of gaunt, ragged men and their animals floating down the river on rafts.

When the men were somewhat restored by food and rest they were supplied with Indian guides who knew the river. These men ran them safely through the rapids below Fort George, even more dangerous than those they had passed. In September they reached Quesnel, the entrance to the Cariboo, four months after they had left Canada. The other party, which had gone overland, went through even more exhausting adventures and lost some of their number before they reached settlements.

At the crude little camp of Quesnel the Overlanders were rejoiced to see miners working at their claims in all the creek beds, but they soon found that claims were hard to get and the country overcrowded with prospectors. There was plenty of work, however, on the government road which was being built, and in the gold camps, at ten dollars a day. While some of the first party of Overlanders became miners many more found their place in other kinds of work and became the first solid citizens of the Cariboo.

Their long route across plains and mountains was followed by other parties of Overlanders, women and children among them. They were the first real pioneers to cross the Canadian plains in the long processions of Red River carts. Some of them noted the fertile land, the thriving wheat fields of the Red River settlements and of Métis villages near Fort Edmonton. They dropped out of the caravans to become pioneer farmers instead of gold seekers.

The Overlanders who reached the Cariboo came from staid, civilized Canadian villages. They were scandalized by the wild doings of the miners, although the firm rule of Governor Douglas and Judge Matthew Begbie kept the towns from being as lawless as the California camps had been. The influence of these law-abiding, church-going Canadians was such that the Cariboo camps evolved with surprising rapidity into respectable towns.

Barkerville, the heart of the Cariboo, was a fantastic place in its early days. Along Williams Creek the gold was so far down under the blue clay that claims were marked by mine shafts and heaps of gravel. The miners even tunneled under the rickety houses of the town itself. A row of log and plank dwellings, built on stilts to save them from spring floods, lined each side of the creek, with plank bridges spanning it at intervals. Every inch of the ground was staked in claims and it was nothing unusual for a man to take out a thousand dollars per foot in gold. Williams Creek in its prime was one of the richest mining grounds in the world.

Prospectors came up the river afoot and with pack horses, by the dangerous trails and along the precipices. From the river they trekked through the resinous pine forests and over high plateaus to reach the Cariboo camps.

Governor Douglas knew that this mining population could not be controlled unless the country was made accessible. So, in 1862, began the building of the famous Cariboo Road. Under the direction of Royal Engineers it was blasted through the Fraser canyons, now by the river bank, now zigzagging around the cliffs hundreds of feet above the roaring stream. Bridges spanned the river to replace the terrifying Indian bridges of poles. On, over plateaus and mountains, the road was built, all the way to Barkerville. It was eighteen feet wide and over four hundred and eighty miles long.

The road was opened in 1865, ushering in the glorious days of the Cariboo. Stagecoaches drawn by six-horse teams, thundered up and down the steep grades and around the precipices in the Fraser canyons, bringing prospectors, storekeepers, gamblers and hurdy-gurdy girls to entertain the miners in the dance halls. Long trains of pack horses and mule teams plodded over the road to bring supplies to camps off the route in the hills. Freight was carried in heavy wagons drawn by bull-teams, with their rough drivers swearing and cracking whips over them.

There were large roadhouses of solid logs along the route — 87 Mile House, 100 Mile House, 150 Mile House — those old stage stops mark the distances on the modern Cariboo Road. One or two of the log stage buildings are still in existence. At the roadhouses passengers slept in log bunks and tumbled out in the cold mountain dawn to breakfast on ancient eggs, hard slabs of ham and slapjacks. Baggage was tied on the roof of the coach and guarded by men with shotguns, for there were desperadoes to watch for in the loneliest places.

Miners, going out with their hoards of gold, tried various devices for safety.   Often fat Indian squaws or hurdy-gurdy girls, rotund in layers of skirts, sat demurely among the rough men in the coaches.   When they reached Yale the bulky females hurried to the bank or express office escorted by bearded men whose gold they concealed under their clothes.   The women, somewhat reduced in girth, departed with handsome presents. From Yale the treasure could be safely sent to Victoria.

Barkerville spread for miles along the creek into other towns named Richfield and Camerontown.   The stagecoaches and freight wagons clattered in clouds of dust past endless rows of plank houses, and the hillsides were sprinkled thickly with miners' tents and cabins.

Pianos for the dance halls and mirrors for the ornate bars were packed in on mule back at tremendous cost.   In the bars, champagne sold for thirty dollars a bottle.   The hurdy-gurdy girls danced to the music of concertina, fiddle or handorgan for the miners' delight.   They were most respectable, with a practical eye on the men's pouches of dust and nuggets.   The rough, shaggy men, hungry for fun, were allowed the pleasure of a wild jig with a hurdy-gurdy girl for a dollar in gold.   Sometimes they paid as high as ten dollars for a dance.   The girls were dancing partners only, and for other favors the men must look elsewhere.   One of these girls married a prosperous Barkerville miner and her descendants cherish her beautiful jewelry and wedding dress of heavy bright blue silk.

Barkerville soon had a newspaper in which the Scot, James Anderson, called the poet of the Cariboo, published his jingles. When one of the dance halls became a theatre for shows by traveling companies Anderson sang his rhymes to the roaring accompaniment of miners' shouts and stamping feet.   He sang of the rise and fall of their hopes:

"*He thinks his pile is made*
An' he's goin' hame this fall
To join his dear auld mither
His faither, friends an' all.
His heart e'en jumps wi' joy
At the thocht o' bein' there
An' mony a happy minute
He's biggin' castles in the air!

"*But hopes that promise high*
In the spring-time o' the year,
Like leaves o' autumn fa'
When the frost o' winter's near.
Sae his biggin' tumbles doon,
Wi' ilka blast o' care,
Till there's no stane astandin'
O' his castles in the air."

The day of the prospector soon passed in the Cariboo, for the greatest wealth of gold lay deep down in the hillsides and mountains. Mining companies with hydraulic machinery and stampmills replaced the individual miner with his pick and sluice box and pack horse.

Meanwhile the colony on the coast and on Vancouver Island had been growing. The Royal Engineers laid out and helped to build the town of New Westminster to be the governing center for British Columbia.

Victoria had changed from a sleepy village to a busy town because it was the outfitting point for the mining country. Its harbor was full of ships coming and going, leaving men of many nationalities in the streets. Thousands of people passed through, and some stayed to buy land from thrifty first settlers who did a lively business in real estate for a while. The small legislature of the colony functioned in a group of wide-eaved buildings called the Birdcages from their shape. In 1858 Victoria had its first newspaper, *The British Colonist*.

The rush to the Cariboo had put British Columbia on the map, and in the wake of the gold seekers came people from England to try their luck in Victoria and New Westminster. They brought with them their English customs and, as some were people with bank accounts in England, they imported comforts for their new homes, such as furniture and pianos, which came by ship around the Horn. The mild damp climate and lush vegetation were pleasing to the English folk. Everything grew with such luxuriance that they were encouraged to order seeds and slips of plants from home. Scotch broom, English roses and foxgloves soon bloomed in the little dooryards of simple wooden houses in Victoria and New Westminster. Cherry orchards and strawberry patches throve in the soft climate. Stately Governor Douglas with his wife and daughters headed a small provincial society patterned on that of home towns in England.

New discoveries of gold on the Kootenay and the Big Bend of the Columbia brought more people to the country. The governor who succeeded James Douglas found it difficult to administer the affairs of two colonies from two towns, Victoria and New Westminster, which were jealous of each other. By royal proclamation, in 1866, Queen Victoria united Vancouver Island and the mainland into the one Crown colony of British Columbia. The island people were placated by having Victoria chosen as the capital of the united colony.

On the mainland, New Westminster spread along the verge of the lush delta lands of the Fraser River. Just beyond, to the north, clustered mountains rose above the primeval forest of mighty trees which covered the hilly land to the water's edge. Sea water poured through a narrow strait between cliffs into a beautiful harbor and the long shining reaches of Burrard Inlet. It was not long before the practical, ambitious men who came to British Columbia saw the value of those hemlocks, spruces, giant cedars and Douglas fir and began to cut them down.

In 1863 a group of men had a water-power lumber mill in operation on the north shore of Burrard Inlet and the little village of Moodyville or Port Moody grew around it. Two years later, another mill was sawing lumber on the south shore of the Inlet. A convivial jag led to the beginning of a village near this mill, when a Yorkshire sailorman, called Gassy Jack because of his volubility, brought from New Westminster a keg of whiskey. The mill workers who helped him drink the keg dry gladly took part in building a little tavern for Gassy Jack. Soon log cabins were built near by and the village was called Gastown in honor of Gassy Jack and his whiskey keg. As it grew the village received the more respectable name of Granville. This little log settlement among the tree stumps was the humble beginning of the great city of Vancouver.

Salmon fishing was an ancient business on the coast, for the Indians had always depended on fish for food. They had invented ingenious nets, spears and hooks for fishing in open waters, and weirs set in the rivers captured great quantities of salmon when they made their great spring migration to the spawning grounds upstream. Men of the Hudson's Bay Company were the first to make commercial use of salmon and halibut. Barrels of fish were salted down to be shipped to England.

Pioneer settlers found the fisheries profitable, so that salmon packing houses grew up along the Fraser delta. Fishing carried white men in their sloops and schooners far up the jagged coast, into inlets and rivers, where Indian villages of painted plank houses and fantastic totem poles stood along the banks. Fur traders had long since brought change to the Indians but the incursion of fishermen and hunters into the distant villages brought further disintegration of their ancient life. Indians worked for the white men and many were drawn away from their villages to the new settlements. In many a deserted village totem poles and weird creatures carved in cedar wood weathered in damp salt air until they were rescued by ethnologists and artists to stand in museums.

The towns and growing settlements had a market for lumber and fish in San Francisco and other American ports. There was a lively trade by sea up and down the coast, and easy communication with the United States, while the people were almost completely cut off from Canada in the east. To reach Canada they must follow the trail of the fur traders over mountain and plain, or make the long journey around the Horn by sea, or sail to San Francisco and travel across the United States by rail. Governor Douglas' dream of a wagon road to bridge the enormous distance to Canada was discussed by many thoughtful men in the eighteen-sixties. Then, when the Dominion of Canada was formed, the question of British Columbia's future had to be decided.

The men who were building civilization in the northwest were vigorous pioneers, thrilled with the possibilities of their magnificent country. Gold, lumber and fisheries made them look forward to a prosperous future. They needed a more democratic government than that of a British colony, more opportunity for advancement. Should they follow the geographical line of least resistance and join with other people of the Pacific coast as part of the United States? Many of the people who had come from the States were in favor of this solution. The strong influence of people of English stock, however, was brought to bear, to keep the link with Britain.

The government of the new Dominion was most anxious to win the Pacific province. After a delegation had traveled from the coast to Ottawa to discuss terms, an agreement was reached. British Columbia joined the Dominion of Canada in 1871 on the promise of the government that a railroad would be built to the coast within ten years. Canada had reached the Pacific, but the new province was separated from the rest of the Dominion by five hundred miles of mountain ranges and over a thousand miles of plain, across which there was neither wagon road nor railroad.

CHAPTER XV

The Epic of the Transcontinental

AN ALL-CANADIAN railroad to span the west and cross tremendous mountain ranges to the Pacific — a mad scheme! So declared Sir John A. Macdonald's political opponents when it was learned that the government had promised the railroad to British Columbia in order to bring the Pacific province into the Dominion. From the end of rail in Ontario to the coast it was necessary to build the line across approximately two thousand miles of wilderness and plains, as well as to find a way through the most rugged and precipitous mountains in North America. This colossal task was asked of a country of four million people, widely scattered, and just beginning their national existence.

Canadians began the adventure under the guiding genius of Sir John A. Macdonald. He and his colleagues had the bold vision of a continent-wide Dominion, made possible by the railroad which would bring population to the empty spaces and provide an outlet to markets for the products of farming and industry. Railroad building must be financed by capital and aided by politicians, and Sir John A. Macdonald with those who believed in this great idea worked for years over financial schemes, as well as against political opposition in Parliament.

The Canadian railroad builders matched the limited resources of their new Dominion against the enterprises of their more populous and richer neighbor. Settlement came quickly to the American west because of the great artery for traffic and trade provided by the Ohio and Mississippi Rivers. Hundreds of steamboats traversed the rivers between the settlements and New

Orleans. Then came the railroads joining the Atlantic to the Mississippi and the Great Lakes — nine of them by 1860. In 1869 the Union Pacific had crossed the continent to San Francisco.

The United States, now expanding westward by rail instead of pioneer wagons, entered a period of wild speculative schemes and the enterprises of financial barons. The Northern Pacific was being built to the coast, close along the Canadian border, and its promoters did not conceal the fact that they intended to divert the trade of the Canadian west to the United States and eventually win that territory for the Republic. Manitoba's railway link with American lines made it inevitable that trade and traffic of that province would be with the United States until there was rail connection in Canada with Montreal. The Dominion needed an all-Canadian route to transport its own goods and people from coast to coast.

Many of the wildcat railway enterprises in the United States were bankrupt before they were completed. One of these was a Minnesota road which had failed due to reckless speculation and fraudulent contractors.

Two Canadians who lived in St. Paul saw an opportunity for profit if they could take over that road and build it to Manitoba. These men, James J. Hill and Norman Kittson, were already prospering with a steamboat transport company on the Red River. Soon they won the support of two more Canadians of outstanding ability. Donald Smith was an important official in the Hudson's Bay Company and George Stephens' financial skill had brought him the presidency of the Bank of Montreal.

The four promoters raised funds, bought the bankrupt road and completed it to join the railway line in Manitoba. It was so successful that within a few years they were millionaires.

Sir John A. Macdonald saw the opportunity for the transcontinental railroad.   Here were Canadians who had succeeded with railway promotion and had new millions to invest.   It was high time that the transcontinental road be finished if British Columbia was not to be lost.   The province had been promised rail connection with Canada within ten years, but most of those years had slipped away and little progress had been made.   Failing to find promoters, the government had decided to build the road itself.   Then had come disastrous political upheavals, hard times in the business world, constant disputes in Parliament over how and where to build the road.   Small sections had been finished, engineers had made long, expensive surveys to determine the best route over plains and mountains.   British Columbians were becoming restive and threatened to secede from the Dominion unless the work was speeded up.   Through it all Sir John and the few who stood with him never lost faith in the great project.

Now, in 1880, the opportunity came.   The four Canadians who had built the St. Paul, Minneapolis and Manitoba railroad saw the vast possibilities of a transcontinental Canadian railroad, when Sir John proposed to them that they form a company to build it.   They had the brains and courage to conquer the difficulties.   George Stephens, Donald Smith and James J. Hill invested their own money and found British and American capital to back the Canadian Pacific Company.

Sir John A. Macdonald announced to Parliament that he had found a group of promoters to finish the railroad on such terms that eventually it would not cost the people of Canada a farthing.   That prophecy proved false, for the money of the government and the citizens was sunk in the project before it was completed.   The results justified it, however.   The Canadian Pacific Railroad was a national project in which the whole country had its share.

Under the charter which was laid before Parliament the Canadian Pacific Company was to receive something over a hundred miles of track already constructed by the government, a subsidy of $25,000,000 and 25,000,000 acres of land along the route, as well as exemption from taxes and import duties on materials for a long period. No competitive road south of the Canadian Pacific line was to receive a charter for twenty years. There was violent opposition to the lavish terms of the agreement. Many felt that the resources of the country were being handed over to a company of private promoters, and few men had the optimism at that time to believe in the future of the undeveloped west. Sir John had his way, however, the charter was granted and work began. Ten years were allotted for the completion of the nineteen hundred miles of track which, with the finished section, would link the Atlantic and Pacific. The story of how the work was done in five years, against incredible geographical obstacles, through financial difficulties which nearly brought ruin to the promoters and Canada, is one of the great dramas of Canadian history.

It was accomplished through the indomitable courage and faith of men who had the ability to plan on a grand scale and never to admit the possibility of defeat, and who were, as well, men of integrity in business. Their spirit inspired engineers, surveyors and workmen to heroic labor and gave them the backing of the Canadian people.

James J. Hill soon left the company, to construct the Great Northern close to the border on the American side, a rival to the Canadian road. When the American railway promoter, William Van Horne, joined the Canadian Pacific as general manager, the company gained the man whose executive ability and driving will could conquer all difficulties in the construction of the road.

The leading men of the Canadian Pacific Company were nation builders but they also thought in terms of empire. The Scotsmen — Macdonald, Smith, Stephens — were alive to Britain's imperial interests in the Orient where she had a colony at Hong Kong as well as an empire in India. Van Horne's mind worked with theirs, for he, too, thought of the Orient. He had great admiration for the feat of Commodore Perry who had opened the gates of Japan to commerce with western nations.

The conception of the Canadian Pacific builders was vast in scope. The transcontinental railroad was to be more than the highway of a nation. It was to be a fast direct route of empire for England over British territory, from the Atlantic across the American continent and on to Hong Kong, India, New Zealand and Australia. By their contract the Canadian Pacific Company had the right to operate ships from any terminus of the railroad, and ship and rail went together in their plans from the beginning.

Five years of exciting expansion and intensive labor began for Canada in 1880. Engineers and construction gangs must contend with the most difficult terrain; they must blast a way through solid rock, carry their tracks over swamp and plain, find a way through mountain passes and over furious rivers. It took astronomical sums to build the road so fast and to carry it completely over Canadian territory. It would have saved time and expense to have linked the road with American lines to avoid the formidable wilderness north of Lake Superior, but it was vital for the young nation to have its transcontinental railroad entirely on Canadian soil.

Over and over again Sir John A. Macdonald used all his skill to win new loans from the government or find financial aid in England. George Stephens and Donald Smith gave their personal fortunes to save the company and the stockholders' investment. At one time the company faced bankruptcy which would have been disastrous for Canada. Then English bankers came to the rescue and the work went on.

Construction under the government had been slow, inefficient and extravagant, but William Van Horne brought to the work American drive, time-saving schemes and the will to conquer the worst obstacles. Every section of the work was planned and must be carried through on schedule, no matter what the difficulties.

As the steel rails pushed on to the west the gangs of graders and track layers, following fast on each other's heels, were a good sight to the people of Manitoba. Winnipeg became a boom town. Foreseeing a great future, when the railroad was finished, its citizens engaged in feverish land speculation. Fortune hunters poured into the place, business streets with gas lights were laid out and the village spread over the prairie in a mushroom growth of raw new buildings.

Every spike, tie and rail, every pound of food for the camps, had to be transported long distances, but so efficient was Van Horne's organization and so effective his direction that the work advanced rapidly. In 1882 two and a half miles of track a day were laid, and more in the next year.

Week by week and month by month the gangs of laborers and their camps advanced over the plains. They had to fight the howling blizzards of winter and work under burning summer sun, but they did not have to be protected by troops from hostile Indians, as was the case when the American railroads crossed the plains. The Northwest Mounted Police had the west under control and a few of these riders of the plains were enough to keep order among construction workers and to prevent trouble with the Indians.

Beside the Mounted Police post at Pile of Bones Creek on the empty prairie grew up a large construction camp of railroad workers. Presently it had become a crude frontier town with the dignified name of Regina; a town which would be the capital of a new province, Saskatchewan.

On went the shining lines of steel over the ancient grassy feeding grounds of the diminished herds of buffalo, scaring away the fleet antelope and disturbing the security of the Indians. In the foothills of the Rockies the engineers and construction gangs had their headquarters in the village of Calgary near Fort MacLeod of the Mounted Police. It was a village which served wandering pioneers and the cattle ranchers who were coming in from the United States. Father Lacombe, head of the mission at Calgary, was known and beloved throughout the country. He had a great influence over the rough gangs of French Canadians, Finns and Scandinavians in the construction camp. It was his friendliness and tact which made it possible for the engineers to win the co-operation of the proud Blackfoot Indians when it was necessary to build tracks across their reservations. After the railroad was completed Chief Crowfoot was honored with a permanent free pass on the trains and was immensely proud of what he called the railroad key which opened the road for him.

The railroad reached the mountains in 1883 but, far in the rear, the tough stretch of country north of Lake Superior had yet to be tackled. That was part of the Laurentian Shield, its adamantine rocks impervious to anything but dynamite. Hundreds of miles of spruce-covered hillocks, granite boulders and bottomless muskeg swamp were intersected by streams and lakes. William Van Horne's engineers found a way through, nonetheless. Supplies, materials and cattle to feed the workers were brought on barges to various points along the lake shore and transported to the camps. Cattle were driven from camp to camp, each cook slaughtering a few and hanging them up for future use. Tracks sank into the muskeg and had to be rebuilt. Bridges and trestles were devised to cross the swamps and streams. When they came to the dark craggy headlands of Lake Superior the road was blasted through and around the cliffs.

The first use for the new tracks across the plains was to transport troops to put down rebellion. Adventurers and speculators had come to the northwest in the wake of the construction gangs. They were planning a land boom along the north branch of the Saskatchewan where Métis and French Canadians had lived for generations. The people, alarmed for their lands, petitioned the government for allotments such as had been granted to their fellows in Manitoba. Their demand was just and reasonable but the government neglected the petition, and the excitable people turned to the former leader, Louis Riel.

He was living in Montana at the time. There Gabriel Dumont, a noted Métis hunter, went to ask his aid. Louis Riel gladly returned to make another try for power. There were only a few mission settlements near the posts of the Hudson's Bay Company and those of the Mounted Police. With his Métis followers and the Indians whom he stirred up to join them, Louis Riel expected to win.

In vain the missionaries, traders and Mounted Police tried to calm the Indians. Several bands went on the warpath; there were raids on the posts and a few settlers were murdered.

Roused at last, the government sent troops to aid the Mounted Police. At places where the railroad was not finished, tracks were laid across ice and snow, or soldiers were transported in sleighs. With their arrival the rebellion soon collapsed and Louis Riel and several Indian chiefs were captured. The uprising was small in itself, but disastrous in the bad feeling it created. It need never have occurred if the government had moved to reassure the Métis and protect their lands. The Indians whose chiefs were executed were saddened and distrustful. Louis Riel was tried and hanged at Regina with the result that he became a martyred hero to the French. Racial feeling once more boiled in Quebec and one more count was chalked up by extremists against the government.

The Northwest Rebellion occurred in 1885, just when the hard-working railroad builders, on both sides of the mountains, were pushing on to the meeting of east and west.

For some time the Pacific end of the road had been under construction by the government aided by American capital. From Port Moody on Burrard Inlet the surveyors and construction gangs worked their way up the Fraser River under the direction of the young engineer, Andrew Onderdonck. Onderdonck's Railway, as it was called, had one of the toughest problems of the whole route, that of laying tracks through the mountainous Fraser canyons.

Hundreds of Chinese had been imported for laborers to the disgust of British Columbians. The staid little town of New Westminster received an exotic flavor from the swarms of yellow men with their strange appearance, speech and food.

Much of the way the tracks were laid beside the old wagon road of the Cariboo. Supplies were brought in by pack train, by barge and Indian canoe. The tracklayers advanced, hewing out the roadbed beside the whirling rapids or high along the cliffsides. Blasts of dynamite roared in the canyons and rocks thundered down into the river. Where men on foot had worn a path and road-makers had created a trail for wagons the engineers could find a way for the road of steel.

On the other side of the mountains surveyors and engineers had searched for years to find a way for tracks through the jumble of mighty mountains, canyons and rivers. They had followed the valley of the Bow River between marching jagged ranges into the lofty world of forests and snow-crowned peaks. They had wintered among snows and glaciers and discovered majestic places never before explored. Yoho Valley, Emerald Lake and the site of Banff were found by exploring surveyors, and Tom Wilson, one of the guides, was the first to see magical, ice-green Lake Louise.

Kicking Horse Pass had been chosen for the route over the Rockies. It was a narrow twisting defile between huge peaks, with the Kicking Horse River roaring over the rocks at the bottom of deep canyons. Engineers found a way for the roadbed through the Rockies by blasting tunnels through the solid rock of mountains, by carrying the tracks in great loops up and down cliffs, and across canyons on lofty trestles. Then they were faced with the Selkirk Range, but they found a way through those mountains, too, came through Eagle Pass and met the track-layers from the west at Craigellachie.

The stupendous project was completed; the "whistle of the steam engine in the passes of the Rockies" was heard, as Joseph Howe had prophesied. There was no fanfare of extravagant celebration such as marked the driving of the golden spike on the Union Pacific. Van Horne declared that the last spike should be a good solid one of iron. Donald Smith, now Lord Strathcona, a stalwart, benign figure with his long white beard, frock coat and high hat, was present to drive it home. Firmly he hammered in the last spike, giving a tap for each town founded as the tracks crossed the country. Then the engine moved over the joining and went on to Port Moody on Burrard Inlet, arriving November 8, 1885. The inhabitants celebrated with flag waving, speech making and a ball.

It was a wonderful day for British Columbia when this final

link of steel joined the province to Canada. Soon, through the scope of the builders' vision, British Columbia was to be linked with the Orient as well.

Port Moody was an inadequate terminus for the Canadian Pacific route of empire by ship and rail. Nine miles down Burrard Inlet the lumber village of Granville sat among the stumps in a forest clearing. William Van Horne saw that it faced a splendid harbor, fit port for the ships that were to sail to the Orient. The tracks were continued from Port Moody and the village, under the new name, Vancouver, became the terminus of the Canadian Pacific Railroad. The first through train left Montreal June 28, 1886, to journey over plain and mountain, 2905 miles, inaugurating service on what was then the longest railway in the world.

The flimsy wooden houses of Vancouver went up in flames during that year of great beginnings, but the inhabitants quickly rebuilt the town in more solid fashion. From that time on Vancouver grew with abounding energy and booming prosperity, matched only by that of the sister Pacific port, Seattle.

The Canadian Pacific builders went right ahead with their imperial route from England to the Orient. Until the company's ships were built Yankee sailing ships brought cargoes from Japan and China to Vancouver. Tea cars and silk cars transported goods of the Orient across the continent to Montreal from which point they were distributed to Canada, the United States and Europe. Before long the first three Empress ships were built for the Orient trade. They were the forerunners of the present great Empress fleet. Later on there was an Atlantic fleet of Duchess ships sailing from England to Halifax, Quebec and Montreal.

The Canadian Pacific was built across almost empty country and settlement followed in its wake. Farmers and cattle ranchers came in from the United States, but they were not enough. The company had to bring in population to grow farm products for the railroad to carry to market, a population needing goods which the railroad would transport. Agents of the company went through European countries spreading the news that there were free farms to be had in a great rich new land. Peasant people, and those who were oppressed or poor all over Europe, heard the news and started for Canada. So began the great stream of immigration which was to people the prairies.

The building of the Canadian Pacific was more than a great achievement in railroad construction, magnificent as that was. It was an epic, the opening of half a continent, a vital part of Canada's history. The vision of its founders was realized as towns and cities grew along its route, as its trains carried the agricultural wealth of the prairies to markets, and its system of rail and ship transported people and goods across two oceans and a continent.

V. Growth of the Dominion

CHAPTER XVI

New Canadians

MEN in sheepskin coats, women in shawls and wide petticoats, with their children and bundles of possessions,
came by the shipload to Quebec and Montreal at the turn of
the century. They filled the railroad stations and crowded into
colonist cars for the long journey to the prairies.

The Canadian government had, in the late nineteenth century,
adopted the policy of encouraging immigration by offering
homesteads to settlers to populate and develop the vast western
territory. From the villages of central Europe, from the plains
of the Ukraine, Poland and other countries, people who saw
no good future at home crossed the ocean, following the lure
of free land in a new country.

At every railroad station on the plains, strange people, bewildered but hopeful, descended from the cars to try their luck
in the great empty land. They took up homesteads on the
plains and in the bush country to the north. Some received
rich land and prospered quickly, others labored with uncom-
plaining courage for years to clear their land and make a living
from their crops. Two new transcontinental railroads were
under construction to make the country accessible north of the
Canadian Pacific line.

The stream of immigration became a flood in the first decade
of the present century. Settlers came from the British Isles,
Scandinavians came into Canada from Minnesota, Wisconsin

and the Dakotas. These people had come from Europe to the mid-western states, moving northward as land prices rose, to take up free land in the Canadian west. Other Scandinavians came directly from Europe.

Some Finns who had come to work on the railroad stayed on, and were joined by compatriots who took up farming in northern Ontario where the country of pines, streams and hills reminded them of home. Many immigrants came to work on the new railroads in the west, or in the mines and factories of Ontario or the lumber camps of British Columbia.

Chinese laborers were among the people imported for railroad work in the Pacific Province. They stayed, to find work in the towns of the province as small shopkeepers, laundrymen, servants and gardeners; and more Chinese, and Japanese as well, came to the province as fast as the government would admit them. Japanese went into fisheries and Orientals of both races became the best of truck farmers.

Companies of Icelanders came to join the first colony of their people at Gimli on Lake Winnipeg, and Icelandic settlements spread along the shores. These northerners who were fishermen by inheritance built up the big business of Lake Winnipeg fisheries. They were intelligent, ambitious folk who soon learned English and began to share in Canadian life, taking pride in becoming citizens of their new country.

Groups of Mennonites entered the country to farm and build villages on the plains. They were serious, hardworking people but their communal way of life and their pacifist religion kept them apart from Canadians. Other sects, such as the Hutterites and Doukhobors found room to practice their peculiar beliefs in the wide-open spaces of western Canada. As the Doukhobors refused to have anything to do with Canadian customs or to send their children to school they have been troublesome. Now they are settling down and some of them begin to work and live like their neighbors.

Canada, at a later date than the United States, became a land of promise for the poor and dissatisfied of Europe. Both these North American nations, whether they like it or not, have been from the earliest times a blend of many races and nationalities. The process of assimilation has not been so rapid in Canada. The American Republic was a haven for throngs of immigrants before the Canadian west was opened to settlement, and everything in their environment urged them to become Americanized as fast as possible. The strong national spirit of Americans roused the ambition of newcomers to become citizens, while in Canada national sentiment was not so developed, and sparse settlements in the west isolated the Europeans from contact with Canadians.

The peasant farmers who came to the plains found themselves in a huge, lonely land where they could not communicate easily with the natives because they did not speak English. They settled in national groups, with their farms near a village center, so they could come together with the comfort of a common language and customs. Thus there were, scattered over the plains, villages of Scandinavians, Poles, Ukrainians and others, each with a national character.

Older inhabitants paid little attention to how the newcomers lived, nor did they make much effort to help them adjust to Canadian ways or to learn English.

In that pioneer period Canadians, and the hundreds of Americans who came into the Canadian west to farm and raise cattle, were concerned in making their own way; increasing the acreage of wheat that brought so much profit, or in building up dairy herds and beef cattle. In the new towns people were excited over the growth of their communities and the building of railroads to connect isolated settlements.

It was through the public schools that the newcomers made contact with Canadian customs. They were ambitious for their children and made an effort to get them to schools. The children learned English quickly and soon adopted the ways of their companions. There was the usual cleavage between the youngsters who were becoming Canadian and their elders who clung to the old customs and language. As the young people passed through school and went into jobs or professions, they did not forget the traditions of their homelands although they did not live by them. The more so, since Canadians were slow to receive these young men and women of foreign stock into the fullness of community life.

Most of the people had valuable contributions to make to the country's life although it was some time before Canadians realized it. Even those who had nothing but their peasant hardihood and persistence in making the earth produce did their part in building prosperity for the new land.

Scandinavians came from a group of small countries, among the most civilized in Europe. They brought to Canada their love of reading, their deep concern for education, their instinct for working together in community enterprises. The Danes came from a land of agricultural co-operation and have been extremely influential in the thriving farmers' co-operatives in the prairie provinces. They have been important in the dairy industry and on dairy commissions. Swedish farmers are intelligent and hardworking with a natural skill in crafts. The Swedish villages have their churches and good schools as well as gymnastic societies. As they become adjusted they make excellent citizens. Talented Norwegians are found on the teaching staffs of provincial universities, and these northern people have done much to create interest in skiing in their new land of snowy mountains.   Another mountain people, the Swiss, found a land to their liking in British Columbia.   They know how to farm on the uplands and have been influential in the Alpine Clubs of mountain climbers and in winter sports.

About fifty per cent of the immigrants of Slavic origin who came to Canada were Ukrainians and the majority of them settled in the prairie provinces.   The first comers were poor peasants but they were followed by prosperous farmers and townsfolk who, with their children and grandchildren, have done well in business and professions, in Manitoba and Alberta. Although these immigrants cherish the memory of their homeland it is their chief ambition to become citizens, and they think of Canada as their land.

Ukrainian villages brought a note of the old world to the plains of Canada and some of them still exist.   The bulbous-domed churches rose above the cultivated fields where women in head kerchiefs and long skirts worked with the men.   The whitewashed log houses with steep dark roofs, surrounded by hayricks and fruit trees, might have been transplanted from the Ukraine.   As farmers became prosperous they replaced their picturesque houses with modern dwellings, which may be a sign of progress but add nothing to the charm of villages. That is only one side of Ukrainian life in Canada, however. In the cities such as Edmonton and Winnipeg they have their cultural institutions, their drama and choral societies, and social gatherings connected with the church.   The Poles are another group with deep national spirit and many talents who have their cultural groups in the cities.

Population was so important for Canada's empty spaces, so necessary for growing industries, mines and railroads, that immigration was fostered up to the period of World War I. Canadians, for some time, did not realize the danger to national unity in the large, unassimilated foreign groups in the country.

Public-spirited individuals and organizations led the way in efforts to help the foreign people feel at home in their new environment. It became the custom to call the newcomers New Canadians, so they would feel they were welcome to a land that would be theirs. The Church of All Nations and All People's Missions in cities of east and west brought the people together in religious meetings, and also helped them with medical care and nursing services. The Y.M.C.A. and Y.W.C.A. were active in organizing study groups and social meetings for young people of all nationalities in their districts. For the children who rapidly became Canadianized, membership in the Girl Guides and Boy Scouts provided comradeship among boys and girls of all nationalities.

Music had been a bond in drawing together the varied groups in Canada, for to most of the newcomers musical expression was an essential part of life. Competitive music festivals, in which choirs of all the schools might join, were started years ago in Winnipeg. At the Civic Auditorium children from a number of schools would sing, in English, before large audiences of interested townsfolk. Competitive music festivals spread from Winnipeg to other western cities.

Most of the national groups in Canada, particularly the Scandinavians, Poles and Ukrainians, kept up among themselves the handicrafts of the homelands, such as weaving and embroidery, and their enjoyment of ancestral folk songs and dances. These were things of beauty all their own to give them comfort in a vast new land.

It was important for native Canadians to realize the gifts of the New Canadians, and for the new citizens it was good to know that they had something to contribute to the cultural life of the country. Folk-song and Handicraft Festivals, when they were first promoted by the Canadian Pacific Railroad that had carried so many thousands of immigrants to the west, were a revelation to all concerned.

The first series of Folk Festivals was staged in cities across the country — in Quebec, Winnipeg, Regina, Vancouver and Victoria. The arts, music and dancing of all the groups in each region brought pride to those who exhibited and pleasure to all spectators. Europeans, in these festivals, became acquainted with one another's arts and enjoyed the appreciation that came to them from native Canadians. Their children realized that this heritage of beauty from the old country was something to cherish, not forget. The idea of folk festivals was taken up by clubs and community organizations all over the country.

These interesting celebrations have brought to the attention of communities not only the cultural contributions of newcomers, but the ancestral arts of the French Canadians and those whose forebears came from the British Isles or from Ireland. The thought that all are Canadians, contributing their arts to national life, is emphasized. French Canadians are encouraged through the Canadian Handicraft Guild to keep up their fine weaving and making hooked rugs and the Europeans to continue their embroideries. Sale for their articles is provided in Guild shops. Here the Indian women also have a market for their fine baskets and bead-embroidered moccasins and jackets.

As the New Canadians take part more fully in art and music, professions, business and farming, they add many characteristics and skills to the nation. Each group is setting its colored stones into what John Murray Gibbon called "the mosaic of Canadian culture." The children and grandchildren of pioneer immigrants have found their places as Canadian citizens, and their feeling of belonging to Canada was intensified by the involvement of their country in two world wars.

The great changes that have taken place in Canada in the post-war decades, since 1945, have brought another flood of immigrants, searching for good jobs in the Canadian economy. These new people have come to work in factories, in mechanized agriculture, in the oil fields or mining towns. Canada now has the task of bringing all these people of many different backgrounds into the national life as true Canadians.

CHAPTER XVII

Ships and Trade on the Great Lakes

CANADA and the United States share the most spectacular cluster of inland seas a continent was ever blessed with, uptilted there in the interior, from huge Lake Superior downward through Huron, Michigan, Erie and Ontario to the St. Lawrence and the ocean. From lake to lake the waters pour, through the rapids of Sault Sainte Marie, through the Detroit and Niagara Rivers, falling from Erie to Ontario in the cataracts of Niagara to swell the flood of the mighty river.

Over the shining waters from Duluth, Fort William and Port Arthur, on the far side of Lake Superior, to busy ports on Lakes Erie and Ontario, pass the fleets of lake freighters. Long low ships they are, built to carry cargoes of grain, coal and iron ore in their capacious holds under the low flat decks. Five to six hundred feet from stem to stern, with the engines aft and the deck houses at the bow, they belong to the Great Lakes and were created to serve the special needs of lake trade.

From April to late November, bucking the ice of spring, sailing the blue summer waters, fighting the gales of autumn, to and fro go the fleets with their long banners of smoke and their deep-throated whistles. During the open season the clustered lakes know also the sleek passenger steamers transporting people for business or pleasure from port to port; small steamers busy with local trade, and slim yachts and sailboats of sailing enthusiasts, almost the only white wings left on the lakes.

The inland seas have known the growth of a continent. Three centuries ago their shores were skirted by the canoes of Indians, explorers and fur traders, and the black-robed missionaries who accompanied them to the farthest wilds.   The Indian canoe route to the west took the French by way of the Ottawa River and other streams and portages to Lake Huron, then through the straits to the Saint Mary's River and its rapids, entrance to vast Lake Superior.   So it was that the two cold northern lakes were among the first to be explored.   The Jesuits built one of their earliest missions near the Sault Sainte Marie, dedicating it to the Virgin and giving her name to the falls and river.   On the bluffs there in the wilderness a Frenchman, De Lusson, claimed a vast unknown continent for Louis XIV.   At the Indians' Great Turtle Island, Michilimackinac, in the straits leading to Huron, the natives and traders met from earliest times.

Men with the itch to see new territory and those seeking furs found their way through Lakes Ontario, Erie and Michigan to the great rivers draining the interior of the continent.   Through the majestic gateway, the St. Lawrence, and the lakes, the French had a route of empire.   The sweet-water seas and the rivers have become since then a great highway of continental and ocean trade.

After the canoes came the flat-bottomed bateaux bringing Royalists to the shores of Ontario to found a new province in the wilderness.   Bateaux and Durham boats made their slow progress up and down Ontario and Erie to serve the new settlements, until men began to build schooners in the harbors of small lake towns.

Then followed an era when the white sails of three- and four-masted schooners, of brigs and sloops, were like flocks of birds over the blue waters from spring to autumn.   Back and forth they went between Canadian and American ports with cargoes of grain, lumber, hides, flour and other products.   Up and down the lakes they served the rapidly growing cities on the

American shores and the smaller towns on the Canadian side. When the first Welland Canal was continued to Port Colborne on Lake Erie, schooners passed through it, across the Niagara peninsula, to carry their cargoes to Montreal and Quebec. In the eighteen-fifties lake schooners, both Canadian and American, crossed the ocean with products of the continent, returning with goods from mills and factories.

They were strong, gallant ships, the Great Lake schooners, built to withstand the treacherous gales and fierce storms of the inland seas. The handling of them bred a race of sailors and captains with their own brand of seamanship, their own chanteys and superstitions. In those days the strong hulls of schooners, with their tall masts and webs of rigging, crowded the harbors of small ports and the inhabitants were acquainted with sailors and ship captains.

Sailors on the Great Lakes were accustomed to danger and spent their lives in hard labor afloat and ashore. They were not only sailors but stevedores, for the ships were loaded by man power. Pushing wheelbarrows, the crews tramped between dock and ship with loads of wheat and coal, or of iron ore from Lake Superior's dark hills.

When the first sidewheel steamers began to puff and churn their way up and down Lakes Ontario and Erie, passengers preferred them to the sailing ships, but the fleets continued to carry the freight of busy farms and towns. The first little steamer on Lake Erie, named *Walk-in-the-Water* after an Indian chief, was not strong enough to sail against the current of the Niagara River, so was dragged through by a "horned breeze" — twenty yoke of oxen.

More and more vessels with chugging engines and streamers of black smoke competed with the graceful wind-ships on the lakes.   Steamers carried colonists to the Erie and Ontario settlements.   On the American side they transported throngs of immigrants to the new middle-western states.   The sailing fleets were queens of the lakes between 1845 and 1862 despite the encroachments of steam vessels.   Soon after that the new railroads along the shores began to take freight, and people were traveling in elegant new steamers with deck cabins and salons fitted with plush sofas and mirrors.   The day of the wind-ships was over, but they left legends of their valiant careers, especially at Sault Sainte Marie.

The Soo, as it is called, is one of the most fascinating and historic spots on the lakes.   There the waters of Superior fall twenty feet in less than a mile in Saint Mary's River causing the rapids.   For countless springs the Chippewa Indians ran the swirling rapids in their canoes with exultant shouts.   Their wigwams stood under the trees of the banks and on the islands, and the families gorged themselves on the whitefish they scooped up in the waters below the falls and rapids.

The Northwest Company had a small trading post at the Soo and later on there was a straggling village of half-breeds, Indians and a few whites on each side of the river.   For generations the huge cold lake beyond the rapids knew no other boat than the Indian canoes and the great brigades of Nor' Westers' canoes, crossing in the lee of the shores to their rendezvous at Fort William.   It was a lake of Indian legend and mystery, awe-inspiring in its vastness, its crags and forest-crowned islands; a place where shimmering mirages confused the vision and made one see the islands floating in the sky.

The fur traders built a few small boats to use between the Sault and Fort William, but there was no need for sailing ships on the immense lake until copper was discovered in the hills.

Copper had been associated with Lake Superior since the distant times when Indians of the region bartered the metal for other things at their trade gatherings.

In the eighteen-forties, when copper companies were developing rich claims on the Minnesota side, they needed schooners to serve their camps on the lake. Somehow they must be transported from Saint Mary's River, past the rapids of the Sault to Lake Superior. It was discovered that the ships could be hauled up on rollers by capstans, then dragged by teams of horses over the portage road. For several seasons strange processions of ships on land crawled inch by inch along the frozen road beside the rapids to go into service on Lake Superior.

Copper mines were superseded by mines to extract the rich ores of the Minnesota iron ranges. Schooners and steamers brought the ore to the Sault, men shoveled it into wheelbarrows and dumped it into flat cars and freight wagons. The wagons and horse-drawn cars transported the ore past the rapids to be loaded on ships for the lower lakes. This was costly and slow. There was an unpredictable store of iron in the Minnesota ranges but it could not be utilized to the full unless there was direct shipping to the lower lakes. The mining companies put all their power behind a project for a canal at the Soo.

The first attempt to lift boats past the rapids had been made by the Northwest Company in 1797. They had built a tiny canal, thirty-eight feet long with one lock and a lift of nine feet to carry bateaux for the fur trade. A model of that little lock is preserved as a historical memento at Canadian Sault Sainte Marie.

The young state of Michigan undertook to build a canal at the Sault, finally obtaining a federal grant after much argument in Congress over spending so much money in such a remote part of the country. After all obstacles were surmounted it was completed in 1855. That first canal, a mile in length, had three lifts of six feet each and the locks were thirty-two feet wide. Later, the first canal was widened and deepened and others were built. With each improvement the procession of ships through the locks grew longer. Schooners were replaced by freighters with iron hulls and those gave way to steel ships.

Canada's twin cities, Fort William and Port Arthur, waked to life long after the bustling copper and iron cities of the American side were sending their products through the locks. The little settlement called Prince Arthur's Landing suddenly became a busy place when a fabulous deposit of silver was discovered on Silver Islet at the tip of Thunder Cape. For a while there was growth and prosperity until lake waters flooded the mine. Port Arthur had to wait for the railroad in order to grow again.

When the transcontinental railroad had connected the prairies with Port Arthur in 1885, there was an efficient outlet to markets for the wheat spreading in green and gold waves over the plains. Every year the harvest of the west poured from freight cars into the tall elevators and from them into grain freighters. Side by side, Port Arthur and the old trading settlement, Fort William, became thriving cities, the country's greatest grain port. Today the ranks of elevators, like white modernistic temples of commerce, flank the harbor, and the long grain-carrying freighters transport the wheat through the locks of the Sault and down the lakes to reach the markets of the world.

It is over one hundred years since the first Saint Mary's Ship Canal was opened, and now hundreds of ships pass through the locks during the season every year. There are five great locks, one Canadian, four American. From April to November the Sault locks handle more tonnage than the Panama and Suez Canals combined.

Canada and the United States co-operated in dredging,

straightening and changing channels in winding Saint Mary's River, to make possible the passing of long processions of ships. In the bulk carriers and the lesser freighters millions of tons of iron ore, wheat, and all the products of Lake Superior cities, pass through the locks and the river to ports of the lower lakes. Beautiful cruise steamers, in summer, are lifted to Lake Superior on their tour of the inland seas.

The frontier village of Sault Sainte Marie, Canadian, has been greatly changed by the modern efficiency of the canals and by commercial enterprises. A pulp and paper mill, power plant and steel mill have brought the industrial world to the Soo. In winter, however, the dark northern wilderness is overwhelming as the town is buried in snow.

For the captains and crews of the lake fleets the short season is a race against time and weather. All the lake channels are frozen in winter. In Saint Mary's River the ice is thirty-six feet deep, and in Whitefish Bay beyond the locks winds drive the ice cakes into deep ridges.

Formerly, when the ice went out of the lakes in April all the church bells in the towns on both sides rang out in rejoicing, and it is still a time for celebration. Far down the lakes the ships have been laid up for the winter. First to sail out are the icebreakers, tough vessels that thrust their broad bows into the ice masses, clearing the channels.

The captains race their ships to gain the prestige of being the first to reach Lake Superior ports in April. At Canadian ports on the lower lakes the first ship is greeted with whistles, horns and speech-making. At Fort William, the end of the trip, a silk hat is presented to the captain, an old custom begun years ago. It is symbolic now, for the topper is placed upon his head, then returned for next year's ceremony. The captain is taken to a shop to choose the hat he prefers. All summer the fleets race back and forth between Lake Superior and Montreal, carrying the products of the plains and bringing in manufactured goods.

When autumn storms begin, the ships buck choppy, dangerous seas and furious gales, and occasionally one of them sinks below the deep waters, as schooners did before them. Late in November the race to Lake Superior intensifies, as the captains try to get out the last cargo before the channels freeze.

The lake traffic in big ships was increased when Canada built the new Welland Canal, opened in 1930. It extends from Port Weller on Lake Ontario to Port Colborne on Lake Erie, a distance of twenty-five miles. In its eight immense locks ships are lifted 326 feet to the level of Lake Erie and pass through the Canal in eight hours.

In the Sault locks and canals at one end of the St. Lawrence Waterways System, and the Welland Canal at the other, the nations sharing the inland seas had one of the outstanding waterways of the world even before the St. Lawrence Seaway was completed.

The International Joint Commission, founded in 1909 and composed of three Canadian and three American commissioners, has charge of all questions concerning the use of boundary waters. Thanks to the intelligence and impartiality of that Commission, its decisions have always been accepted and the two nations continue to use effectively their inland seas and canals. Despite the narrow St. Lawrence canals there has been ocean trade with Europe by transshipping cargo from big ships at Montreal to smaller vessels for the lake journey.

Montreal is an ocean port a thousand miles from the sea, receiving ocean-going ships since the St. Lawrence channel has been widened and deepened. All the waters of the inland seas pour out through the St. Lawrence River in a constant swift flow, navigable for quite large ships except for the rapids. In three sections the river narrows and roars over rocks in furious, tossing waves.

For years the dream of a Great Lakes-to-ocean seaway, deep enough to bring ocean ships to lake ports, occupied the minds of men in government and of farmers, industrialists and manufacturers on both sides of the lakes. It was a project of tremendous potentialities, the kind of audacious undertaking that North Americans, both Canadian and of the States, had carried out during their history with ingenuity and courage. It was a vision to stir them again — that of a stream of ships passing from Duluth, Port Arthur and Fort William across the ocean and back again with the commerce of the world.

There were long negotiations between Canada and the United States over a joint project; intense arguments pro and con in both countries. The middle west, both in Canada and the United States, wanted ocean shipping for their products, to increase trade with coastal ports and Europe. Buffalo, Boston and New York feared the reduction of their own shipping trade; the eastern railroads and the Canadian Pacific thought the Seaway would undermine their business, and Montreal feared the loss of its position as the head of ocean navigation. Many Canadians felt strongly that the St. Lawrence should remain completely Canadian.

In 1932 the two nations got so far as to work out a contract providing for the deep waterway, with a section devoted to plans for building locks, canals and power plants, and provisions for the costs to be borne by each nation. Then world conditions worsened and both Canada and the United States became involved in World War II. The actual building of the St. Lawrence Seaway had to wait until the 1950's.

The construction project for the Seaway and power plants was the greatest and most complicated operation for constructing a waterway since the Panama Canal was built. It required the expert skills of modern technology and engineering to construct dams, locks and canals, to build power plants, and the use of hundreds of monstrous machines for hauling, excavating and construction. More than a thousand men altogether, engineers, technicians and laborers, were involved in the colossal undertaking. It was completed in four years after struggles with the ice and snow of winter, of spring floods and tremendous obstacles and setbacks. Canada and the United States poured $470,000,000 into the vast enterprise.

Men with their machines cut canals through rock and earth, they moved whole villages, they diverted the river while they constructed dams, and drowned the worst rapids of all, the Long Sault. The rocks lie under a new lake, named St. Lawrence, created by a huge cement spillway dam and power dam to furnish power for a great hydroelectric plant in the International Section of the rapids. Ships are lifted to the level of Lake St. Lawrence in two large locks. The International Rapids power work for the dam and the Moses-Saunders Power Plant was paid for jointly by the Hydroelectric Power Commission of Ontario and the Power Authority of New York State. Both nations will share equally the use of the river and resulting hydroelectric power. The Moses-Saunders Power Plant is one of the six largest in North America.

At Montreal, ocean ships which used to transfer their cargo to smaller vessels for the lakes, are now lifted up the 46-foot fall, past the Lachine Rapids, to continue their journey. The Seaway has replaced twenty-two small locks with a water stairway of seven big steps, and has created two new lakes. Ships up to 9000 tons can pass through the locks, and tankers or other lake vessels of even greater tonnage can pass through because they are not so deep in the hull.   Canada built five of the locks, the United States two.

In April of 1959 icebreakers moved slowly up the river from Montreal, breaking up and pushing aside the thick winter ice to make a channel.   They were followed by a number of vessels flying the flags of various nations, which proceeded on their voyage to inland cities on the shores of the lakes.

In June of 1959 a shining yacht with Queen Elizabeth II and her husband, Prince Philip, on board led another procession of ships to the St. Lambert Locks above Montreal.   There they were met by President Eisenhower of the United States and Prime Minister John G. Diefenbaker of Canada, for the simple ceremony that officially opened the St. Lawrence Seaway.

Two nations co-operated to bring ocean shipping to the heart of the continent and both nations share in the great advantages brought to commerce, industry and transportation.   By working together for their mutual benefit they strengthened the ties of their long friendship.   Canada and the United States are an example to the world, in proving that two nations may co-operate peacefully in the use of natural resources in which they both have rights.

CHAPTER XVIII

The Pacific and Prairie Provinces

GEOGRAPHY causes British Columbians to turn their backs on Canada, for tremendous mountains lie between them and the rest of the country. Their outlook is toward the Pacific. Early settlers came chiefly by sea; fisheries and lumber of the coastal area created prosperity for the young province and these products went to market by sea.

The building of the Canadian Pacific Railroad brought this far-western province into the Dominion of Canada, thus increasing trade with the prairies and the east. But British Columbians, still looking seaward, built up their greatest prosperity through shipping. This trade developed after the opening of the Panama Canal that permitted ship commerce with Europe.

The people of Vancouver Island and the great port of Vancouver think in terms of waterways. It is by steamer that they reach the pulp mills and canneries on the bays of the wild, jagged coast, and the lumber mills that are the outlet for logging camps of the forests. Steamers ply between Vancouver and the island capital, Victoria, and between Vancouver and the sister American port, Seattle. It is by boat that commuters and visitors go back and forth between Vancouver and settlements or camps in gorgeous coastal country.

It is only about eighty years since the busy modern city was a lumber village among tree stumps, but Vancouver has always been a pioneers' town, attracting people from all over the world. It has become one of the most cosmopolitan cities in Canada and the third in size. Canadians from the east came in search of new opportunities, many Americans came from the States.

Europeans have come to work in the lumber and pulp industries, in canneries and fisheries. Shipping connections with the Orient brought some Hindus, many Chinese and Japanese to swell the population.

Spread over hills above the harbor and intersected by waterways, the thriving modern city is close to the wilderness out of which it grew. Although there is a skyline of skyscrapers and industrial structures, the forest is at the end of city streets; sea and forest are within reach of city dwellers. They have, in the wooded peninsula called Stanley Park, acres of ancient cedars, firs and hemlocks preserved for their delight. Often open-air plays are given under the great trees. The people look out across the harbor to Lions Gate Bridge, spanning Burrard Inlet, and to mountains beyond. Vancouver, lively and proud, stands between the mountains and the sea, blessed by the beauty of its setting as well as in the commercial advantages of its position.

The harbor is filled with shipping from the ports of the world; from the United States, Europe, Australia and the Orient. The wharves are piled with lumber, canned fish, products of the pulp and paper mills, among other exports. Graceful passenger liners steam out to the Orient, tugs, ferries and barges add to the busy scene.

There are many similarities between Vancouver and American Seattle. Indeed, Canadians think of Vancouver as being quite American in its business activities and way of life. There is constant going back and forth between the two coastal cities and people of Vancouver are perfectly at home in cities and resorts of the American West Coast.

Many citizens of British or Scottish stock, however, have a deep affection for the mother country from which they, or their forebears, came. The position of Canada in the British Commonwealth of Nations means much to them and to the retired English people of Vancouver Island.

Victoria, the island capital, has long had a reputation for being "a bit of old England" and the natives have acquired both pride and profit from the English customs, the stately Empress Hotel, the grace and charm of their flower-decked city. Indeed, every islander of both town and country is a gardener, working happily in the earth and enjoying outdoor life. The soft climate produces a wealth of greenery and flowers. In the 1960's even the quiet island shares with the rest of the province the influx of new people and the growth of a great lumber industry.

British Columbians began their prosperity with salmon fishing and lumbering, two industries that remain of vital importance. The province has the greatest stand of timber in the British Empire. For centuries the forest giants grew in the mild, moist climate of the coast — cedar, hemlock, Douglas fir. From the forests of the Island and the mainland the huge logs come down to the lumber mills and smaller timber to the pulp mills. Forest giants cannot be replaced, but the national and provincial governments realize the necessity for conservation and re-foresting of their woodlands.

The delta valley of the Fraser River is a peaceful rural scene of cultivated fields, grazing cattle and comfortable farms. This area and the famous apple orchards and other fruits of the Okanagan Valley present a region of agricultural plenty in a land so largely composed of mountains and wild rivers.

There are great cattle ranches on the plateaus of the Cariboo, the region that was once swarming with prospectors and miners. The discovery of gold brought people to the interior, but after the easy gold was exhausted some inhabitants went into cattle raising, others found work in deep mines.

The old hazardous road to the Cariboo through the Fraser
River canyons was rebuilt to become a highway that opens up
the country. The tracks of the Canadian Pacific were also laid
with difficulty through the rugged gorges.

The two greatest enterprises of contemporary British Columbia are the extraction of mineral wealth from the mountains
and the taming of wild rivers to provide hydroelectric power.

The harnessing of rivers for a huge hydroelectric plant made
possible the amazing aluminum-processing town of Kitimat,
far up the coast. The smelter at Trail, on the Columbia River,
is one of the greatest metallurgical works in the world for the
refining of ores, especially lead and zinc. Eventually the furious
Fraser River will be trapped for the use of man. Bargaining
is going on between Canada and the United States for the construction of a dam and hydroelectric plant in the Canadian section of the Columbia. The Canadians want the United States
to pay the cost of the project which, when finished, will make
power available to the United States. The plan is still in the
stage of negotiation.

In building dams on its rivers British Columbia must consider
the welfare of the fine sock-eye salmon so important to the
economy. The fish, by atavistic instinct, go up the rivers each
year to their chosen spawning grounds. They can swim through
rapids, leap up falls, but they die in attempts to get over dams.
Fish ladders must be built at strategic places on rivers to help
the fish reach their goal.

The rough, primitive section of northeastern British Columbia
was the scene of a monumental road-building project in 1942 —
the Alcan, or Alaska Highway. For the defense of North
America in World War II the governments of Canada and the
United States co-operated to build a much-needed military road

away from the coast, through northern Canada to Alaska.   Supplies were brought by rail to the tiny railhead, Dawson Creek, in northeastern British Columbia.   From there, and from the Alaska end, men and machines carved out a road through the wilderness; plowing down forest trees with bulldozers, laying out miles of corduroy road over quaking muskeg bogs, spanning rivers by pontoons and bridges.   The men struggled through mud, dust, rain, winter cold and summer heat.   The road crossed a section of British Columbia, a slice of the Yukon, then proceeded through Alaska to Fairbanks.   It was completed in eight months, and was a triumphant conquest of primitive wilderness by skillful engineering, combined with human courage and endurance.

After the war Canada bought the United States' interest in the Alaska Highway.   It has become a practical road of travel over which stream trucks transporting supplies, cars dragging house trailers, settlers with their household goods piled on their cars, or adventurous tourists who enjoy unspoiled northern country.

A land of great rivers, lakes and mountain ranges, of spectacular peaks and glaciers, British Columbia is perhaps the most dramatically beautiful section of Canada.   Its fascinating indented coastline, with deep bays between mountain walls, was the result of partial sinking of coast ranges eons ago.   The tops of another sunken range form a long string of islands, protecting the coastal waterways through which ships pass all the way to Alaska.

An immense mountain wilderness, unmatched for primitive grandeur in all North America, contains a series of National Parks set aside by the government.   Hundreds of tourists every year enjoy Jasper Park and exquisite Lake Louise.   Some of the parks lie in British Columbia, others in Alberta province across the mountains. A good deal of territory is so inaccessible that only gradually is it being opened up for recreation.

East of the Rocky Mountain rampart the plateaus and plains had to wait for railroads to be built and for settlers to arrive. Alberta and Saskatchewan became provinces of the Dominion in 1905 when the people of farms and towns were ready for their own government.

With Manitoba, an older province, they form a distinct region of Canada, separated from British Columbia by the Rockies, and from eastern Canada by a thousand miles of rock, woodland and water. It is a region where, for many years, life has revolved around the success of the wheat crop, the price of wheat in world markets; around the breeding of stock, of dairy industries and truck farming. In a word, it is the Canadian West, the farmers' world.

Alberta is a plateau land, sloping gently toward the foothills of the Rockies, running without a break into the American state of Montana on the south. Southern Alberta became Canada's great ranching country when the cattlemen, moving up from the American plains, brought their herds into the rich grazing lands of plains and foothills. When the railroad arrived, there was an outlet for beef on the hoof so that bonanza days came to ranchers and cattle barons, who made fortunes as Americans had done on their plains. Eastern Canadians speculated in land and cattle, younger sons of English gentry found a new exciting life in the ownership of great ranches and herds.

Calgary was the supply center and the cowboys' town, the place for their hilarious Saturday-night celebrations. It is still a cowtown, famous for its annual rodeo, the Stampede, but the discovery of oil and gas under the soil of southern Alberta has changed its character. Calgary is now a bustling industrial city, headquarters for a number of Canadian and American oil companies.

Modern technology, scientific exploration for petroleum and gas, combined with money and enterprise of both Canadian and American corporations, have brought a greater wealth than that from farms and cattle ranches. The rural scene is invaded by oil rigs and refineries. From the refinery at Pincher Creek, on the slopes of the mountains, natural gas is piped all the way to Montreal. The Turner Oil Fields supplied a great deal of oil for a while. Then in 1947 the discovery of rich deposits of petroleum near Edmonton brought into production the Leduc Oilfield, and a boom in the industry.

Historic Fort Edmonton, set on bluffs above the north Saskatchewan River, saw a frontier town grow up beside it as settlers came in. When a rail line reached it in 1891 Edmonton became the outfitting center for Klondikers rushing to the Yukon. The prospectors gave the town its first boom as they bought up all available supplies and started with carts, pack horses and dog teams for the Klondike mines.

In these days of great enterprises the citizens of Edmonton are thrilled to have their town develop into a modern city, headquarters for rail and air lines that serve regions which are growing in the use of their resources. One rail line runs to the Peace River country, a splendid farming region, another runs north to carry freight to waterways where connection may be made with steamboat transportation "down North" on the Mackenzie River. Edmonton is on the airline to Alaska and is headquarters for planes that serve the mining camps in the Northwest Territories.

In neighboring Saskatchewan province the dramatic story is that of wheat; of the plowing and planting of rich deep soil, thousands of acres of it, with the wheat the world demands and will pay for. Farmers of various nationalities took up their homesteads on these plains, broke the sod and planted it, worked for their harvests, made money and planted more acres in wheat. A Dominion cerealist, Charles Saunders, developed a hard spring wheat, the Marquis, quick in maturing, so that planting could be extended farther north. The growing season is short on the northern plains, but the long days produced more hours of sunshine than elsewhere. So the spring tide of rippling green and the summer tide of ripe gold spread ever farther over the land.

Every little market center wanted rail connection to ship its crops. Various western railroads, as well as some in the east, were combined in the Canadian National Railways, a great transcontinental system, publicly owned and operated. Branch lines were built to link the farming communities. Stark little prairie towns with tall, hump-shouldered elevators beside the tracks, were landmarks in the wide sea of the plains. The farmers prospered and bought new machinery, built new houses and barns. Fine Canadian wheat flowed from the terminal elevators into lake carriers, and money flowed back to prairie farmers.

They looked forward to unbroken prosperity but the Canadian wheat farmers had the same troubles as those in the American West; droughts that withered the crops and blew the soil away in dust storms, business depressions and poor world markets. There were years when wheat was plentiful but the world market was not good and the surplus was unsold. Now there has been a demand for the surplus and the 1962 crop is so fine that the farmers are happy and look forward once more to prosperity.

An interesting story of the prairie provinces is that of farmers' co-operatives. In pioneer days, when labor was scarce and farm machinery hard to come by, the farmers helped each other by exchanging work; getting together to reap the harvest and to share the few tractors, reaping and threshing machines.

This neighborly helpfulness was a good background for the growth of co-operative associations, when the western farmers were faced with the complex problems of marketing agricultural products and dealing with powerful groups such as railroads, elevator companies and market commissions. Saskatchewan took the lead and is the banner province with its large number of associations of producers and consumers.

The marketing of wheat was, of course, the most important problem. The farmers organized the Saskatchewan Wheat Pool, the largest collecting agency in Canada; owned and operated by members of the association.

Hard times, that brought rising costs of living, reduced farm incomes. Then the people carried the co-operative principle into purchasing associations, Consumers' Co-operatives. Not only have the people learned to reduce living costs by purchasing foods through their own organizations, but they have others for buying farm implements and handling petroleum products. Co-operation seems to be the answer for farmers in the big prairie provinces.

Now that mechanized agricultural work has replaced men and horses to a certain extent, fewer hands are needed and there is less work for owners. Many prosperous farmers with large wheat acreage spend part of their time in the nearest town or even live there entirely, supervising the work on the farms when necessary. A good many men have given up farming as they find well-paid industrial jobs in towns. The women enjoy the shops and social doings, the children do not have to be transported long distances to school. The prairies are becoming more and more urbanized.

Regina, the capital city of Saskatchewan, is the goal for those who want to live in town, or to visit for a change from farm life. It is a friendly, tree-shaded city that is growing from oil and manufacturing interests as well as being the market center for farmers. Near by, at Fort Macleod, the famous Royal Canadian Mounted Police set up their first headquarters as they undertook their great work of bringing law and order to the huge, half-empty country.

In the province of Manitoba only two per cent of the land in the southern section is good for wheat farming. On the map the big province, extending into the north, seems to be made up of lakes, large and small, in a territory that is covered with spruce forest and rocks, where moose and caribou roam. Lake Winnipeg is larger than Lake Ontario and it is only one of a number of large sheets of water. Fur farming is big business in the forest region. Indians and half-breeds raise mostly silver fox, mink and muskrats. Trappers take to the snowy wilds in winter, setting their traps and collecting furs to trade at the Hudson's Bay Company posts in the summer.

The southern part of the province has history to remember if the busy people stop to think about it. Seventy years before the railroad reached the plains the Selkirk settlers came from Hudson Bay to establish their farms at the junction of the Red River and the Assiniboine. The Red River was a pathway of travel by boat to settlements in Minnesota, and the fur trappers also took their pelts by carts along the banks to trade with American settlers. French voyageurs, the first people in the region, intermarried with Indian women and were called Métis. Their town, St. Boniface, across the river, is as French as Quebec.

The railroad brought conservative Canadians from Ontario to pioneer in the big land and to found the city of Winnipeg. Since then people of many nationalities have come to the city and province. They helped Winnipeg grow into the large, bustling city of modern times, the hub of the prairies in business and transportation.

Roads and railroads lead north from Winnipeg into the region of lakes, rocks and forest. The Pre-Cambrian Shield that spreads over two thirds of Canada in the north covers the upper part of Manitoba and lies in a big curve around cold Hudson Bay. These ancient rocks contain untold wealth in minerals that are now, in the twentieth century, being extracted. Prospectors discovered rich ores in northern Manitoba and mining camps cropped up in almost inaccessible wilderness. Flin Flon, the great copper mine of picturesque name, was prospected by air and everything for the operation of the mine was brought in by plane, and ore carried out the same way. Mining in northern Manitoba is part of Canada's twentieth-century pioneering by air.

This inland province has a seaport on Hudson Bay. Churchill was, and is, a post of the Hudson's Bay Company. To that bleak settlement huddled among enormous boulders and muskeg swamp, the Indians and Eskimos brought their furs. Hudson Bay, icebound for four or five months of the year, was too remote to come into the schemes of Canadians until after the wheat of the west was going to market. Then the government became interested in constructing a short route to England, by shipping grain from Hudson Bay. A rail line was built to Churchill over many miles of rocky wilderness and muskeg swamp and its harbor was prepared for shipping grain by a modern elevator and system of conveyors for loading ships. From 1931 to 1937 freighters with cargoes of grain left the port for Europe. Then business depression and other causes brought an end temporarily to Churchill's usefulness. The tiny settlement of railroad workers, Hudson's Bay employees and trappers existed quietly in a place that seemed like the end of the world to outsiders. There was a government wireless station and a post of the Mounted Police.

World War II brought changes to Churchill. From the Bay, during the season when the ice was out, it was a short, relatively safe route to Europe, so once more the elevators were filled with grain, and ships carried this and other products across the sea. An air strip was built, quarters for the airmen and some soldiers, and these have continued to operate since the war. An air force called Arctic Wings sends planes off to scan the bleak glacier lands and islands at the top of the world. In summer, the supply ship sometimes brings tourists to take a look at the far north, and hunters come to catch the great white whales that enter the Bay in summer.

From farms to wilderness, from cities to trappers' huts and mining camps the prairie provinces are an interesting, growing section of Canada. Out of their varied heritage the people have created their own culture. They have their provincial universities, their choral societies and orchestras, and the festivals of those with foreign background. These people have the vigorous, democratic instincts of those who have created civilization in a great new land. They are a strong influence in making Canada a North American nation.

The western cities such as Winnipeg, Edmonton, Regina, Calgary have the vigor of young communities and each has its individuality. It is in this new region of Canada that most of the independent political movements have had their inception. There is the same sort of opposition of farmers' interests to those of financiers and industrialists in the east as exists in the United States; a criticism of activities of politicians in Ottawa similar to that of American farmers to the management of political affairs in Washington.

Feeling that their interests were neglected by the historic parties, Liberals and Conservatives, farmers of the west and of Ontario organized groups to go into politics at the close of World War I. Out of these associations grew the Progressive Party which did not last very long. Some of its members became supporters of the Liberal Party.

The business depression that was upsetting the world by 1929 hit the prairies hard. Out of the poverty and anxiety of the people, their feeling that radical change was necessary, grew two new political parties. One was the Co-operative Commonwealth Federation founded by J. S. Woodworth, a social reformer and labor representative from Winnipeg. It was a socialist movement in the beginning, but as the party gained in strength and was joined by white-collar and professional people, its program became more practical. The C.C.F., attempting to unite labor and farmer groups under one banner, called for a large measure of public ownership of financial institutions and industries.

The troubles of people in Alberta raised up a political prophet who took the province by storm. William Aberhart was a schoolteacher whose social credit schemes were half-digested from those of Major Douglas of England. The people of Alberta saw in these ideas the cure for all their ills. Their prophet headed a political party, the Social Credit, and became premier of the province in 1935.

The financial schemes of the party were too fantastic to be successful; the rest of the country scoffed at this socialist government and called the premier Funnymoney Aberhart. Many Albertans, however, believed that the province gained under his regime. They pointed to four hundred miles of paved roads to replace rutted dirt roads, to labor legislation revised, rural schools reorganized and help given to struggling farmers.

The plains were first brought into relation with the rest of the nation by the railroads, and now they are linked to the whole country by the network of airlines that spreads from east to west and far into the northlands.   One more link was needed in this age of motor travel and that has been provided by the completion of the great Trans-Canada Highway.   Before this was accomplished motorists had to make long detours in crossing the country, into territory south of the border, in order to avoid huge wilderness areas with inadequate roads or none at all. Now Canadians may drive from the newest province, Newfoundland, across 5000 miles of forests and farmlands, through towns and over mountains.

To build the road over the Rockies through Rogers Pass, to join roads in British Columbia, was the most demanding and expensive part of the enterprise.   There, in September 1962, the Trans-Canada Highway was officially opened by Prime Minister John G. Diefenbaker.   For years the national and provincial governments had worked to bring this to pass and it had cost them one billion dollars, but now the whole width of the huge country is open to motor travel, and all on Canadian soil.

CHAPTER XIX

From Ontario to the Maritimes

IN THE United States no geographical barrier separates the west and middle-west from the east, although there are differences in people's points of view and manner of living. On the other hand, a visitor to Canada is struck by the way in which geography accentuates the psychological differences between the provinces of mountains and prairies and those of the east. Ontario's western boundary extends beyond Lake Superior, but hundreds of miles of unspoiled country of lakes, woodlands and streams lie between Winnipeg and busy, populous southern Ontario.

That barrier is no longer important for motorists since the completion of the Trans-Canada Highway; also rail lines and airplanes make transportation easy.

After skirting the north shore of Lake Superior the Trans-Canada Highway passes Sault Sainte Marie and continues along the shore of Lake Huron, through a lovely countryside that has been changed by the discovery of vast sources of uranium ore, and the building of mines and the planned town of Elliott Lake. Near by is the bleak smelter town of Sudbury where ores from nickel and copper mines are processed. These mines supply 87 per cent of the world's nickel as well as some platinum and palladium.

Then the Highway skirts the shore of Georgian Bay, opening from Lake Huron. This delightful region is Ontario's resort country, cool and bracing in the summer, a popular retreat for fishermen, campers and other vacationers. From that section travelers enter the populated industrial region of southern Ontario on the north shore of the lake of that name.

Old Ontario, lying between Lakes Huron, Erie and Ontario and extending to the border of Quebec, was formerly Upper Canada. In the arrow-shaped section of southwestern Ontario are centered the financial, industrial and political power of Canada. There, in the towered Parliament Buildings at Ottawa, above the Ottawa River, the nation is governed. The big businessmen of Toronto together with the financial magnates of Montreal over the border in Quebec Province, control the nation's economy.

Smoking chimneys and humming factories in towns along the shores of Lakes Erie and Ontario are turning out the manufactured products of Canada. The north shore of Lake Ontario is a string of towns and industries. The immense power plant, Ontario Hydroelectric, at Queenston, created electric power to serve farms and towns of the province and is an example of successful public ownership.

The productive farmlands of southwestern Ontario are still the nation's richest food basket in their varied agriculture. From those fields and orchards crops of grain and vegetables are harvested, fruits are gathered and dairy products sent to market. Niagara Peninsula is fragrant with blooming orchards in spring and luscious with the later harvest of fruits. Ontario cornfields and wheat fields, the meadows shaded by wine-glass elms, the prosperous farmsteads with silos and capacious barns, are quite like the American farming country across the lakes. The tremendous growth of cities because of industry has made many changes, but there are still small, quiet towns with solid old houses of gray stone and maple-lined streets that retain the quality of an earlier Ontario.

Canada's industrial age has changed the scene along Lake Ontario and the waterway of the St. Lawrence. From the eastern end of the lake to Montreal, the river has been completely made over by the St. Lawrence Seaway. Channels were deepened in the enchanting section of the Thousand Islands, and from there new locks, new lakes, the Moses-Saunders Power Plant and dam, have created a man-made landscape. Ships of all sizes from freighters to ocean vessels proceed through these locks and lakes to Lake Ontario, to Toronto and the upper lakes.

The wealth and pride of Ontario are centered in Toronto, a city as American as any across the lakes in its skyscrapers, business and industry. Wealthy people have fine homes, the best of motor cars, in a city that is completely modern in shops and offices. Toronto is growing so fast in industry, commerce and population that it possesses an American type of energy. Large suburbs, with houses identical in design, spread from the city in every direction. Yet many older inhabitants take satisfaction in what remains of a city of homes with the freshness of trees and gardens.

The Americanized surface of life is the most evident to visitors, but this is also the city where the spirit of the United Empire Loyalists, devoted to Great Britain, is most alive, and the memory of the founders of the province is most revered. There are people who have what Canadians call "the colonial mind" — that is, they are so imbued with respect for British culture and institutions that they fail to think as independent Canadians. This is true, of course, only of a minority, but they impress their attitude on Canadians from other sections of the country.

Older Toronto, near the beautiful campus of the University, has the charm of great trees shading streets of conservative brick houses. Students from all over the country are drawn to the justly famous University which is a scientific center. It was here that Sir Frederick Banting gave his discoveries of insulin to the world. Research workers rely on the splendid resources of the University Library and the great Public Library near by.

Like any important metropolis Toronto is many-sided. The city has a reputation for snobbery and self-satisfaction with Canadians in other regions, but even its critics must admit that this is a place where intellectual pursuits and music may be enjoyed to the full. It is a city of publishing houses and good books, with a winter season of plays and symphony concerts; the home of the Royal Ontario Museum, the Art Gallery, the Mendelssohn Choir and the Conservatory of Music. People of intelligence and progressive spirit are responsible for the good schools, the library system and social services.

Even the children of isolated settlements in the northlands are reached by traveling schools — the School Cars. The Department of Education and the railroads co-operate in the enterprise. Coaches equipped with blackboards, desks, books and phonograph records, with living quarters for the teacher, are hooked to trains and spend the winter season visiting remote settlements on the line. The trains leave the School Car on a siding at each settlement for a week at a time while classes are held and homework given out. Then the car is moved to other stations, stopping again on the return trip for another session of work. The teachers who give their winters to these traveling schools are as much social workers as teachers. Parents enjoy the books and records, instruction in English is given to foreign workers, and the people of scattered homes are drawn into more neighborly association.

The northern primitive country is the largest part of Ontario, much of it in the massive, ancient rock cover of the Pre-Cambrian Shield. It is in this rugged northern country that minerals, timber and water power are sources of future prosperity for the province. These resources are now being developed gradually by mining companies and hydroelectric corporations.

Mining and industry have brought people of many national-ities to Ontario in recent times, to work in the big enterprises or in the cities. This is also the province where the two main stocks of Canada, the French and those of English, Scottish or Irish ancestry rub elbows uncomfortably. The Protestant Irish of Ontario, the Orangemen, find no common ground with French Catholics of Quebec. Intolerance and prejudice on both sides of the border are more prevalent here than elsewhere in Canada. The French and English are rather reluctant neigh-bors, and the old antagonisms between the provinces have not been eliminated.

Toronto and Montreal are commercial rivals, the Ontario city challenging the supremacy of Montreal's bankers and capitalists. Traveling from Toronto to the great bilingual, cosmopolitan city encircling Mount Royal, a visitor passes into another world. Here are sparkle, glitter, a sophisticated spirit, the ripple of French speech, the pleasure of French food. There is great wealth, sometimes ostentatious, in both French and English upper-class circles and each has its own region of beautiful homes on the slopes of Mount Royal.

For Canadians from the faraway provinces Montreal is the city of sophistication and color, with beautiful shops, luxurious hotels, and the only gay night-club life in Canada. Americans, too, love it for its shops, restaurants and touch of foreignness.

What other great modern city has had such a fascinating history as this, sprung from little Ville Marie founded by re-ligious crusaders! From the trading post of French and In-dians, and the town of the British and Scottish fur lords, it has gone on to become the metropolis of French and English com-mercial and social life. The two branches of the Canadian stock live side by side, each in its own section of the city, in rather distant friendliness, mingling comparatively little.

Montreal is unique among great cities in having a wooded mountain springing from the center of its island, billowing with green in summer, patterned with the black and white of snow and bare branches in winter. From the terrace on Mount Royal one looks down upon mile after mile of streets; the docks, ships and warehouses of an ocean port a thousand miles from the sea; acres of industrial sections with factories and bleak workers' homes; handsome modern buildings towering among clustered trees just below the mountain; bridges swarming with traffic that connect the island with the mainland.

On the French side of the city, and in old Quebec, a French culture exists, nourished by bonds with the classic literature of France and its scholarship. The old country means nothing politically to French Canadians, but culturally it has been a homeland.

The educational system of Quebec is based on that of France. Upper schools for boys, called classical colleges, are more like French lycées than English Canadian high schools and junior colleges. In addition to the importance of Catholic training, the system is centered on the Latin idea of all-around culture in the classics and humanities, rather than specialized training for scientific and technical work. McGill, the University of Montreal, differs somewhat from other institutions. It has one of the most distinguished medical schools in the world, and a school of physics. Scientists of this University invented the detection devices and the operation of "McGill's Fence" as it is called, the Mid-Canada Early Warning Line. But still, medicine, law and the Church are favored careers.

Ancient gray Quebec has taken on a veneer of tourism that is unbecoming to the aristocratic mother of Canada. The French-ness of Quebec is something profound, rooted deep in the people and clung to, but it is also an asset for the tourist agencies.

Behind the stately gray-stone walls of convents, the Séminaire and Laval University, there is an intensely Catholic spirit and great scholarship. Charming French social life goes on in homes discreetly removed from public view behind their blank street fronts and solid doors. All this however is a closed door to tourists who do not have the open sesame of the proper introductions. English Canadians in the city, who have their own residential districts, school system and churches, also need a special introduction to the French homes.

Quebec is something unique in North America, preserved there on its lofty cliff in narrow, winding streets, steep slate roofs and gray walls, as a memento of old France. None of the modern activities or political excitements destroy the fundamental strength and quietude of the ancient city on the cliffs. Its walls and towers look down, as they have for centuries, on the swift-flowing, mighty river, bringing the commerce of the world to Canada, as it brought the little French ships of old.

For Americans the French province has the attraction of visits to a foreign land, just by crossing the border. The French ways and speech, the gayety of winter sports in Montreal and Quebec, the delightful ski resorts in the Laurentian Mountains, draw crowds of Canada's neighbors each year.

The fishing settlements of sea-beaten, rugged Gaspé Peninsula and the Laurentian countryside with its gay little villages and whitewashed farmhouses has always possessed great charm for visitors and Canadians, but change has come to the traditional life of farm and village during the post-war decades. The industrial age has come to this once peaceful rural region.

The acreage of habitant farmers extended back from the St. Lawrence in long strips, for each farmer wanted a frontage on the river. Farmers divided the land with their sons but now there is not enough for young families. Young men leave the farms to find jobs in the pulp and paper mills, or they go to towns to become mechanics, or find work in the big mining and lumber industries of the far north. More people in Quebec province now earn their living in towns and industries than on farms and that is indeed a change from the ancestral pattern of life.

Highways pass the farmers' doors; mill towns and shipping ports change the scene along the river. The women like enameled cookstoves for their old-time kitchens and dresses bought from the mail-order catalog. Few of the fine old wood-carvers are left and young people are weaned away from the old songs and legends.

Fortunately, the School of Handicrafts in Quebec is saving the ancestral folk art of French Canadians by training women and girls in the techniques of their grandmothers' work. Students of this school go out to the villages, encouraging the handicraft workers to keep the traditional quality of their hooked rugs and weaving. The Canadian Handicraft Guild also helps to preserve the distinctive handiwork by providing a market for the articles.

Quebec Province, huge in territory, and wealthy in forests and water power, is rapidly becoming industrialized. Along the St. Lawrence and on the upper reaches of the Saguenay River, pulp mills snort and puff, chewing up millions of logs from the forests to make pulp and newsprint for export. From the paper mills tons of newsprint are exported to the United States and Europe.

Far in the interior, between Hudson Bay and the Laurentians, a vast primitive region of forests and waters was for generations the haunt of fur trappers and big-game hunters. The greater part of it is still wilderness, but in recent years industry has penetrated to the country around the Upper Saguenay and Lac

St. Jean. The swift, untamed rivers have been trapped in hydro-electric developments to furnish power for machinery in pulp and paper mills and aluminum plants. Old villages have become busy towns and new ones have grown around the mills. The model town of Arvida in this region is one of the most important centers of the aluminum industry of Canada. The great Shipshaw Dam provides electric power. The rivers of this ancient wilderness, now made accessible, are capable of generating incalculable power for industry. Farmers, as well as industrialists, are finding the Lac St. Jean region profitable for living.

From Chicoutimi, at the head of navigation, the Saguenay remains the stream called by the Indians the "dark, mysterious river." Its black waters flow between forests and mountains to join the St. Lawrence at the traditional trading post of Indians and fur traders, Tadoussac.

Although people travel by train, and now by the Trans-Canada Highway from the St. Lawrence to the Maritimes, those small provinces are still separate from Canada in thought and life. Older people speak of "going up to Canada" when they are traveling to the inland provinces. There are people who are doubtful if the Maritimes gained advantages by joining the Dominion.

Dr. D. C. Harvey, Archivist of Nova Scotia, and a distinguished son of the Maritimes, has said that the special heritage of these provinces is the all-pervading presence of the sea. In this they differ from any other part of Canada, and they keep for the Dominion its direct association with the Atlantic.

The full force of the stormy ocean breaks on Nova Scotia's rocky coast, and the deep funnel of the Bay of Fundy thrusts between Nova Scotia and New Brunswick, sending its phenomenal tides into every creek and inlet, then sucking them

out again. Prince Edward Island and Cape Breton are surrounded by the sea.

Even more beaten by winds, seas and mists is Canada's newest
province, Newfoundland. It is an island extending into the
ocean, but the coast of Labrador is also part of the province.
This bleak land of dark rocks, rough seas and fogs remained a
Crown Colony of Great Britain after the Dominion of Canada
was established. It was the landfall for the first white seafarers
from Europe who sailed the northern seas to catch codfish.
The Newfoundlanders, through the centuries, have been hardy,
sturdy people who have lived mostly by codfishing.

During World War II Great Britain permitted the United
States to build a naval base beside the harbor of St. John's, the
principal town, and the base is still there. After the war the
people were no longer satisfied to be under a British Commissioner, and the question of Newfoundland's destiny came up.
The Canadian government discussed with the chief men of the
island the advantages of joining the Dominion. A plebiscite
was held in 1949 and the people voted to become a province
of the Dominion with its own provincial government.

Codfishing is no longer a secure means of livelihood, but these
men who have battled the seas all their lives have the courage to
adapt themselves to whatever means of earning a living presents
itself. Newfoundland has a lumber industry, and great quantities of iron ore are being extracted from mines in Labrador.

Maritimers have lived with the sea and from it throughout
their history. Their fisheries, from the time of the French, have
been an important contribution to the life of Canada. Their
shipyards and ship designers gave to the age of sail hundreds of
fine schooners, barks and clippers. The Grand Banks codfishers
of Lunenburg, in their sturdy schooners, are famous among
deep-sea fishermen. Saint John in New Brunswick and Halifax

in Nova Scotia give to eastern Canada two ice-free winter ports.

Nova Scotia has the distinction of being the oldest English province of Canada and the first to have a representative assembly. Halifax was always a direct link with England and always a seafarers' port, busy with seaborne commerce between wars.

In World War I the town was a naval base and port of embarkation for Europe. In World War II it was even more important. The town was thronged with sailors, soldiers, war workers and officers. Naval vessels of the United States and Canada were among the long gray ships that lay in the harbor. The freighters were to be escorted by war vessels in convoys that slipped out of the sheltered waters for the dangerous voyage to Europe.

Aside from Halifax, life is very quiet in the Maritimes. In Nova Scotia the apple orchards of lovely Annapolis Valley yield a crop every year. There is a big trade with New England in fish and lobsters, there are important coal mines on Cape Breton, and some business and shipbuilding. For many years one of the important products of Nova Scotia has been the great number of important men in education, statesmanship and business contributed by the province to Canadian life.

Prince Edward Island, the smallest province, is a little world in itself, with intensively cultivated fields sprinkled with white farmhouses, barns and grazing cattle. The people, who live mostly by fishing and farming, are quite content to remain aside from the hurly-burly of modern life. It was in Charlottetown, the capital, that the Fathers of Confederation first met in 1864 to discuss founding the Dominion of Canada. The islanders take pride in that first meeting, although their forebears did not join the Dominion until 1873.

Scottish Highlanders of Catholic faith settled in Cape Breton and eastern Nova Scotia. Their descendants are small farmers,

fishermen and coal miners. In Antigonish, Scottish professors
founded St. Francis Xavier University to be an educational center
for Scottish and Irish Catholics. The professors were anxious
to help the people of villages and mines, whose lives were
grim with economic struggle, by widening their horizon through
adult education projects. It was difficult to persuade the hard-
headed, laborious people that study would be useful to them,
but the professors worked with great faith. Groups were
brought together to discuss what they would like to study, then
books were provided for them by the University. From study
groups the professors went on to co-operative schemes based
on the English Rochdale co-operatives. Education was necessary first, to show the people how they could improve their
lives by working together for the common good. Fishermen
increased their income by marketing their fish and lobsters on
a co-operative basis and farmers did the same with their produce.
One community built and ran a successful cannery, another a
sawmill. Co-operative stores and credit unions were established.

In small villages and mining communities the inhabitants
learned that, by their own efforts in working together, they
might be "masters of their destiny" as Dr. Coady of the Extension Department in the University phrased it. These Nova
Scotians, separated by thousands of miles from the western
farmers, have a common interest with them, and an exchange
of ideas through co-operative associations.

Women of Nova Scotia and New Brunswick have skill in
handicrafts, particularly in weaving and hooked rugs. Their
native ability is put to use in co-operative groups in Nova Scotia
and in the cottage industry of New Brunswick. The lovely
rugs and soft homespuns have a ready sale and the women are
able to add to family income by their work.

Always there has been close association between Maritimers and New Englanders, though sometimes they came to fight rather than to trade and make friends. The folk of the North Atlantic coast live in the same sort of country, many of them came from the same ancestral stock, and New Englanders helped to populate Nova Scotia.

There is no appreciable difference between the forests and rivers of New Brunswick and those of Maine, nor between the weatherbeaten houses and slow-spoken men of fishing villages in Maine and Nova Scotia. Close neighbors as they are, Maritimers and New Englanders have the mutual understanding and friendship of relatives who appreciate each other.

CHAPTER XX

The Great Northland

CANADA is a huge country, second only to Russia in size, extending from the American border to the Arctic Circle and beyond into the frozen territory of icy seas and islands at the top of the world. Without a study of the map it is difficult for most Americans to understand that so much of the country lies in the cold northlands, because they know their neighbors in a strip of territory about two hundred miles deep, extending from the Atlantic to the Pacific. Indeed, about 90 per cent of Canada's population lives in this southern strip where civilization developed.

Americans may wonder why the English, French, and immigrants of many nationalities in pioneer periods, were so much slower in settling their land than was true of pioneers in the United States. Geography gives the answer, for the huge Pre-Cambrian, or Canadian, Shield covers much of the northern territory. This tremendous, thick mass of rocks — granites, gneisses, basalts and others — contains some of the oldest rocks on earth that go back billions of years in earth's story. The whole area was subjected to geologic upheavals in bygone eons of time; the granite surface was scraped, gouged and deformed by glaciers during the Ice Ages when ice caps covered the whole upper portion of North America. These ancient rocks show up in a few places in the United States but in Canada they are laid bare.

The melting of glaciers left behind countless lakes, ponds and streams that make a good part of the Canadian Shield a watery land, the huge boulders interspersed with muskeg bog and stunted fir forests. Other sections are barren tundra, the thin soil and rocks covered with mosses and lichens.

This wilderness of the Canadian Shield reaches from the Atlantic coastline, under the waters of Hudson Bay, and over eight hundred miles of forest, lake and tundra, all the way to the shores of Great Bear and Great Slave Lakes in the North-west Territories. The upper part of each province — Manitoba, Saskatchewan, Alberta — is an extension of this strange country, a most difficult land to explore and settle.

The Pre-Cambrian Shield, through the centuries, has been a block to settlement, but it is also Canada's storehouse of wealth in minerals; copper, zinc, lead, silver, iron, gold, nickel, uranium. There is also a source of hydroelectric power in its fierce rivers.

The Dominion of Canada divided its immense northland into two territories, the Yukon and Northwest Territories. The Yukon had a short boom in exploration and settlement when thousands of prospectors rushed to the Klondike gold fields, and risked their lives on the wild Yukon River to reach Alaska. The gold rush left a few small settlements; Dawson City which became a quiet ghost town after the miners left, and the sizable settlement of Whitehorse in the Yukon. Another period of activity came when men and machines came through to build the Alaska Highway. Airdromes built along the Highway brought the airplane into the primitive country. The North-west Territories remained chiefly the domain of fur traders and missionaries until the air pioneering of the twentieth century.

Sir Wilfrid Laurier once declared: "The twentieth century belongs to Canada." It was a brave prophecy, for no one could foresee how rapidly growth and prosperity would be increased by the exploitation of the northlands that is now under way. It is the last North American frontier. That tremendous undertaking had to wait for the swift advance of air power in the world during World War II and after, also for the developments in modern technology and engineering that made possible the extraction of minerals in rugged terrain.

In the second half of the twentieth century, the discovery of immense ore deposits, the build-up of efficient mining enterprises, the ingenious taming of rivers for hydroelectric power, constitute an absorbing adventure for modern Canadians. They are joined by other men who have the hardihood, intelligence and love of the wilderness to undertake this kind of pioneering. Canadians throughout their history have been men of the north, undismayed by the privations and dangers of wilderness exploration, able to cope with the furies of nature in that realm of cold and storm that is frozen up much of the year. They had curiosity, ingenuity, combined with hard-headed good sense. The work that is going on at the present time is the final phase of Canada's dramatic story of exploration; the development of rich resources in their land.

The first flights of pioneer airmen into the wilds of the Northwest Territories took place in the 1930's. It was an exploration by air, the transportation of men and machines by plane, that began the build-up of mines.

Those indomitable men, the "bush pilots" were the twentieth-century pioneers. In their small planes, without radio, flying in the worst of weather, these cool, resourceful men went exploring in a primitive, half-empty land. They were entirely on their own, and had to take care of themselves and their planes under all conditions. They carried cooking apparatus, food staples, rifle and fishing rod so, if they were forced down on a lake with engine trouble or other accidents, they could exist while they made repairs to continue their flights. The bush pilots were exploring rough country of scrubby woodland and rocks, impossible for landings, but there were plenty of lakes on which to set down their planes. In winter, with skis on their machines instead of pontoons, they sat down on the ice. They flew prospectors to Great Slave Lake and Great Bear Lake, enormous bodies of water in the Northwest Territories. When valuable claims had been staked, planes carried in mine machinery, lumber, fuel, food supplies and men to build the mines and operate them.

Many of the intrepid fliers were veterans of the Royal Canadian Air Force. Others were men who were bred to the north, with a knack for existing in the wilds. They made reconnaissance flights for the government to photograph the territory, or for mining companies and individual explorers. The aerial mosaics made from the thorough photographing of the terrain were invaluable to geologists and mining experts in their study of mineral deposits.

In the years of pioneering only one or two pilots were killed and only a few planes cracked up. Already the bush pilots are a legend, though some of them are still working. The present well-organized schedules, radio equipment, weather reports, seem pretty soft to the old-timers. They are slightly scornful of pilots who don't like to risk flying in storms, or who expect to find a comfortable bed and food at the end of the run. The work of the bush pilots was a splendid achievement, for they pioneered before the air knowledge of the present time, when men have flown to the remote corners of the earth. Their successors profit from their work.

The present-day pilots continue the services of the past in flying out sick or injured people — white, Eskimo or Indian — or in searching for men lost in the bush. Despite all the aids to safe flying, pilots and engineers in the north must be extremely resourceful, well-trained men, capable of dealing with any emergency.

Before the age of air travel the great Mackenzie River was the water route into the Northwest Territories. Men have followed that route ever since Alexander Mackenzie made his pioneer journey down it to the "frozen north" in 1789. Next to the Mississippi, it is the largest river of North America; it flows northwestward across the Northwest Territories to the Arctic Ocean. The Peace and Athabaska rivers as well as lesser ones flow into Athabaska and Great Slave lakes and make part of the chain of waterways which carry boats from the Athabaska River into the lake of that name; by the Slave River into Great Slave Lake, and thence by the Mackenzie proper to the Arctic. Although the river's flow is stilled under ice for a good part of the year, it has built the largest delta, except for the Mississippi, on the continent.

Lonely posts of the Hudson's Bay Company have existed along the river for about a hundred years. Near the posts missionaries made settlements and all these outposts were served by canoe, dog team and York boats. Later, supplies for the scattered settlements were hauled from Edmonton to Athabaska Landing and loaded on small boats to reach the portage between Fort Fitzgerald and Fort Smith. There a pioneer steamer of the Hudson's Bay Company transported men and supplies to Fort McPherson on the Peel River.

Everything, including passengers, had to be portaged over the sixteen miles beside the rapids in the Slave River between Fort Fitzgerald and Fort Smith. A corduroy road was built by two enterprising Irishmen, the Ryan brothers, to carry people and goods across by horse or ox team. That trail has become a road over which busses, tractors and heavy freight, passengers as well, are taken over the road to Fort Smith.

Then a railway was built from Edmonton to Waterways and stern-wheel steamers went into service on the river, making it easier for freight and passengers to travel "down north" on the Mackenzie. On its summer trips, a steamer chugged along over the broad river, pushing a fleet of barges ahead of her, struggling with winds, currents and sandbars. Frequently she sidled up to the bank to take on a load of wood for the engines or to transfer cargo. While tied up the crews were tormented by the swarms of insects and fierce hungry dogs of Indians and half-breeds. Old-timers found river transport useful, but they feared the encroachment of the world "Outside." They were prospectors, trappers, traders who loved the spacious solitudes of the northlands and had nothing in common with the "chech-akos" as they called men who had never seen the ice go out.

The Mackenzie River Transport now operates a fleet of stern-wheelers, modern steamers, motor ships, tugs and barges "down North" to transport quantities of freight and machinery during the summer months to the mine and oil settlements. The Mackenzie Basin also proved to be a good air route to the Arctic, for the atmosphere is clear and dry, less cold than other parts of the Northwest Territories.

When Imperial Oil Ltd. of Canada, a subsidiary of Standard Oil of New Jersey, sent its men scouting for new sources of petroleum for Canada, they traveled on stern-wheel steamers to Fort Norman near the Arctic Circle. Not far from that old settlement they struck oil in a fine gusher well. There was petroleum in that region, plenty of it, but no way to market it.

It was in 1929 that an experienced prospector, Gilbert Labine, made his discovery of gold, silver and pitchblende ore, source of uranium, at Echo Bay on Great Bear Lake. He had prospected on foot around the shores of the lake; he was one of the few men in Canada at that time who could recognize radium and uranium in the gray-blue pitchblende ore. He was flown in by a bush pilot and staked his claim to a gold and silver mine, but he soon found he had something more valuable in the pitchblende ore of the Eldorado Mine he undertook to develop. He sold ore for the production of radium.

Soon after his discovery, bush pilots flew in prospectors to Great Slave Lake where gold was discovered at Yellowknife, in the 1930's. A large company undertook to work the mines and prospectors flew in to stake claims. Everything for the operation was transported by bush pilots. Carefully they set down their pontooned planes on the shallow lake near shore, to unload lumber, machinery, barrels of gas and oil to fuel the machines, food supplies for the miners. In 1935 a rough settlement of huts and tents was scattered among the boulders and scrub pines as mines were built up.

Norman Wells then had a market, to supply oil needed for the mines on Great Slave and Great Bear Lakes. Later it supplied oil to service the building of the Alaska Highway. Norman Wells is now an established town with the farthest-north oil refinery in North America.

Yellowknife is one of Canada's phenomenal mining towns, supplied with civilized comforts in the wilderness. It grew into a sizable town as more gold mines came into operation. There are shops, restaurants, a school, a hotel and movie theater. Wives of men who work in the mines cheerfully keep house for their families in good dwellings supplied with modern appliances. They wear fur parkas in winter, slacks in the brief summer; their children have a healthy life and good schooling.

Living in the sub-Arctic, their short summer has warmth and almost continual daylight, only plagued by black flies and mosquitoes. In the bitter cold of long winters they live in a semi-twilight, their night skies brightened by the shifting banners of the northern lights.

The hardy families of miners like it; there is something about the spaciousness of the great land, the simplicity and camaraderie of existence that appeals to them, as the lure of the north has always drawn men in the past. The people are content with occasional visits "Outside" by air.

Muskeg, tundra and bush make roads almost impossible. In the winter, when the whole land is frozen hard under the snow, tractor trains, made up of flat cars on runners, caboose for the crew and tractor for motor power, rumble over the land and the solid ice of lakes, carrying supplies and machinery to many settlements impossible to reach in any other way except by air. Tractor trains serve the mines in winter, planes fly back and forth in summer and winter, but the people are cut off from communication during the spring thaw when the ice goes out of the lakes. Then the permafrost, the eternally frozen land, thaws out a few feet down in the muskeg, creating a mass of mud and water. Eventually engineers will manage to build roads over the treacherous muskeg and landing strips for planes at the lakes.

During World War II, when uranium was becoming important, the government took over Gilbert Labine's Eldorado Mine on Great Bear Lake, and the Eldorado Mining and Refining Company developed the big mine called Port Radium, at the foot of the cliffs where Labine had first seen the pitchblende ore. After the war Labine made other discoveries and staked claims on Athabaska Lake. Uranium City was developed from his claims.

When scientists discovered that the nucleus of the uranium atom could be split, the fission process was developed to yield vast quantities of nuclear energy. That was the beginning of the Atomic Age, demanding huge stores of uranium ore.

Prospecting along the north shore of Lake Huron in Ontario led to the discovery of uranium deposits between Blind River and Elliott Lake. The whole area is believed to have one of the most extensive bodies of uranium ore in the world. In 1935, when uranium was discovered in this region, the greatest prospecting rush in the history of the province began. Mining companies soon bought individual claims, and these mines were consolidated under Eldorado Mining and Refining Ltd., a federal Crown corporation. At that time uranium was being mined only in the Belgian Congo and Czechoslovakia besides Canada.

When Canadian corporations were planning great mine operations in primitive regions, far from any practicable transportation, it was decided to build planned towns, not rough mining camps or company towns, in order to attract the skilled workers and technicians they needed. These men would not go to the wilderness unless they could bring their families to well-built towns where they would have a civilized existence. The government also decided that the new communities must be developed under provincial government guidance, to protect the inhabitants and to prevent exploitation by the corporations. Elliott Lake was one of the newest and most modern of these towns built through co-operation of the provincial government and the mine company. Each of these towns was to be set up with municipal government like any other kind of town.

Elliott Lake grew and flourished, with a large population of people who lived as comfortably with community services as in any older town. Most of the workers lived in the community

and commuted to their work in busses or cars on roads built
by the company. The mines boomed after the company received from the U.S. Atomic Energy Commission an order for
more than a billion dollars' worth of uranium ore, to be delivered between 1957 and 1962. Then in 1959 the Atomic
Energy Commission informed the Company that it would not
take up the post-1962 uranium options, but would spread delivery until 1966. The reason for this decision was that the
search for uranium had been going on in a number of countries,
including the United States, and Canada's reserves of the ore
were no longer so all-important.

Elliott Lake, which had been supplying twenty-four per cent
of the world output, was suddenly reduced in production;
hundreds of miners were laid off and people began to move
away. The mines are continuing production, however, and
new needs for uranium, for peaceful uses of atomic energy
in the future, may save Elliott Lake from becoming an atomic-
age ghost town.

The construction of hydrolectric power plants is another of
the great enterprises being carried on by industrial corporations
in Canada's northland. Water power is needed for many industrial projects, but electricity is especially necessary for the
refining of aluminum from its native ore, bauxite, which is
mined in some places in the United States or in Jamaica and
sent to processing plants. Aluminum is processed by means of
electro-metallurgical means that require enormous quantities
of electricity.

The Aluminum Company of Canada, Alcan, had mills in
Ontario but not enough electrical power. The company selected a site on the northern coast of British Columbia where
the Skeena River breaks through the mountains to reach the sea
at the fishing port of Prince Rupert. The whole coastal region

is mountainous, covered with dense forests, with some lakes and small rivers. There was one rail line to connect the coast with the interior.

In this inaccessible, rough region the engineers and technicians of Alcan carried through one of the most complicated engineering projects ever yet undertaken. A huge dam was constructed in the interior at the eastern outlet of the Nechako River to create a very large reservoir. Then a ten-mile tunnel was cut through the mountains to carry this water on a down grade, in a waterfall sixteen times higher than Niagara, to a power house that was carved out of a mountain. The electric energy produced by the rushing waters was carried over mountains and glaciers by a transmission power line, built under great difficulties, to the smelter constructed at Kitimat. This village, on the Douglas Channel, had a harbor for the shipping purposes of the company. Deep-sea docking facilities were constructed to serve ships bringing in ore, and to ship out the aluminum.

Here, between mountains and sea, another of the planned towns was laid out and built, by co-operation of the company and the provincial government. The sturdy families of Kitimat, who live there because of their husbands' jobs in the aluminum industry, do not mind their remote location. The community is efficient and comfortable, their children have a healthy life, and the people enjoy the mountainous country along with the easygoing tempo of life, so far from big cities.

Enterprising corporations, Canadian and American, are constantly searching by air for available deposits from which to extract the Pre-Cambrian Shield's wealth of nickel, zinc, copper, lead, iron and uranium. One of the most exciting and difficult of these enterprises is being carved out in the desolate, forbidding country of naked rock and stunted trees along the border of Quebec Province and Labrador which is part of the Province of Newfoundland. It is cold, windswept, completely barren country, labeled by explorers long ago "the land of Cain." But those rocks contain some of the most profitable minerals of the Shield, particularly iron. Even in this unpromising country geologists and surveyors, over a long period, have searched, sampled ores and reported the great deposits of iron ore.

The Labrador Trough, one of the channels gouged out by retreating glaciers, is a mass of high-grade ore. The rocks containing the minerals, iron oxide and others, have been washed and softened throughout the ages so they are quite porous. The ore can be dug out by open-pit methods.

After a long study by geologists, work crews and miners, it was decided that the deposits were so valuable that the enormous cost of mining the ore would be practicable. Iron was in great demand after the war years and United States steel companies were among those in need of it. The project interested Jules Timmin, a Canadian mine expert, head of a great gold-mining company and a millionaire. He decided that his company, Hollinger Consolidated, would undertake the project, and several United States steel companies went in with him in a company called Hollinger-Hanna, Ltd. Iron Ore of Canada, a subsidiary company, undertook the building and operating of the mines. An airlift was established, based on a small Laurentian village, because the site was inaccessible by road. The airlift was a tremendous operation until a rail line was built from Sept-Îsles, a fishing port on the St. Lawrence. By tunnels through mountains, along the edges of cliffs and over the plateau, the rails were laid to the mine region. There the town of Schefferville, another planned community, was constructed to be the housing and administration center for the mines.

In that bleak wilderness technicians, miners and their families have a civilized existence with well-built houses and electricity for every purpose. The mining area is a great land shimmering with reds, browns and purples of earth among stunted firs. The huge open-pit mine is carved out in deep terraces of earth and rocks, where enormous steam shovels gobble up tons of crimson ore to be dumped into trucks and carried to the surface to flat cars. All operations go on in a haze of red dust.

Tons of ore are constantly on the railroad moving to Sept-Îsles, there to be dumped into conveyors that carry the mass to the holds of ships. The ships transport the ore up the St. Lawrence to the Great Lakes or down the Atlantic coast to United States steel mills.

Everywhere in the great northlands Canada's storehouse of mineral riches is being discovered, studied and brought into production. These enterprises require colossal sums of money and the most expert skills in planning, operation and technology, as well as the most modern machinery. The work is made more difficult than it might be in other parts of the world because of the harsh climate, the sparsely inhabited wilderness, and the fact that the mineral treasures are far down in the rocks of the Shield.

Only large, wealthy corporations are able to carry through such costly operations. Most of the enterprises are carried on by a combination of Canadian and American capital. Industrial organizations in the United States are better prepared to take the risks involved, they have more available money, but both nations have the technicians and engineers. Some mining companies are operated by Canadian corporations that are subsidiaries of parent companies in the United States; some are entirely Canadian but partially financed by American capital.

Some people in Canada are worried by the economic domination of the United States because of these extensive investments. It is the policy of the Canadian government to welcome the investments but to require that a Canadian company be formed, incorporated in Canada, with a percentage of stock available to Canadian investors. Industrialists of the two nations can pool their resources in vast undertakings, for the benefit of both countries and to satisfy world demand for minerals, because they have close, friendly relations and each is the other's best customer.

The Canadian giant is stirring; this northern nation is beginning to bring into use the huge reserves of natural resources which will make it one of the most important of nations in the latter half of the twentieth century.

CHAPTER XXI

Canada's Arctic Realm

IT WAS Vilhjalmur Stefansson, Arctic explorer, scientist, and an Icelandic Canadian by birth, who first exploded the old belief in the silent frozen North. He predicted Canada's move into the northlands. By argument and successful living, by exploring throughout the far north, he made known what he called "the friendly Arctic."

Stefansson told the world about the hot days of the brief Arctic summer, the grasses and flowering plants that grew above the Arctic Circle, the abundance of birds and animals. The Barren Lands of the Northwest, said Stefansson, are in reality good grazing grounds for the herds of valuable native animals, musk-ox, reindeer and caribou.

The Canadian government maintains a large reindeer herd, tended by Eskimos, that produces meat and hides for the subsistence of the natives. Inhabitants of the Northwest Territories watch every year for the migrations of the herds of caribou, for these animals are the most useful of all to Indians and Eskimos. They eat the meat, use the fur for hides, blankets, clothing and shoes, make the scraped skins into kayaks, buckets, dog harness, and use the sinews for fish and harpoon lines. The animals have been hunted so persistently by natives and whites that the government has installed some measures of protection to keep the caribou from extinction.

People who live in the northern land learned long ago that the short summer was a good growing period. Wives of the traders at fur posts, or missionaries, had their summer crops of potatoes, a few vegetables, even some flowers. In building they had to cope with the frozen land called permafrost that thaws only a few feet in summer to create watery mud. Permafrost cannot be dug into except by drilling so houses were built on top of the ground. In Aklavik, the old fur trading post that became a town after steamers on the Mackenzie and airplanes brought in people, the houses were built on delta land. These were slowly sagging and sinking as warmth from the buildings thawed the surface underneath and turned it into mud. The government proposed to move the whole town to a site on higher land, and to build houses on stilts with air space underneath to keep the ground from thawing. An airstrip was also built on high frozen land so the runway would not sink into summer mud.

In the ordinary line of duty many Canadians — strong, resourceful and sensible — are well acquainted with the problems of life in the far north. On many a bleak island, on the lonely coast or in distant wilderness settlements, the Mounted Police have their posts. Generally two men are stationed together, though there may be more at stations where there is a great deal of work. At the most remote stations, the men are sometimes cut off from the outside world for a year at a time. They have books, comfortable quarters, radio equipment for their reports and for exchanging news with their fellows at other posts. These officers of high repute are trained to shoulder responsibility and to deal tactfully with any crisis that may arise. The Mountie is governor, doctor, judge, and protector of the natives in the Canadian wilds and the people respect him.

The men at the Arctic posts of the Hudson's Bay Company have also learned to live efficiently without the social contacts of civilization. Wives often accompany their husbands to remote stations; children are born there and as youngsters play with young Eskimos until their father returns "Outside." On the shores of Hudson Bay and the Arctic Islands the task of the Company is to collect and pack the furs brought in by Eskimo or Indian hunters. Up to the value of the furs they bring the hunters choose what they need and want from the Company store. Post managers, along with the Mounties, are the men who look after the natives, and they are the ones to whom the people look for help with their problems.

Every summer the stout icebreaker ship sails from Montreal to make the rounds of the northern posts, to deliver supplies and mail, and collect the bales of furs. It is the big event of the year when that steamer appears in Hudson Bay or pushes her strong bow through the drifting ice to the Arctic posts.

The Eskimos trek in with their families from far and near to camp around the post. The settlement is lively with their laughter and fun and the yelping of their sledge dogs. Before the steamer leaves there will be a celebration with games, prizes and feasting provided by the Company. The ship brings new employees, a few tourists, sometimes scientists who wish to study some aspect of the Arctic. These last men are more likely now to reach their objectives by air.

When white men first penetrated the icy northland they found the intelligent, active Eskimo people well established in the Arctic, from Alaska to Greenland. They are good-natured, easy-going people, whose culture, customs and occupations are well suited to their frozen territory. Anthropologists have long studied the question of when and from where the Eskimos reached the Arctic. They believe from evidence they have acquired that Eskimo traditions and culture drifted with people across Asia, through Siberia, from Stone Age Europe in several migrations thousands of years ago. They have found artifacts of several groups of Eskimo people who once lived in the Arctic but have disappeared.

Eskimos of the twentieth century prefer their own way of life, hunting seal and walrus, or trapping fur-bearing animals, but they also adapt themselves readily to the techniques of white men. They are delighted with airplanes, they learn quite easily to run motors in trucks or boats, for they have great mechanical ability. A few prosperous Eskimos have abandoned the old-time kayak for their sea hunting in favor of a motor-driven small boat.

White men brought them a source of livelihood in selling furs to the Hudson's Bay Company, but that source is less profitable now. The fur business is declining, partly because of the increase of fur farms for raising mink and muskrat, also due to the rise of synthetic furs and changes in fashion. It will not hurt the Company badly, for Hudson's Bay Company has gone into the mercantile business in a big way. Every large Canadian city has the glittering, modern department store of the Bay and whenever a new town grows the Bay store comes in to provide the things people want.

It is hard on the Eskimos and Indians to lose their secure trade in furs. The native people are under government care, and efforts are being made to help them. Their health is looked after, there are some schools for children, relief payments are issued to families in need. But the Eskimos are proud people who prefer to earn their way if they can live by it. Their mechanical skill helps them find jobs at the growing number of air stations in the Arctic. These merry people, so alive to all that is going on, and their noisy sledge dogs, are part of every settlement.

The mysterious lure of the Arctic has drawn explorers for

centuries.   The search for the North Pole and for the legendary Northwest Passage brought expeditions by ship to contend with ice floes in the waters, often to be frozen in for months by the inexorable Arctic cold.

One of the most tragic attempts to find the Northwest Passage in the past was that of Sir John Franklin, an experienced Arctic explorer.   In 1845 he headed an expedition with two ships to search for the Passage, a journey from which none returned.   The ships were caught fast in the ice and never released.   For three years members of the party survived, trying to find a way out over the ice, but they all died.   Bones and bits of equipment were found by later explorers but the remains of Sir John Franklin were never discovered.   Numerous expeditions, sent in search of the lost Franklin party, added greatly to the knowledge of Arctic seas and islands.

Later in the nineteenth century various corridors between the islands were explored by navigators without success.   Then, in 1852, Captain Kennedy and Lieutenant Joseph Bellot discovered a narrow strait twenty miles long, running east and west between Somerset Island and Boothia Peninsula.   This is Bellot Strait, named for the discoverer.   It proved to be the key corridor, but it is shallow, narrow and clogged with ice.

The first passage from Atlantic to Pacific in one ship was completed in 1906 by Roald Amundsen, the explorer, in his sloop *Gjoa,* after an exploratory voyage of three years.   The explorer and his companions had left the Atlantic in 1903 and did not emerge at the western end until 1906.   In 1940 a sergeant of the Mounted Police, Henry Larsen, who had been a Danish seaman before he joined the Mounties, sailed with eight companions in his 80-ton schooner, *St. Roch,* from Vancouver, B.C., through the Passage to the Atlantic and returned from east to west.

The Northwest Passage is navigable for ships of shallow draft which can elude the ice floes, but it has been discovered too late to be of much practical value.   Nevertheless, when the Distant Early Warning radar stations (Dew Line) were being constructed across the Arctic shores from Alaska to Baffin Island in Hudson Strait, the Northwest Passage proved useful. In the late summer of 1957 it was decided to attempt the delivery of heavy equipment by ship to as many stations as possible. A Canadian icebreaker, the *Labrador,* which had been the first ship of deep draft to sail through the Passage in 1954, took the lead in escorting U.S. supply ships from Southampton Island in Hudson Bay through the ice pack of the treacherous Passage. They succeeded in landing equipment for various stations of the Dew Line.

It remained for the post-war Atomic Age and the completion of nuclear submarines by the United States Navy, to cross the top of the world under the thick, treacherous ice of the Arctic Ocean.

In 1958 the U.S. submarine *Nautilus,* captained by Commander William R. Anderson, blazed a sea route from Pacific to Atlantic under the ice of the Arctic Ocean.   A few months later the U.S.S. *Skate,* captained by Commander James F. Calvert, made the next voyage, from the Atlantic, and surfaced within forty miles of the North Pole — 90° North — on March 17, 1959.   *Skate's* job was to experiment with the problems of surfacing among ice floes.   Then in 1960 the U.S.S. submarine *Sea Dragon* traveled by way of the North Pole in transferring from the Atlantic to the Pacific fleet.

The commanders and crews of these submarine ventures had learned a great deal about the mysterious depths of the Arctic Ocean; its submerged mountain ranges, the thickness of the undersurface of the ice pack over their ship.   They were equipped with the most advanced, delicate instruments for navigating in the dangerous depths. The crews lived in their ship which was like a metal box with built-in comfortable atmosphere. Only atomic submarines can do this, for conventional undersea ships must surface at frequent intervals to refire diesel engines and recharge batteries, but the nuclear engines make this unnecessary.

On August 22, 1962, the veteran atomic submarines, U.S.S. *Skate* coming from the Atlantic and the U.S.S. *Sea Dragon* coming from the Pacific, held a historic rendezvous at the North Pole. They were both able to surface through small openings in the ice pack. The commanders of the ships and their crews stepped out on the ice, exchanged colors and memorial plaques in the glimmering white of the ice-covered sea, so startlingly silent at the top of the world.

That was more than half a century since the date of April 9, 1909, when Commander Robert E. Peary, after so many hazardous explorations, stood at last on the ice at the North Pole.

Undersea crossing over the top of the world is too difficult to advance very fast, but the ever-alert airlines recognized that the shortest route from North America to Europe was over this frozen north. The intrepid airmen worked it out and now fly back and forth over the Great Circle Route. Several European airlines now fly passengers over this route from Europe to the Pacific coast at Los Angeles and return; the latest thrill in air travel.

The air age has indeed come to the Arctic region with air strips, well equipped, built at various strategic places in the frozen land. At Frobisher Bay on icy Baffin Island there is a large efficient airport. Human activities go on below massive, glacier-clogged peaks covered with snow. This station was built originally as a refueling stop for planes during World War II.

It was reopened in 1951 and built into a big airport equipped with weather and radar stations, with buildings to house men, fuel, repair shops, trucks — everything needed for assistance to planes. It is manned by 200 airmen, mostly American, and a large crew of construction workers. Frobisher Bay is the eastern anchor of the Dew Line. It is also a refueling base when necessary for planes flying the Great Circle Route.

In the uneasy period since World War II, known as the Cold War, this northern route took on dangers, when the Soviet Union, once a partner, adopted the policy of Communist conquest for which Russia was well supplied with atomic weapons and planes. It was realized that an easy way for Russia to send war planes over North America was over the top of the world. This led to a massive undertaking that could only be completed by employing the most modern engineering and technology combined with colossal sums of money. That was the establishment of radar warning stations from Alaska to Baffin Island — the Distant Early Warning (Dew Line) — over three thousand miles across the far north.

The radar stations were built under the most difficult conditions in the frozen Arctic regions. Transportation was one of the major problems in country with no roads. Everything had to be flown in, straining the resources of Canadian airlines. Dew Line was financed and built by Americans, is manned by men of both nations, as are the stations of the Mid-Canada Line or "McGill's Fence" as it is called, farther south. This line was financed entirely by Canada, the detection devices were invented and operated by Canadians. Again, everything had to be flown in, even supplies for a whole year to each station.

All the stations of the two warning lines, where a few men at each post operate the radar and other communications in isolation, have comfortable quarters, books and recreation facilities for the lonely men. In the event of an enemy attack the Dew Line and Mid-Canada Line would flash instant warning to the combined Canadian-United States headquarters in Colorado, from which orders would flash to send bombers of both countries into the air.

These radar lines, built between 1955 and 1957, may soon become obsolete because intercontinental ballistic missiles are more likely to be the threat than bombers. The experience and knowledge gained through construction and operation of scientific posts in the Arctic regions has not been wasted, nonetheless. This knowledge has already been used in the projects for further development of resources in this immense cold territory. Old-timers, observing the comfortable stations, the rapid communication between them, the constant criss-crossing of planes, say somewhat regretfully that the Arctic will never be the same again.

It is true indeed that the Canadian northlands are constantly changing; huge mining and hydroelectric projects, a network of airlines flown by experienced pilots, air strips and efficient airports dug out of the wilderness. It is a frontier of adventure for hardy, scientific-minded young men of various nationalities who have the determination and skill to open up and bring to civilization Canada's unique, valuable northlands.

VI. Contemporary Canada

CHAPTER XXII

Canada: a North American Nation

IN THE turbulent, anxious world of mid-twentieth century, Canada has her place as a nation making her own decisions and policies, although the link with the mother country still exists. Canada is a self-governing nation among the others of the British Commonwealth of Nations. Generally, at the present time, the "British" part of the title is dropped and this remarkable group of co-operating nations is called simply the Commonwealth.

These important developments in the Dominion of Canada have taken place in the twentieth century. Gradually, with respect on the part of both Canada and Great Britain, the relationship has changed; partly because of world conditions and partly because a sense of nationhood has grown among the citizens of the huge sprawling Dominion of ten provinces.

In Canadian politics the two important parties have been the Liberals and Conservatives though a few other parties have risen at times to satisfy convictions of various groups in the provinces. As in England, the Prime Minister of the winning party is the most powerful man in government, but he and his cabinet are responsible to the House of Commons, the body that represents the will of the people. Canadians have been able to retain the technicality of their relation to the mother country through the office of the Governor-General who represents the Crown.

Under their chosen system, during the first decade of the present century, Canada made tremendous national progress through the peopling of the prairies by immigration and the beginning of the great wheat crops that meant national prosperity. This growth created a spirit of energy and confidence, and the desire to build their economy on an east-west axis, united by all-Canadian transportation. Also, in the east, the increase of manufacturing and the movement of people from farms to cities, began to change the country from an agricultural nation to an industrial one.

In this period of national energy the leader was the Liberal Prime Minister, Sir Wilfrid Laurier, the first French-speaking government leader. His was a brilliant, elegant personality, with great appeal to politicians and people. Sir Wilfrid Laurier strengthened the idea of development east to west instead of south toward the United States. He wanted to make Canada one nation from sea to sea with a strong tie to Great Britain, to counteract the economic pull of the United States. His party was defeated in 1911 and Sir Robert Borden, leader of the Conservative party, became Prime Minister.

He was the Canadian leader during the trying period of the War of 1914–1918 which changed the sentiment of the people. They had wished to remain free of Great Britain's policies in Europe, but when the mother country was involved in the world-wide struggle they responded with the belief that they must participate in defense of the Empire. They gave without stint of their strength, money, supplies and men. Canadian troops won honor on many battlefields and thousands died in the struggle.

During those years of travail and sacrifice the country grew in strength and maturity, emerging into complete nationhood. Sir Robert Borden, the Prime Minister, represented the feeling of the citizens when he insisted that Canada, participating loyally with money and men, should have a voice in war strategy. Lloyd George agreed with him and Canada was represented on the Imperial War Council.   It was due to Sir Robert's insistence, too, that Canada and the other Dominions were invited to be members of the peace conference.   Canadian delegates signed the treaties for their nation which were accepted by the Dominion after they had been ratified by the Parliament at Ottawa.   Canada, as well as the other Dominions — Australia, New Zealand, South Africa — became members of the League of Nations as separate nations.

Canada, the senior Dominion, led the discussion after the war that changed the British Empire, with its subordinate countries, into the British Commonwealth of Nations.   Feeling in the Dominions had become national and they were not satisfied with an inferior position in the Empire.   Canada had no wish to break from the mother country, but felt the need of being recognized as a nation, equal in status with Great Britain.

This was achieved in the Imperial Conference of 1926. Arthur Balfour drafted the declaration defining the new relationship of the British family of nations, stating: "The British nations are equal in status, in no way subordinate to one another in any aspect of their domestic or internal affairs, though united by a common allegiance to the Crown, and freely associated as members of the British Commonwealth of Nations." This principle was ratified by the British Parliament in the Statute of Westminster in 1931.

In this free association for their mutual benefit each Dominion is a self-governing nation on an equal footing with other nations of the Commonwealth, including Great Britain.   The people of the Commonwealth countries join with those of the

United Kingdom in giving their allegiance to that symbol of unity, the "King who reigns but does not govern."

Quietly but firmly the Canadian government worked for the right to make its own treaties, especially with the United States, and to maintain separate legations in foreign capitals. Canada now has its ministers in Washington and all other important capitals and there is an American minister in Ottawa. Canadian interests in England are represented by a High Commissioner.

Canadians share with those of the same Anglo-Saxon stock in the United States a North American political inheritance, deeply democratic, with an instinct for equality. So says the well-known Winnipeg editor, John W. Dafoe, in his book, *Canada: an American Nation*. Consequently in their relations with the Empire they persisted until they had attained autonomy in the Commonwealth of Nations. And in their experiments with national government they did not rest until they had achieved the form of political democracy that satisfied their instinct to be free, self-governing people.

There is no doubt that Canadians have a deep love for their own land. In addition, the citizens of British or Scottish ancestry cherish a bond of sentiment and loyalty to the old country. It is something very deep, not easily defined or reasoned about — it just exists. The French Canadians do not have this sentiment, for Canada is their land, but they are a part of the Dominion politically and in crises the French province joins the national action.

In the 1920's there was a great surge of prosperity in Canada. Wheat poured from the prairie farms to markets of the world; manufacturing increased, new highways and airlines improved transportation. Canadians were discovering the valuable resources of the northlands as minerals were extracted by big mining companies and hydroelectric projects were underway.

Then came the disastrous market crash of 1929 and the great depression that had a crushing effect in both Canada and the United States. The decline of world markets and disasters to crops made an end of the thirty-year Canadian "wheat boom" and brought misery and distress to the prairie provinces. Prosperity in industry had created strong labor unions, and the workers from farms and factories joined in demands for government aid to help them over the breakdown of earning capacity.

In the early 1930's economic anxieties led the people of the provinces to form new political parties: the Social Credit party of Alberta; the Co-operative Commonwealth Federation of the plains and eastern farmers. Among the people there was great unrest, confusion and questioning of government policies. They began to talk of a social service state as they learned of President Franklin D. Roosevelt's New Deal in the United States. Prime Minister Richard Bennett of the Conservative party tried to introduce some New Deal ideas into his government plans, and the federal government spent great sums to aid the provincial governments in taking care of their people.

In the election of 1935 the Liberals won and William Lyon Mackenzie King became Prime Minister. He was the grandson of the highly honored, fiery political rebel of the past, William Lyon Mackenzie. Mackenzie King was a Liberal who believed in social reform and public ownership, but he was also an extremely cautious, experienced politician, always striving to maintain unity among the differing political groups.

While Canadians were paying little attention to the increasing dangers in troubled Europe, King George VI and his queen, Elizabeth came to make a royal tour of Canada in the early summer of 1939, the fateful year. The personal appearance of the royal pair, who represented loyalty to the Crown, roused a responsive feeling in the Canadian people. The visit renewed for them the pride of their heritage in the proud British Empire.

It was brought home to them again that fall, when Hitler's drive for conquest involved the mother country, and Great Britain declared war on Germany, September 3, 1939. There was no question in most Canadian minds as to where they stood in this war; they must join in defense of their own country as well as England. Parliament met to debate the country's stand, and when a declaration of war had been decided upon Ernest La Pointe, the French-Canadian associate of Prime Minister Mackenzie King, made the final appeal for the declaration, ending with the words of farewell spoken by Queen Elizabeth when the royal pair left Canada — *"Que Dieu bénisse le Canada"* and an appeal to his French Canadian people to accept the national decision. He said, "Yes, God bless Canada, God save Canada's honor, Canada's soul, Canada's dignity, Canada's conscience."

In the terrible years of the world-wide struggle Canadians contributed wholeheartedly with all their resources. Munition factories turned out shells, bombs, ammunition, tanks, airplanes and military vehicles. Canadian farmers stepped up the production of all foods to feed the nation and send quantities overseas. The British Commonwealth Air Training Plan was put into operation in Canada to train thousands of pilots and crews; men from England, the Commonwealth countries, Canadians and other nationalities. The Royal Canadian Air Force administered the complicated project. The Navy increased its usefulness with corvettes and destroyers that guarded the Atlantic convoys transporting food and supplies to England.

Canada sent four divisions to Europe to join in the deadly struggle with the Axis powers.

The United States, a friendly, sympathetic neutral until the day the Japanese attacked Pearl Harbor, then declared war and joined the colossal conflict. Canada and the United States found themselves partners in defense of what was called "fortress America." Canada provided locations for American bases and communications on her territory. Together the two nations built the Alaska Highway and the Canol project, the pipeline that carried oil from the Yukon refineries to Whitehorse, Skagway and Fairbanks. They built air fields and weather stations for three northern air-supply routes that ferried hundreds of new bombers and fighters to Europe. The two governments learned to work together for the necessities of war, and in the post-war years of the Cold War they have continued to plan the defense of America against the threat of the Soviet Union with its schemes for Communist conquest.

In 1945 Mackenzie King led a delegation to San Francisco to participate in the conference that resulted in the founding of the United Nations. Canada became a member of the United Nations as an autonomous nation. Another post-war event of importance was the completion of Canadian territory by the admission of Newfoundland to the Dominion, as the tenth province. In a referendum, in 1949, the people of the province had voted to join the Dominion of Canada. The territory was now complete, from this Atlantic outpost to the Pacific, and there was great satisfaction over this achievement. Mackenzie King, who had led the nation for a quarter century, now retired. The French Canadian, Louis St. Laurent, became Prime Minister in his place.

The end of World War II marked the end of an era in history. The nations of the world now entered the Atomic Age and the Space Age. The second half of the century has found the nations of the world in a revolutionary period; the rise of nationalism in colonial territories brought about the independence of numerous new Asian and African nations, as colonialism under the great powers approached an end. In many underdeveloped countries the spirit of "rising expectations" among the people led to revolutionary upheavals.

Canada entered the new age as a nation with her own place in international affairs, her seat on the councils of the United Nations, her membership in NATO. The country was richly endowed with essential minerals and water power, and the population, in 1958, had risen to 17,000,000 people.

In the United Nations Canada began to take an important part in international affairs. At the time of the Suez crisis, when France and England threatened war over the Suez Canal, Lester B. Pearson, head of the Canadian delegation, proposed a compromise; an international UN force to bring about a cease-fire. Canada took the initiative, the crisis abated, and Lester Pearson emerged as Canada's first international statesman. He was awarded the Nobel Peace Prize for this achievement.

Industrial, mining, and agricultural advances had made this country one of the important trading nations of the world. Canada had won autonomy within the Commonwealth, and now wanted to attain survival on the North American continent, resisting the dominance of the more wealthy and powerful United States.

Canadian people and their government faced many problems in the strengthening of their nation. The country had been settled and had grown prosperous through the hard work and intelligence of numerous nationalities, as was true in a general way of the United States; but the assimilation of a great number of nationalities had been completed in the big neighbor country, while Canada was still in the process of becoming a united nation. The citizens of English or Scottish ancestry, with their strong ties to the mother country, were no longer the majority in the population. The economic prosperity of the prairie provinces had been built up by citizens of diverse national backgrounds. They are today people of vigor and independence, more inclined to favor American ways in business, agriculture and community life than the typical Canadian ways. In politics they make their convictions heard and do not intend to be dominated by the federal government in Ottawa. British Columbians, also, are now people of varied backgrounds, who intend to manage the affairs of their province first, with secondary attention to the plans of the federal government.

The most serious problem in attaining national unity is the basic fact that Canada is, and probably always will be, a nation of two cultures — English and French. Canada has been like a tree with two strong branches sprung from a single trunk — the two great racial stocks. The branches have grown side by side but not symmetrically. The story of Canada reveals how troublesome have been the problems of attaining understanding and unity between the French and English branches.

The amazing vitality of the Norman stock has kept Quebec Province French in language, customs and thought for more than a century in an Anglo-Saxon country. The French were the first Canadians; they had made the land theirs by toil and devotion before they were deserted by France. Since that time Canada has been their own native land, their beloved *terre canadienne*.

Many thoughtful, forward-looking Canadians, both English

and French, speak and write on behalf of unity and equality between the two stocks. There are also intense French nationalists who speak more loudly for their point of view than do the progressive men who believe in unity and co-operation. Some of them even cherish the unrealistic idea of a French state in North America. Narrow-minded extremists on both sides make themselves heard, spreading prejudice in regions where the two races do not come in contact. Some of the provincial French regard English Canadians with dislike and suspicion, but such attitudes are just as prevalent among English Canadians who are ill-informed.

The rapid industrialization of the northlands in Quebec and other provinces is all to the good in mingling people of the two racial stocks. French Canadians leave their province for industrial jobs; French and English work together in mining enterprises or other jobs. The sharp edges of prejudice are worn down as people live and work together.

One of the most important points of contact is language. Canada is a country with two official languages, French and English, yet few English Canadians are bilingual. English is the daily language, of course, in most of Canada. French Canadians who live among their compatriots of English stock become proficient in both languages and politicians of the French province are equally eloquent in both, but English-speaking Canadians are not such good linguists and often do not take the trouble to attain fluency in French.

In the midst of political controversies between the two branches of the Canadian tree, the traditional tie to England was brought home to the people by the death of King George VI, in 1952, and the accession of his daughter as Queen Elizabeth II, ruler of the United Kingdom and the symbol of the Crown to the Commonwealth nations.

Canadians were reminded of their membership in the Commonwealth and their loyalty to the Crown when Queen Elizabeth and her husband, Prince Philip, came to Canada in the autumn of 1957. The young Queen, so friendly in personality, won all who saw her. For the first time in history the reigning monarch, as Queen of Canada, assisted at the opening of Parliament. It was an occasion carried through with truly British ceremonial dignity. To the music of bands and the pealing of church bells, to the enthusiasm of crowds, the Queen and her husband rode in an open carriage to the stately Parliament buildings. They were escorted by Royal Canadian Mounted Police in scarlet tunics, mounted on black horses, and passed between lines of bandsmen and Canadian guards.

Queen Elizabeth spoke to the assembled Parliament with characteristic simplicity when she made the Address from the Throne. "I greet you as your Queen. Together we constitute the Parliament of Canada." Her sincere, understanding praise of Canada, its resources, its development into a nation with its own identity, won a warm response. Perhaps the visual image of the Queen, who represented the Crown, reminded the younger generation of independent Canadians of their dual allegiance; to the United Kingdom and to their own nation.

Within a few years the Commonwealth faced a crisis that might break up this group of co-operating nations, united by their tie to Great Britain. This was the rise of the European Economic Community, E.E.C. or the Common Market. It is composed of six nations: France, West Germany, Italy, Belgium, the Netherlands and Luxembourg. In the years since World War II these nations have made an amazing comeback from the devastation of war, aided first by the Marshall Plan from the United States, then by their own determination and skill. They put aside their political enmities and economic rivalries to pool their resources in an economic plan of trade among themselves for their common benefit. It has resulted in a prosperous, expanding block of nations, a new power in the latter half of the present century.

Prime Minister Macmillan of England determined that it was best for Great Britain to enter the Common Market, a group of nations that would rival the United States in wealth, population and skills. The Prime Minister has met great opposition to this plan from the labor movement, farmers, and some members of Parliament.

It was necessary to consult the Commonwealth nations, for they feared the loss of their preferential market in the British Isles. If Great Britain was a member of the Common Market the Commonwealth countries would be subject to tariffs imposed for all nations outside the E.E.C. Australia, Canada and New Zealand were especially concerned over loss of income from their agricultural products.

The Prime Ministers of the Commonwealth were invited to London for a conference in September, 1962. It was a tremendous gathering, representing about half the people of the free world; the full-fledged Commonwealth nations and many new associated nations.

Canada was represented by Prime Minister John G. Diefenbaker, whose Conservative party had won a large majority in the last election. There were days of meetings, discussion, and sharp comments from the Prime Ministers. Some of them did not agree with Macmillan's argument that the Commonwealth countries would profit from trade with this expanded Europe, others feared that the Commonwealth, as a group of nations, would not survive. John Diefenbaker's comment was that for one hundred years Canada had resisted "the American magnet" but under the Common Market the country might be driven into "the American orbit."

The Prime Ministers agreed that the mother country should do what it thought best, but they gave only reluctant consent. Negotiations between the British government and leaders of the Common Market went on for several months. Then the question was settled (or at least postponed) for the time being, when President De Gaulle of France, in January, 1963, declared that Great Britain did not belong in the group of European nations and vetoed the entry of the English nation into the Common Market.

Canadians had greater worries than E.E.C., for the financial and economic affairs of the country were not in good shape; there was dissatisfaction with what was considered the Prime Minister's lack of firm policy for improving conditions, and with the fact that no budget had been brought down in Parliament for two years; normally this is a yearly occurrence in mid-March. There was controversy in the Cabinet and three members resigned. Though Diefenbaker had been elected in 1958 with the largest majority in Canadian history, 208 of 265 seats; after the elections of June 1962 he was heading a Conservative Government that held only a minority of the votes in the House of Commons. To add to the confusion, the extremists in French-speaking Quebec were exerting their perennial pressure on Ottawa for more autonomy for the Province, and Real Caouette, the fiery leader of the Social Credit party there, was apparently making a strong impression on Quebec voters.

The usually friendly relations between the Canadian and United States governments were severely strained in the discussions over Canada's share in North American defense, and by Diefenbaker's delaying tactics in accepting nuclear warheads for the Canadian bombers and missiles that were part of the joint defense system. The Social Credit and New Democratic parties were also opposed to nuclear weapons and their "ban-the-bomb" demonstrations were attracting some anti-nuclear support.

A statement issued by the U.S. State Department in the winter of 1963 caused a storm in the Canadian Parliament. The statement was to the effect that Canada was failing in defense co-operation and had refused nuclear weapons. Although President Kennedy and the Secretary of State were not responsible for its publication, and Dean Rusk hastened to send a note declaring there was no intention to criticise the Prime Minister, Diefenbaker's anger was not soothed. He accused the United States of "unwarranted intrusion" in the politics of Canada. The incident resulted in a vote by the House of Commons of no confidence in the government and the dissolution of Parliament.

Elections were set for April 8, 1963. Prime Minister Diefenbaker and the Conservatives opposed the Liberals, headed by Lester B. Pearson, with the younger Social Credit and New Democratic parties hoping to strengthen their positions in the House of Commons. It was a bitter and bewildering campaign of invective and accusations by both leaders. Pearson had been opposed to nuclear weapons for Canada, but since Diefenbaker, in 1958, had promised to accept them, Pearson felt that Canada must stand by its commitments. The Liberals won, but without a clear-cut majority of seats in the House of Commons. Pearson needed 133 seats of the 265 in the House and lacked only five. Five Social Credit members from Quebec offered Pearson their support, then later withdrew it, causing a rift in that already shaky party. Surprisingly, both the Social Credit and New Democratic parties lost seats.

Without a majority government Pearson would find it difficult to carry through his program of stable government for improvement of the economy and the maintenance of Canada's place in international affairs. On Saturday, April 13, the completed count of votes from servicemen, veterans and their families was heavily pro-Liberal. It would give that party two more Parliament seats to add to the 128 won in civilian voting. The Liberals were short three seats from a majority. Prime Minister Diefenbaker then conceded defeat and wired congratulations to Lester B. Pearson. The Liberals, with Pearson as Prime Minister, were ready to form a government, even though without a clear majority.

The stormy Canadian election wakened Americans of the United States to the need for more understanding of their neighbors' problems along with the necessity for closer cooperation between the governments in the precarious world of the present time. Each nation needs the other. Lester B. Pearson is a firm friend of the United States, a statesman of integrity and international standing. The anti-Americanism roused by Diefenbaker's campaign oratory, while appealing to some, was by and large rejected by the Canadian electorate. Traditionally a bit wary of their far larger neighbor to the south the Canadian people realize the importance of close co-operation between the two nations.

Canada and the United States must work out many problems to adjust to the expanding, shifting world of the present era. They are both North American nations, interdependent through geography, through historical experience as pioneer countries in the western hemisphere, and through many common interests in language and culture. Can they continue to work together as friendly equals on the problems of trade, economics and politics, or will they go separate ways? Canada, in particular, faces a crucial period in her history; over the relations with the Commonwealth and the United States, and over the national ambition to be a united nation of free people in North America.

CHAPTER XXIII

National Culture and Arts

THE Canadian people, in the nineteenth century, were too preoccupied with the hard work of exploring, settling and building a nation to concern themselves consciously with cultural expression. Yet all the nationalities, by adding joy to their lives with music, and satisfaction in handicrafts, were laying a foundation of culture for their country. The French Canadians and various new nationalities had their folk songs and dances, their embroideries, weaving and wood carving, and their legends as well. The aboriginal inhabitants, Indians and Eskimos, had their ancestral chants, their songs and primitive dance to the beat of drums to express their thoughts and feelings.

It takes time for people of new countries, whose ambitions are set upon the future, to realize they have a valuable heritage in the culture of the primitive inhabitants. That time has come for Canada. In their scholarly work on the tribes of Canada, and of all North America, Diamond Jenness and his associates of the National Museum at Ottawa have done splendid work. Going out among Indians and Eskimos, this museum staff and those of other museums have made fascinating collections of primitive handicrafts, music, clothing and implements.

At the present time the delightful carved stone figures made by the Eskimos, who live around Hudson Bay and on Baffin Island, are admired as a genuine native art form. Throughout their history Eskimos have carved the creatures of their world and their magical images on stone, bone or ivory. The small figures of the modern Eskimos are carved from gray-green or black stone that takes a high polish. The forms of seals, polar bears, walrus, caribou, Eskimo hunters or mother and child, have a primitive strength, action and humor that a modern sculptor might well admire. The carvings are passed from hand to hand, receiving polish from each one who caresses the smooth stone, for the worth of a figure is judged by the sense of touch. The woman's art is to make skin pictures by cutting out figures from thin black sealskin, then appliquéing them to a large hide of bleached white sealskin or caribou. The Eskimo carvings, so unusual and appealing, are popular in galleries and shops, but there is no danger of mass production in this tribal art. Each man carves what he wishes and each small sculpture is individual.

In the long period when Canada was French, along the St. Lawrence, the settlers from France created a wealth of lovely folk songs that have been saved from oblivion by the work of scholars such as Marius Barbeau and E. Z. Massicote, who went out among the villages to collect songs and legends to be recorded for posterity. In the old days French Canadian wood carvers created statues for the churches and some of these have been preserved in museums, also examples of the women's weaving.

Through the devoted work of scholarly men there exists, in museums, invaluable source material for researchers on the cultures of primitive people and of the French Canadians.

In English Canada, during the nineteenth century, painters were producing serious, conventional canvasses, but the only painter of that period whose work receives recognition today was Cornelius Krieghoff of Dutch extraction. His gay, lively paintings of winter festivities in Quebec, Montreal and the countryside are practically documentaries of social life in old French Canada.

It was the first surge of national feeling, at the beginning of the present century, that inspired a group of artists to give a vivid interpretation of Canadians' newfound pride in their own land. These young men, later on called the Group of Seven, discarded the conventional painting of the period, and the European influences to portray the space, luminosity and strength of the Canadian landscape. They set out from their base at Toronto to explore the northern country of Quebec and Ontario, camping in the wilderness wherever they found stimulating subjects. With bold fresh color and strong brush strokes they painted the forest trees, the rocks and waters, the birds and animals of the northland. These young artists were Lauren Harris, Arthur Lismer, J. E. H. MacDonald, T. Y. Jackson, F. H. Farley, Frank Carmichael, Frank H. Johnson, Tom Thomson.

Their work was interrupted by World War I, but they came together again after the war, minus one member, Tom Thomson who had died. When the Group of Seven exhibited their paintings in a Toronto art gallery, they met opposition and criticism, as so often happens when new ideas in art are presented. This did not daunt them, and it was not long before their fresh, individualistic work brought them fame at home and recognition abroad. The Group of Seven became almost legendary and their work was an inspiration to later artists.

At the same period, in Victoria, B.C., a deeply imaginative artist, Emily Carr, was following her lonely creative path, absorbed in the spirit of the Pacific Coast Indians and the landscape. She made friends with the Indian people, visiting their villages where the weird, gaunt totem poles stood before stark plank dwellings. She learned their legends and the meaning of their ancestral culture, painting their life and legends in colorful compositions. Her interest in the Indians was further carried out in a book called *Klee Wyck,* a series of written sketches drawn from her visits among the people. Emily Carr was also an interpreter of her Pacific coast country; the forests, storms and swirling mists were painted in sweeping rhythms and strong forms in her canvasses. Today Emily Carr is honored as one of the truly creative Canadian painters.

The work of these early painters gave a tremendous boost to those who came later. Artists are now at work in every part of the country. There are galleries in some of the cities for the display of their work, but Canadian artists have the same problem as those in the United States — how to live from their art. Often they must keep painting for a part-time activity while they earn money at something else.

The National Gallery at Ottawa is a source of inspiration and assistance to art for the whole country. It houses the finest collection of Canadian painting in existence, and has revived the Annual Exhibition of Canadian Art, intended to show the best painting of the year, selected by regional committees. The Gallery raises the understanding of art for the people by traveling exhibits, by sending out lecturers, and producing film strips of Canadian artists to be sent to schools and art groups. The Gallery also has a fine collection of European painting. Art is brought to the people in instruction classes at important galleries. There are summer schools, of which the School of Fine Arts at Banff is most popular.

Modern painters in Canada are following the international trends in experimentation through abstraction and non-objective theories, though realistic painters also have their audience. Groups of French and English painters in Montreal, and others in Vancouver, are doing stimulating work in the field of experimentation.

More important than painting in Canada's cultural growth has been the love of music that runs like a thread through the story of its people. From the folk songs of the French habitants, and the song and dance of European groups, to the choral and orchestral societies of cities, Canadians of various backgrounds have made music an integral enrichment of life.

Artists and musicians have found it easier to interpret their country than have the writers. English Canada, to be sure, has had poets, men such as Charles G. D. Roberts and Bliss Carman of New Brunswick. One literary figure of Nova Scotia, in the nineteenth century, was Thomas Chandler Haliburton who put his caustic, witty comments on the life of his time into the mouth of Sam Slick, a Yankee clockmaker. Haliburton ranks with such masters of humorous literature as Artemus Ward and Mark Twain.

In historical studies Canadian scholars have done notable work, to which French Canadians have contributed histories of the French period in North America and of their province. French Canada, in its own closed circle, has its poets and novelists whose works find a market in the French province and in France; but they are seldom translated into English. It is limiting to Canadian literature that there is so little translation of English or French books into the other language. English Canadians receive most of their books from English or American publishers, because costs of production for a rather limited market make it too difficult for many publishing houses to exist in Canada.

In principal cities public libraries are established and maintained, notably in Toronto and Vancouver. In some western provinces where town centers with libraries are few, the libraries make use of bookmobiles to bring books to the scattered population. The universities have excellent libraries in every province, and collections of books for research are a joy to scholars in Toronto and Ottawa.

It was part of the rising spirit of nationalism after World War II to question Canada's cultural advances; what did they have, what was needed to promote creative activities of all sorts. Artists, writers and workers in the dramatic arts were struggling to break free from European and American influences. They needed help and encouragement from the government to provide opportunities for development of Canadian talents. For this purpose the government established the Royal Commission for National Development in the Arts, Letters and Sciences, with Vincent Massey as Chairman. Vincent Massey, a man of many accomplishments, who became the first Canadian-born Governor-General, did more for Canadian culture than any other one person in his period.

Thoughtful Canadians were searching for their own cultural identity. They had for so long followed English ideas and productions in literature that they lacked confidence in their own work, and English literary men were inclined to consider Canadian work "colonial," not to be judged equally with their own productions. American publications also, books and many magazines, entered Canada in great numbers and were a further detriment to Canadian writing. There are so few publishers in the country that authors sought publication of their books in London or New York. Often a Canadian edition was then issued, or the foreign edition went on sale. Thus Canadian authors felt they must win publication outside their country before they were recognized at home.

Canadian journalism uses the work of numerous good writers; specifically, Bruce Hutchison interprets his country delightfully both in books and in journalism. One magazine,

Maclean's, has been a successful publication, dealing with all aspects of Canadian life. *Saturday Night* is another good periodical.

Canada has had, in the person of the late Stephen Leacock, a national literary figure who endeared himself to all Canadians. Stephen Leacock devoted his delightful satire, humor, and deep understanding of his people to many books that interpret the people, their nation and their problems, to themselves. Even he doubted whether Canada could attain a national culture, placed as the country is between the two large English-speaking nations, Great Britain and the United States. However, Canada does have good novelists, writers such as Hugh MacLennan, Morley Callaghan, Mazo de la Roche, who interpret regional Canadian life in excellent novels. There is a modernistic stir of thought and experimentation among young poets in university cities — Toronto, Montreal and Vancouver. Poetry, in fact, has received more recognition internationally than prose writing. All creative writers find it as difficult to make a living from their work as their fellows in the United States.

Government encouragement and support stimulated creative people in all the arts through The Canada Council, established a few years later than the Royal Commission by the urging of Vincent Massey. Great sums were voted to "foster and promote the study of, and production of, works in the arts, humanities and social sciences." Money was spent to aid in the construction of university buildings, concert halls and theaters in some of the provinces, and to give federal aid to provincial galleries, museums and libraries. The offer of financial aid brought many requests from cultural organizations or individuals in the arts. There was plenty of dramatic talent among Canadians ready to respond to the opportunity to work in little theaters, in ballet companies, or in opera. In Toronto and

Montreal there were also young composers at work. Canada forged ahead in cultural activities with a spirit of vitality that is on the way to refute Leacock's doubt of a Canadian culture.

The most exciting advances have been made in the fields of music, ballet, theater and opera. The Canadian Opera Company was founded in Toronto. When this company goes on tour through the provinces the performances are welcomed in every city where they play, even though they must often rely on a piano as sole support for the singers, because of the cost of transporting an orchestra. The National Ballet of Toronto and the Royal Winnipeg Ballet have attained a high level of accomplishment. There is also *Les Grands Ballets Canadienne* in the French province.

Large cities have their symphony orchestras and other musical organizations. The Canadian Youth Orchestra, composed of young men and women performers, gives performances in various centers. Little theater and repertory companies have sprung up in a number of metropolitan centers. Every year since 1953 the Dominion Drama Festival has organized groups to put on plays in cities across the country. Provincial actors and musicians have an opportunity to show their talents and to bring delight to audiences. Montreal has a professional theater, the *Théâtre de la Comédie Canadienne,* that produces plays in both French and English, with special attention to the works of Canadian playwrights. A new enterprise, the National Theater School, is flourishing and sending its graduates out into professional work.

The most successful and best-known of Canadian cultural enterprises is the Stratford Shakespearean Festival. The idea originated in the mind of a young man, Tom Patterson, of the small town of Stratford in Ontario on the banks of the Avon River. Why not a Canadian Stratford-on-Avon? he questioned.

NATIONAL CULTURE AND ARTS

In his enthusiasm he raised money from townsfolk and obtained funds from wealthy men in other communities. Tyrone Guthrie, former manager of the Old Vic in London, was so captivated by the young man's idea that he consented to be the first director. He and Patterson collected a company of actors, some English, some Canadian. The townsfolk pitched in with money and help to build a huge tent, and here, in the summer of 1953 the first Shakespearean Festival was presented. The performances attracted audiences from Canada and visitors from the United States. After four seasons Patterson and his associates put on a campaign to raise money for a permanent playhouse, and the townsfolk contributed seven dollars from each man, woman and child in the community. A Toronto architect designed an unusual circular theater seating 2200 people.

At first it was difficult to convince the Canadian public that the Shakespearean Festival was really good, for they could not believe that Canadians could produce such excellent theater. The Festival has won its way, however, and is the pride of the Canadian people. At first the directors used imported stars and Canadian supporting actors, but now almost all are Canadian and it gives the actors an opportunity to increase their skill and reputation. In the lovely Ontario summer, streams of natives and visitors pour into the little Canadian Stratford where the townspeople devote themselves to making it pleasant for them. They witness delightful professional performances in a charming New World setting.

The Canadian Broadcasting Company, CBC, has drawn the people together through radio and television. Broadcasting in Canada is a combination of public and private enterprise. CBC gets about half its income from the government and half from commercial advertising. There are private stations but all are under the supervision of the CBC Board of Governors. There is strict oversight of commercially sponsored programs and advertising, so Canadians do not receive as many, or as irritating, commercials as is the case in the United States.

A TV network was established by the CBC that covers the whole country, making it possible for Canadians to receive a large number of programs. People of the provinces who do not have the chance to see live performances of drama, opera or ballet may view some of these arts on television. CBC plays an important part in encouraging workers in the arts by employing actors, musicians and ballet dancers.

Films made in Canada by the National Film Board are shown by this worthwhile organization. It produces documentaries exclusively that depict Canadian life. Their film, *The City of Gold,* on the Klondike Gold Rush, won the 1957 Cannes Festival Award for short films. Interesting aspects of Canadian life come to the people in visual form through these film programs. The CBC French station in Montreal broadcasts to the province lively programs in French to suit the point of view and interests of the French-speaking population.

Through exciting activities in all the arts, going on in every part of the country, Canadians are most certainly finding their cultural identity. They are taking pride in the talents of their own people and are ready to extend their productions in the arts to win recognition abroad.

CHAPTER XXIV

Neighbors in North America

CANADIANS are people quite like us," many Americans say casually, and do not search further to learn about the character of their northern neighbors, nor do they bother to learn much about their history, their ambitions and desires in the modern world. Americans are rather inclined to take their neighbors for granted, as they might consider relatives whom they like, but with whom they may often have differences of opinion.

As people pass back and forth across the border, with only slight inspection from customs officers, they meet each other with real friendliness and feel at home each in the other's country. They share not only language but many ways of thought and feeling and a common standard of living in such things as motor cars, comfortable homes, labor-saving equipment, sports, movies, radio and television.

To Americans traveling in Canada for vacations, or working in business, the surface of life seems much like home, but they discover differences in point of view and the tempo of living. Canadians are more conservative than Americans, slower and more cautious in action. They instinctively resist the dynamic self-confidence of their neighbors' spirit and perhaps emphasize British elements in their thought and life in order to counteract the overwhelming influence of the American way.

The "American invasion" now regarded with distrust by many Canadians is that of customs, a materialistic outlook, too much control of Canadian industry and finance. They do not want to see Canada Americanized, but it is difficult to avoid it in surface ways when Canada receives hundreds of American products, when the country is bombarded with radio programs, receives its screen plays from Hollywood and its magazine diet from the United States. The Canadian Broadcasting Company, however, is counteracting the influence from across the border, in entertainment and information, by their own radio and television programs, attuned to the Canadian people's interests and culture.

The press of the United States gives little space to news from Canada unless there is an international crisis which involves both countries. Canadians, on the other hand, are well aware of what is going on in the United States in politics, economics and financial affairs.

Canadians have been drawn as by a magnet to the greater prosperity and opportunities of the big neighbor so that thousands have come to live in the United States to carry on careers in the professions and arts. Americans have always enjoyed travel and visits in the Rocky Mountain resorts, in Vancouver and Victoria, in Montreal, Quebec and the Laurentian countryside. During the postwar years more and more Americans have been living and working in Canada; hundreds of airmen are stationed there; technicians and businessmen are involved in the big industrial projects such as mining and oil fields. It is natural that there should be some worry among Canadians over the dominance of the United States in their affairs.

Ever since Canada has been able, as a nation, to negotiate directly with the United States, through the governments and the International Joint Commission, the settlement of crucial questions has been a triumph of reasonableness and fair dealing. And, as Canada has become influential in international discussions, their political leaders find they can help in controversial issues between Great Britain and the United States, because they have links with both nations and may interpret one to the other. Crises in the affairs of the United States have always affected Canadians, and the relations of British North America with the mother country have always been of importance to the Americans across the border.

Throughout their history the two peoples have been closely linked; there have been disagreements, politicians have grown hot and angry over controversial questions, but the governments have always managed to work things out through discussion and compromise because they had the will, fundamentally, to be good neighbors. Both peoples are proud of the famous undefended frontier, and war between the two nations under any circumstances is unthinkable.

Pioneer ancestors of both peoples, by their adventurous spirit, their character, and faith in what they were doing, opened up a continent. Their descendants pushed on westward until they had reached the Pacific and created two nations extending from sea to sea. Each of those nations received a flood of immigrants from Europe, seeking opportunity in the New World, and they have both experienced the problems of assimilating many nationalities.

Each in their own way, the peoples of both nations have followed their profound instinct for freedom and self-government. Their will to control the government under which they live takes the form of political democracy in both countries. With all its shortcomings and difficulties, it is the way of life they have chosen, so that both Canadians and Americans have the job of making democracy work.

The time has come for North Americans south of the common border to take their fellows in Canada more seriously, to learn their history, to respect their achievements and increase their understanding. As individuals and in groups the two peoples instinctively like each other and find many things in common. As nations, they have managed to co-operate constructively on great projects for their mutual benefit, such as the St. Lawrence Seaway and traffic on the Great Lakes. Canada and the United States have proved that adjoining nations can live side by side in constructive peace and good neighborliness.

Here in the western world the will of free men to control their own destinies has been the guiding principle in the development of two nations created out of a vast new continent. They now have the responsibility of using their influence in councils of many nations so that the dream of man for peace, freedom and equality may come true.

Bibliography for the First Edition

Armstrong, Elizabeth H. *French Canadian Opinion on the War, January 1940–June 1941.* (Contemporary Affairs Series No. 12) Toronto: Ryerson Press, 1942.

Barbeau, Charles Marius. *Downfall of Temlaham.* Toronto: Macmillan Co. of Canada, 1928.

—— *Kingdom of Saguenay.* Toronto: Macmillan Co. of Canada, 1936.

—— *Quebec, Where Ancient France Lingers.* Quebec: Librairie Garneau; New York. The Macmillan Co., 1936.

—— and Saipr, Edward. *Folksongs of French Canada.* New Haven: Yale University Press, 1925.

The Beaver: Magazine of the North.

Beston, Henry. *St. Lawrence.* (Rivers of America) New York: Farrar & Rinehart, Inc., 1942.

Brebner, John Bartlet. *The Explorers of North America, 1492–1806.* London: A. C. Black Co., 1933.

Bryce, George. *Remarkable History of the Hudson's Bay Company.* London: S. Low, Marsten and Co., 1900.

Burt, Alfred Leroy. *A Short History of Canada for Americans.* Minneapolis: University of Minnesota Press, 1942.

Call, Frank Oliver. *Spell of French Canada.* Boston: L. C. Page and Co., 1926.

Canadian Steamship Company. *Tadoussac.*

Carr, Emily. *Klee Wyck.* Toronto: Oxford University Press, 1941.

Cartier, Jacques. *Bref Récit et Succincte Narration de la Navigation faite en 1535 et 1536 par le capitaine Jacques Cartier aux îles de Canada, Hochelaga, Saguenay et autre.*

—— *Relation Originale au Voyage de Jacques Cartier au Canada en 1534.*

Cartwright, Steven. *Population: Canada's Problem.* (Contemporary Affairs Series No. 11) Toronto: Ryerson Press, 1941.

Champlain, Samuel de. *The Voyages of Samuel de Champlain,* ed. by W. L. Grant. (Original Narratives of Early American History) New York: Charles Scribner's Sons, 1907.

Chronicles of Canada, ed. by George M. Wrong and H. H. Langton. 33 vols. Toronto. Glasgow Brook & Co.

Cooper, John Irwin. *Montreal: the Story of Three Hundred Years.* Toronto: Macmillan Co. of Canada.

Dafoe, John Wesley. *Canada: an American Nation.* New York: Columbia University Press, 1935.

Davidson, Charles Gordon. *The Northwest Company.* Berkeley: University of California Press, 1918.

Dollier de Casson & Brehant de Galinée. *Exploration of the Great Lakes 1669-1670.* Toronto: Ontario Historical Society.

Dollier de Casson. *History of Montreal, 1640-1672.* New edition with English translation and notes. Toronto: J. M. Dent & Sons.

Dufferin and Ava, Marchioness of. *My Canadian Journal 1872-1878.* New York: D. Appleton & Company, 1891.

Duncan, Dorothy. *Bluenose: a Portrait of Nova Scotia.* New York: Harper & Brothers, 1942.

—— *Here's to Canada!* New York: Harper & Brothers, 1941.

Ferguson, George Victor. *How We Govern Ourselves.* (Contemporary Affairs Series No. 1) Toronto: Ryerson Press, 1939.

Finnie, Richard. *Canada Moves North.* New York: The Macmillan Co., 1942.

Gibbon, John Murray. *Canadian Folksongs Old and New.* New York: E. P. Dutton & Co., 1927.

—— *Canadian Mosaic. the Making of a Northern Nation.* Toronto: McClelland & Stewart, 1938.

—— *Steel of Empire: the Romantic History of the Canadian Pacific, the Northwest Passage of Today.* Indianapolis: Bobbs Merrill, 1935.

Guillet, Edwin Clarence. *Early Life in Upper Canada.* Toronto: Ontario Publishing Co., 1933.

Harvey, Daniel Cobb. *The Colonization of Canada.* Toronto: Irwin & Co., 1936.

Havighurst, Walter. *Long Ships Passing: the Story of the Great Lakes.* New York: The Macmillan Co., 1942.

Healy, W. J. *Women of Red River.* Gathered by Woman's Club of Winnipeg.

Hudson's Bay Company, Incorporated 2nd May, 1670. *A Brief History of the Hudson's Bay Company.* London, 1934.

Hutchison, Bruce. *The Unknown Country; Canada and Her People.* New York: Coward-McCann Co., 1942.

Irving, Washington. *Astoria.* New York: E. P. Dutton & Co., 1902.

Jameson, Anna Brownell. *Winter Studies and Summer Rambles in Canada, 1836–1837.* London: Sanders and Oakley.

Jenness, Diamond. *Indians of Canada.* Ottawa: National Museum of Canada Bulletin 65.

Jesuit Relations. *Relation de ce qui s'est passé en la Nouvelle France en l'année 1626.*

———— *Relation de ce qui s'est passé en la Nouvelle France en l'année 1638.*

———— *Relation de ce qui s'est passé en la Maison des Pères de la Compagnie des Jesus aux Huron pays de la Nouvelle France aux années 1648 et 1649.*

———— *Relation de ce qui s'est passé en la Maison des Pères de la Compagnie de Jesus aux Huron pays de la Nouvelle France aux années 1662 et 1663.*

———— *Relation de ce qui s'est passé de plus remarquable aux Missions des Pères de la compagnie de Jesus en la Nouvelle France en années 1662 et 1663.*

Jesuit Relations and Allied Documents; *Travels and Exploration of the Jesuit missionaries in North America 1620–1791,* ed. by Edna Kenton. Toronto: McClelland & Stewart.

Kane, Paul. *Wanderings of an Artist among the Indian Tribes of North America.* Toronto: The Radisson Society of Canada, 1935.

Knight, James. *Founding of Churchill, being the Journal of the Governor-in-chief in Hudson Bay, 1717;* ed. by James F. Kenny. Toronto: J. M. Dent & Sons, Ltd., 1932.

Lescarbot, Marc. *Canada; History of New France.* Toronto: Champlain Society, 1907–14.

———— *Neptune's Theatre,* tr. by Edna B. Holman. London: S. French, Ltd., 1927.

Louisburg in 1745; the anonymous *Lettre d'un Habitant de Louisburg,* narrative by an eye witness of the Siege of Louisburg; ed. with English tr. by George M. Wrong, Toronto.

MacCormac, John. *Canada; America's Problem.* New York: The Viking Press, 1940.

MacDougall, John. *Saddle, Sled and Snowshoe; Pioneering on the Saskatchewan in the Sixties.* Toronto: Ryerson Press.

MacKay, Douglas. *Honourable Company; a History of the Hudson's Bay Company.* Indianapolis: Bobbs Merrill, 1937.

Mackenzie, Sir Alexander. *Voyages from Montreal through the Continent of North America to the Frozen and Pacific Oceans in 1789 and 1793.* 2 vols. Toronto: The Radisson Society of Canada, Ltd., 1927.

MacMechan, Archibald McKellar. *Book of Ultima Thule.* Toronto: McClelland & Stewart, 1927.

McWilliams, Margaret. *Manitoba Milestones.* Toronto: J. M. Dent & Sons, Ltd.

Maheaux, Abbé Arthur. *French Canada and Britain; a New Interpretation.* (Contemporary Series No. 13) Toronto: Ryerson Press, 1942.

Makers of Canada; ed. by W. L. Grant, 1926 ed. 12 vols. Toronto: Oxford University Press.

Miner, Horace. *St. Denis, French Canadian Paris.* Chicago: University of Chicago Press, 1939.

Nute, Grace Lee. *The Voyageur.* New York: D. Appleton & Co., 1931.

Parkman, Francis. *Count Frontenac and the New France under Louis XIV.* Boston: Little, Brown & Co., 1897.

—— *Half-Century of Conflict,* 2 vols. Boston: Little, Brown & Co., 1893.

—— *Jesuits in North America in the Seventeenth Century.* Boston: Little, Brown & Co., 1902.

—— *La Salle and the Discovery of the Great West.* Boston: Little, Brown & Co., 1907.

—— *Old Regime in Canada.* Boston: Little, Brown & Co., 1902.

—— *Pioneers of France in the New World.* Boston: Little, Brown, & Co., 1903.

Repplier, Agnes. *Mère Marie of the Ursulines.* New York: Doubleday, Doran Co., 1931.

Scott, F. R. *Canada Today; a Study of Her National Interests and National Policy.* Toronto: Oxford University Press, 1939.

Siegfried, André. *Canada.* Tr. by H. H. and Doris Hemming. New York: Harcourt Brace and Co., 1937.

Skinner, Constance Lindsay. *Beaver, Kings and Cabins.* New York: The Macmillan Co., 1933.

Stefansson, Vilhjalmur. *Friendly Arctic; the Story of Five Years in Polar Regions.* New York: The Macmillan Co., 1921.

───── *Northward Course of Empire.* New York: Harcourt, Brace and Company, 1922.

Stewart, Andrew. *More Farmers for Western Canada.* (Contemporary Affairs Series, No. 9) Toronto: Ryerson Press, 1941.

Vaillancourt, Émil. *Knots.* Montreal: G. Ducharme, 1939.

Veillées du bon vieux temps, a la Bibliotèque Saint Sulpice. La Societe Historial de Montreal.

Vestal, Stanley, pseud. *King of the Fur Traders; the Deeds and Deviltry of Pierre Esprit Radisson.* Boston: Houghton Mifflin Co., 1940.

Waldo, Fullerson Leonard. *Down the Mackenzie through the Great Lone Land.* New York: The Macmillan Co., 1923.

Wittke, Carl. *History of Canada.* New York: F. S. Crofts Co., 1941.

Wrong, George M. *Canadians; the Story of a People.* New York: The Macmillan Co., 1938.

Contemporary Canada

Anderson, Commdr. William R. USN. "The Arctic as a Sea Route of the Future." *National Geographic Magazine,* January, 1959.

Berton, Pierre. *The Mysterious North.* New York: Alfred A. Knopf, 1956.

Boyer, David S. "Alberta Unearths Her Buried Treasure." *National Geographic Magazine,* July, 1960.

───── "Kitimat: Canada's Aluminum Titan." *National Geographic Magazine,* September, 1956.

Brown, Andrew H. "New St. Lawrence Seaway Opens the Great Lakes to the World." *National Geographic Magazine,* March, 1959.

Calvert, Commdr. James F. USN. "Up Through the Ice of the North Pole." *National Geographic Magazine,* July, 1959.

Chapin, Miriam. *Contemporary Canada.* New York: Oxford University Press, 1959.

Creighton, Donald. *The Story of Canada.* Boston: Houghton, Mifflin Co., 1960.

Department of Northern Affairs and National Resources, Ottawa, Canada. *Canadian Eskimo Art.*

Gilmour, G. P. ed. *Canada's Tomorrow.* Toronto: The Macmillan Co. of Canada, 1954.

Hannon, Leslie F. ed. *Maclean's Canada. Portrait of a Country.* Toronto: McClelland & Stewart, Ltd.; New York: Hawthorn Books, 1960.

Horne, Alastair. *Canada and the Canadians.* Toronto: The Macmillan Co. of Canada, Ltd., 1961.

Hutchison, Bruce. *Canada: Tomorrow's Giant.* New York: Alfred A. Knopf, 1957.

LaFay, Howard. "Dew Line, Sentry of the Far North." *National Geographic Magazine,* July, 1958.

Lalor, Lt. William G. Jr. USN. "Submarine Through the North Pole." *National Geographic Magazine,* January, 1959.

Peart, Hugh W. and John Shaccer. *Winds of Change.* Toronto: The Ryerson Press, 1961.

Phillips, Alan. "Canada, My Country." *National Geographic Magazine,* December, 1961.

Taylor, Griffith. *Canada.* London: Methuen & Co.; New York: E. P. Dutton, 1961.

Robinson, Ira M. *New Industrial Towns on Canada's Resource Frontier.* University of Chicago Press, Dept. of Geography, 1962.

Wilson, Phyllis. "Queen of Canada." *National Geographic Magazine,* June, 1959.

ABOUT THE AUTHOR

Anne Merriman Peck was born in Piermont, N.Y., but her New England family soon afterward returned to Connecticut where she grew up. With a keen interest in art, she intended to make painting her career and studied in Hartford and New York. Then she spent several years painting, and illustrating children's books. Marriage and a little boy added home life to her career. Mrs. Peck managed several vagabond trips to Europe for painting, study of galleries and architecture. Through these trips she became interested in people of other nationalities, their habits of daily life, their cultures, art, literature and music. She had keen pleasure in getting off the beaten track to hobnob with simple people in small places. Mingling with ordinary citizens in day coaches and busses quickened her knowledge and interest in the people. European travel was the foundation for writing travel books with historical background for young readers.

Wide travel in Europe was followed by long visits in Mexico, Central America and South America, and she followed her usual habit of visiting and traveling with the people except for some important trips by air that gave her a bird's eye view of the magnificent countries. Out of her deep interest in Latin America grew a compelling desire, through her books, to try to help advance understanding, cooperation and friendship among all the peoples of the Americas.

Study of neighbor countries was continued with the exploration of Canada and the resulting book on our northern neighbor. She remembers with special pleasure two trips to little-known parts of Canada: one by busses through the mountainous Cariboo country in British Columbia, with a day spent in the old "ghost town" of Barkerville; another was a roundabout, amusing trip to reach Churchill on Hudson Bay, an adventure that opened the eyes of this observant American to real wilderness.

Her three *Pageants* are *The Pageant of Canadian History, The Pageant of Middle American History,* and *The Pageant of South American History.*

Mrs. Peck now makes her home in Tucson, Arizona. The varied peoples and dramatic history of the Southwest have provided material for more study and have resulted in two books: *Southwest Roundup,* and *The March of Arizona History.*

Index

Parrtown (St. John, N.B.), 164-66
Parsnip River, 121, 132
Pas, The, 226
Passenger steamers, 274
Patriotes, 197-98, 202
Patterson, Tom, 358
Pays d'en haut, 110
Peace River, 120-21, 132, 316
Pearl Harbor, 341
Pearson, Lester B., 342, 348-49; awarded Nobel Peace Prize, 342; elected prime minister, 348-49
Peary, Commander Robert E., 332
Peltrie, Mme. de la, 42, 43, 44, 47, 48
Pembina, 234
Penobscot River, 14
Pepperell, William, 90, 91
Perche, 69
Permafrost, 319, 327
Perry, Oliver Hazard, 179, 258
Peru, 23
Peter the Great (Russia), 124
Petite Hermine, Cartier's ship, 17
Philip, Prince, consort of Elizabeth II, 284, 345
Phips, Sir William, 84, 85
Picardy, 69
Pile of Bones Creek, 259
Pincher Creek, Alberta, 291
Pioneering, in northern Canada, 314
Pitchblende ore, discovered, 318, 319
Pitt, William, 92, 94, 97, 155
Place d'Armes, 75
Plains of Abraham, 97, 159
Platinum, 299
Poets, Canadian, 355
Polish immigrants, 266, 268, 270, 271
Political movements, independent, 296-97
Politics, Canadian, structure of, 335
Pompadour, Mme. de, 92
Pontgravé, Sieur de, 26, 27, 31
Pontiac (chief), 154, 157
Population, increase in twentieth century, 266-73
Port Arthur, 279, 282
Port Colborne, 281
Port Moody, 251, 262, 263, 264
Port Radium, 319
Port Royal, 27-31, 84, 88
Port Rupert, 321
Port Weller, 281
Portland, Me., 211
Portugal, 14, 15
Poutrincourt, Baron de, 28, 31
Power Authority of New York State, 283
Prairie provinces, 285, 290-98

Prairies: development of, 285, 290-98; settlement of, 232-36, 266-73
Pre-Cambrian Shield, 2, 295, 302, 312-13, 322-23
Près-de-Ville, 160
Press, U.S., attention of, to Canadian news, 362
Prime minister, powers of, 335
Primitive culture, 1-10
Prince Arthur's Landing, 279
Prince Edward Island, 164, 166, 219, 220, 308, 309
Prince William Sound, 129
Progressive party, 297
Prosperity, in the 1920's, 338-39
Province House, Halifax, 192
Puget Sound, 126, 128, 129
Pulp mills, Quebec, 306

Quadra, Don, 130
Quebec, 19, 27, 35-37, 58, 110, 264, 303-7; attacked by Americans, 158-61; described, 63-64, 75, 174; education in, 214, 304; English in, 85, 95-99, 152-55; English-French rivalry in, 343-44; first legislative assembly, 171; founding of, 32-33; Franciscans in, 40, 50-51; geological formation of, 2; government, 62, 66-68, 93; Indians at, 81-82; Jesuits in, 40, 50-51, 57, 67; life in, 58-76, 214-15; natural resources in, 323; Norman stock in, 69-70; political reform in, 196-97; Recollet friars in, 40; Roman Catholic Church in, 60-61, 75-76, 156; shipbuilding, 190; Ursulines in, 41-46
Quebec Act (1774), 156-57, 169, 170
Quebec Conference, 219-20
Quebec Gazette (Chronicle), 155
Queen's College, Kingston, 214
Queenston, Ont., 184
Queenston Heights, Battle of, 179
Quesnal, Jules, 133, 241, 242, 245
Quinté, Bay of, 183

Radar stations, in Arctic, 331, 333, 334
Radio, 359-60
Radisson, Pierre Esprit, 101-6, 110
Radium, in pitchblende ore, 318
Railroads, 210-13, 234, 255-65, 267; to Churchill, Man., 295; transcontinental, 279
Rainy Lake, 107, 115
Ranching, in Alberta, 290
Rebellion of 1837, 201-4
Rebellion Losses bill, 208-9
Reciprocity Treaty (1854), 210